D0850473

Status and Respectability in the Cape Colony, 1750–1870

A Tragedy of Manners

In a compelling example of the new cultural history of South Africa, Robert Ross offers a subtle and wide-ranging study of status and respectability in the colonial Cape between 1750 and 1870. He describes the symbolism of dress, emblems, architecture, food, language and polite conventions, paying particular attention to domestic relationships, gender, education and religion, and analyses the values and the modes of thinking current in different strata of the society. He argues that these cultural factors were related to high political developments in the Cape, and offers a rich account of the changes in social identity that accompanied the transition from Dutch to British overrule, and of the development of white racism and of ideologies of resistance to white domination. The result is a uniquely nuanced account of a colonial society.

ROBERT ROSS is coordinator of African Studies at the Rijks Universiteit Leiden, The Netherlands. He has written widely on South African history, and his books include *Adam Kok's Griquas: A Study in the Development of Stratification in South Africa* (1976); *Cape of Torments: Slavery and Resistance in South Africa* (1982); *Beyond the Pale: Essays on the History of Colonial South Africa* (1993); and, most recently, *A Concise History of South Africa* (1999).

African Studies Series

Status and Respectability in the Cape Colony, 1750–1870

A list of recent books in this series will be found at the end of this volume

Status and Respectability in the Cape Colony, 1750–1870

A Tragedy of Manners

Robert Ross

 CAMBRIDGE
UNIVERSITY PRESS

PUBLISHED BY THE PRESS SYNDICATE OF THE UNIVERSITY OF CAMBRIDGE
The Pitt Building, Trumpington Street, Cambridge CB2 1RP, United Kingdom

CAMBRIDGE UNIVERSITY PRESS
The Edinburgh Building, Cambridge CB2 2RU, UK   http://www.cup.cam.ac.uk
40 West 20th Street, New York, NY 10011–4211, USA   http://www.cup.org
10 Stamford Road, Oakleigh, Melbourne 3166, Australia

© Robert Ross 1999

First published 1999

Printed in the United Kingdom at the University Press, Cambridge

Typeset in Times NR MT 10/12 pt. in QuarkXPress® [SE]

A catalogue record for this book is available from the British Library

ISBN 0 521 62122 4 hardback

For Jatti, Susie and Nigel
friends and colleagues

Contents

Illustrations

Acknowledgements

My main debts in the writing of this book are to my colleagues working in the field of pre-industrial Cape history. The names of those on whose work I have drawn most are to be found in footnote 3 to chapter 1. More specific debts are due to Patricia van der Spuy, who engaged in valuable digging on my behalf in the Cape Archives and the South African Library, and to Thomas Lindblad who translated a newspaper report from Swedish for me. All other translations are my own, at least when the source cited is in a language other than English.

A number of friends have been so kind as to read the manuscript and give me comments on the basis of which, I hope, I have made improvements. They are Dmitri van der Bersselaar, Jan-Bart Gewald (both of whom were able to get their own back), Adam Kuper, Susie Newton-King, Kathy van Vliet, Nigel Worden and the Cambridge University Press's putatively anonymous reader.

Throughout the period of this research I have been grateful for the support from the Faculty of Arts of Leiden University. The drafting of the last two chapters and much of the final editing were completed while I was a research fellow at the Netherlands Institute for Advanced Study, Wassenaar, a wonderful environment for academic research, and I am most grateful to its rector, director and staff for their assistance.

Abbreviations

ARA	Algemene Rijksarchief, The Hague
AYB	*Archives Year Book for South African History*
BPP	British Parliamentary Paper
CA	Cape Archives
CMM	*Cape Monthly Magazine*
CPP	Cape Parliamentary Paper
DR	Dag-register
DRC	Dutch Reformed Church
JAH	*Journal of African History*
JME	*Journal des Missions Evangéliques*
JSAS	*Journal of Southern African Studies*
LMS	London Missionary Society; also the archives of that body, now the Congregational Council for World Missions, held in the School of Oriental and African Studies, London
LMS-SA	LMS archives, incoming letters, South Africa
NZAT	*Nederduitsch Zuid-Afrikaansche Tijdschrift*
PA	*Periodical Accounts Relating to the Missions of the Church of the United Brethren*
PEMS	Paris Evangelical Missionary Society
QBSAL	*Quarterly Bulletin of the South African Library*
RCC	G. McC. Theal (ed.), *Records of the Cape Colony*
RCP	Resolutions of the Council of Policy
SACA	*South African Commercial Advertiser*
SAHJ	*South African Historical Journal*
SHCT	*Studies in the History of Cape Town*
SSA	*Collected Seminar Papers of the Institute of Commonwealth Studies, London: The Societies of Southern Africa in the Nineteenth and Twentieth Centuries*
UCT	University of Cape Town
UNISA	University of South Africa
VOC	*Vereenigde Oost-Indische Compagnie* (Dutch East India Company); also the archives of that body in the ARA

Griqua wedding party (*W. B. Philip collection: Jagger University Library, University of Cape Town*)

1   Introduction

In December 1979 I was working in the Cape Archives. Together with a number of other researchers, I would often drink coffee at about 10.30, not in the Gardens Cafe, then the usual resort of Cape historians, but in a small coffee bar in a nearby arcade. I suppose that, in the heart of summer, it was cooler than under the trees in the open air.[1] Now, before their move to the old Roeland Street gaol, the Cape Archives were in the centre of the city, very close not only to the South African Parliament but also to the law courts. One day, as we came out of the cafe, we passed a group of about five people. Leading them was a tall, fairly elderly man who was walking, slowly, upright and sedately. The others were all shorter than he was, or at least they made themselves appear so. They were all dressed in the robes of barristers, and I suppose that if I had been sufficiently attuned to the niceties of legal dress, I might have noticed the details which distinguish the chief from the acolytes. But I did not need to have such additional signs to recognise the hierarchy within that little group, as they walked through the passage after having come down from the advocates' chambers higher in the building to the court. The four lesser mortals were walking with short, somewhat hurried strides at least half a pace behind their leader, hanging onto his words, and when they entered the conversation they did so with evident deference. Obviously, I did not hear their conversations but from their body language it was quite clear what the relationship between them was.

This incident has stuck in my mind for a number of reasons. The first relates to their complexions. The man at the front had a light yellow-brown face and his hair, though greying, had obviously been dark black and somewhat curly. The others' hair was in various shades of brown and off-black and their skin was what has been called pinko-grey. In Cape Town, in 1979,

---

[1] William Beinart, who was also working in the Cape Archives at the time, is unsure whether we went to the cafe in the arcade because it was cheaper than the Gardens or because there was some sort of informal boycott of the Gardens as a segregated public amenity. Personal communication, 23 July 1987. This confusion between the dictates of economy and the symbolism of racial and political struggle might be seen as a (somewhat trivial) metonym for South African history and historiography as a whole, provided that the 'ecological' explanation that I have given is not entirely forgotten.

as before and since, it was most exceptional to see the racial hierarchy, which confined those considered to be so-called 'coloureds' to a position below the erroneously so-called 'whites', so evidently reversed.

The second reason is that I recognised the barrister. He was Benny Kies, an inspirational teacher at Trafalgar High School on the edge of Cape Town's District Six (he had taught a number of my friends) and political leader, who had turned to the law after a banning order from the South African Government had made it impossible for him to continue as an educator. It was the first time that I had seen him, and it was to be the last. He was then engaged on a political trial of temporary notoriety – there were so many – and was to collapse and die in court a few days later. This perhaps fixed the incident in my mind.

Nevertheless, it is on the first reason that I wish to dwell. Body language largely is outside the vision of historians, at least of those of us who deal with the world before the invention of the movie camera.[2] This is an unfortunate fact of life, because our physical postures are perhaps the clearest way in which in our normal life we express our position relative to those other people with whom we interact. Any foreigner who has ever seen South Africans in a documentary film or watched a black South African actor portraying a downtrodden fellow countryman or woman will have noticed the attitudes they strike, as expressive as anything they say. But there are many other ways, in terms of rituals, language, dress, spatial arrangements, religion, even food, by which we express or mark our status. These can be reclaimed historically, if with difficulty. In this book, I wish to investigate some of these, with reference to the Colony of the Cape of Good Hope in the eighteenth and nineteenth centuries.

This book has been long in the writing. There have been a number of reasons for this. Aside from the normal (and not always convincing) excuses of an academic – pressure of teaching, administration and so forth –, a variety of other projects, all with relation to the Cape, but not specifically to this book, have diverted me from this piece of writing. Subliminally, however, they were closely connected to it, particularly the work which I have done, especially in collaboration with Elizabeth Elbourne, on the history of mission Christianity at the Cape. At the same time, the recent burgeoning of historical work on the colonial history of the Cape, particularly in the nineteenth century, has allowed me to proceed with more confidence than I otherwise would have had.[3] Equally, I have absorbed

---

[2] For an attempt, see Jan Bremmer and Herman Roodenburg (eds.), *A Cultural History of Gender*, Ithaca, N.Y., Cornell University Press, 1991.

[3] I am thinking in particular of the researches of Andrew Bank, Henry Bredekamp, Clifton Crais, Wayne Dooling, Elizabeth Elbourne, Katherine Elks, Natasha Erlank, Martin Hall, Alan Lester, Kirsten McKenzie, Antonia Malan, Candy Malherbe, John Mason, Susan

through a process of osmosis,[4] if at all, those changes in international intellectual fashions which have probably made the choices of material to be presented rather easier.

In retrospect, the serious problem I had was in deciding what I actually wanted to say. I had a subject, or at least a field. To those who I expected could expand such shorthand, I described this book as 'a semiotic history of the Cape', or more prosaically and less pretentiously, as a history of the markers of status. I also thought of it as being located within the semantic fields covered by two Dutch words, both of which have wider, or at least more varied, meanings than any English equivalent. The first of these is 'etiquette', which means the same in Dutch as it does in English, but has also retained its original meaning of 'label'.[5] The relationship between codes of behaviour and the assignment to categories which exists within the Dutch word is a fruitful source of reflection.[6] The second is 'voorstellen/voorstelling', a pair of words with such a wide set of references that the tidy-minded would do well to avoid them. 'Voorstellen' can mean to introduce (someone to someone else), to propose (that something be done[7]), or to imagine something as being possible. 'Voorstelling' can mean an idea of how things are and thus a way of seeing things in the mind's eye or a performance (of a play, for instance). The closest English word to at least these last two meanings might be 'interpretation'. Obviously, again, the connections which are set up within a single set of words can potentially increase understanding. To try to reduce them to concepts which can be 'used', on the other hand, would probably nullify the effect.

Newton-King, Pam Scully, Rob Shell, Patricia van der Spuy, Russel Viljoen, Kerry Ward and, last alphabetically, but properly first as he has taught and inspired many of the others, Nigel Worden. In many cases, I have been privileged to make use of their work while it is as yet unpublished, or indeed incomplete. For this, many thanks.
[4] And therefore do not feel competent, or inclined, to give a full theoretical exposé of what lies at the back of my work in this sense. Anyway, I have been warned off by many examples of a tenuous relationship between the exposition of fashionable ideas, to prove that the author is aware of the latest trends, and the main body of the work.
[5] In its original meaning, this word was indeed absorbed into English from French, but in the process transmuted into the 'ticket'. Apart from professional etymologists, there can be few English-speakers who appreciate the historical identity of the two words.
[6] This collaboration was made easier for me by a long association with Dik van Arkel, one of whose most fruitful concepts for the analysis of racial behaviour has been 'labelled interaction', or in Dutch, 'geëtikketeerde interactie'. In this book, as it happens, I do not use this concept, although the insights it offers are great. See Dik van Arkel, 'The Growth of the Anti-Jewish Stereotype: An Attempt at a Hypothetical Deductive Method of Historical Research', *International Review of Social History*, 30, 1985, 270–307 and Chris Quispel, *Dienaar en Bruut: Studies over laat-negentiende-eeuws racisme, in het bijzonder in het Zuiden van de Vereenigde Staten*, Leiden, Centrum voor Moderne Geschiedenis, 1995, 191.
[7] *Not* 'to propose to do something'. This is the word-for-word translation of the Dutch construction, a source of considerable and damaging confusion.

This is all very well, or perhaps not, but a subject is not a plot, and authors need plots, in order to select what material to use, and in what order. It was only slowly that I came to realise what the basic arguments of this book should be, and how they could be used to provide limits to what might otherwise be a virtually boundless enterprise. I must admit, though, to allowing myself on occasion to include material which I feel to illuminate the history of Cape society, even if it is not strictly relevant to those central plot-lines. Such indulgences aside, this book is now about (in two senses of that word) the following propositions:

1 During the eighteenth century, the Cape colonial society knew a wide range of interconnected, and not always consistent, statuses, which were proclaimed in a wide variety of ways.

2 During the course of the nineteenth century, these were overlaid, and in most cases came to be dominated, by the power of ideas of the social order deriving from Great Britain, and by a considerable stress on English ethnicity.

3 These ideas entailed the imposition of British ideas of respectability onto the Colony, which was particularly apparent in matters of gender.

4 This gave those outside the inner core of society the opportunity to make a bid for acceptance, by adopting the behaviour and the outward signs of respectable society.

5 Ultimately, the acceptance of such bids was conditional and partial. It relied on the denial of identity politics, and on the individualisation of society which was at the heart of Cape liberalism. However, such individualisation ran counter to the ethnicisation of political life, initially based on feelings of English superiority and then taken over by what was to become Afrikaner nationalism. In such a context, claims for acceptance could only be made by groups of people, defined on some criteria other than that of their individual respectability and in practice that which came to be seen as race. This process was exacerbated by the fact that many claims were negated, at least temporarily, by an ethnic exclusiveness hardening into racism.

6 These matters came to a climax in the mid-century political crisis. This intertwined the uprising of the disappointed, known somewhat erroneously as the Kat River rebellion, with the revulsion of many of the whites against colonial oligarchy. In this crisis, the deep politics of gender and respectability came together with the high politics of constitutional change. Out of it came the liberal constitution of 1853, one of the most 'democratic' in the world at the time, which recognised the achievement of respectability within its theory, at the cost of maintaining the ex-slaves and Khoi in a subordinate position.

7 There is a further argument which is implicit in all this. Respectability

was the outward manifestation of a specific class ideology. Because it was so successful, it came to be seen widely as part of the natural order of things. In the jargon it had become hegemonic. The result was to defuse class-based conflict within the Colony.[8]

The contours of this plot are specific to South Africa, as might be expected from a colonial society which united in itself so many elements usually only found singly. All the same, in this as in so much else, what went on in South Africa was part of a much wider process. The establishment of respectable society, on terms essentially established in Great Britain, was a global undertaking, an insidious, because totally informal, expression of cultural imperialism.[9] As such, it was the direct precursor of the attempted Americanisation of the world in the later twentieth century.

This drive for respectability had to begin by transforming the society of Great Britain itself. As such, of course, it was far from totally successful. All the same, a large proportion of nineteenth-century British social history has been written in terms of 'the rise of respectable society'. Even those who start from a Marxist point of view, when they are not primarily concerned with labour history, usually end up with much the same concerns.[10]

Just how successful the British were in spreading their ideals globally is a mute point. However, at least throughout the rest of the anglophone world, similar processes can be discerned. Richard L. Bushman has written about *The Refinement of America* in terms which are comparable, *mutatis mutandis*, to what was going on in Britain and South Africa.[11] Indeed the great cleavage of American history in the nineteenth century, which led to the Civil War, was in part the North's attempt to impose not merely its economic but also its cultural values on the South, and after emancipation (and indeed before it) many of the freed slaves came to embrace at least some parts of the northern ideology, much to the chagrin of their erstwhile masters. Something very similar can be discerned in the British Caribbean, notably in Jamaica. There the post-emancipation conflicts which culminated in the Morant Bay rebellion had many causes. The planters attempted to maintain the economic system they had dominated in as

[8] Many of these ideas were at least implicitly present in my first book, *Adam Kok's Griquas: A Study in the Development of Stratification in South Africa*, Cambridge, Cambridge University Press, 1976. It is thus perhaps surprising that I took so long to realise how applicable they were to what I was now attempting.

[9] One of its early, and most explicit, statements was in the Report of the (British) Parliamentary Select Committee on Aborigines, BPP 638 of 1837.

[10] See e.g. F. M. L. Thompson, *The Rise of Respectable Society: A Social History of Victorian Britain*, London, Fontana, 1987; Leonore Davidoff and Catherine Hall, *Family Fortunes: Men and Women of the English Middle Class, 1780–1850*, London, Hutchinson, 1987 and, in general, Miles Taylor, 'The Beginnings of Modern British Social History?', *History Workshop Journal*, 43, 1997, 1–76.

[11] *The Refinement of America: Persons, Houses, Cities*, New York, Alfred A. Knopf, 1992.

unchanged a form as possible. Ex-slaves took empowerment from religious movements, whether the reconstructed African faith known as Myalism or the forms of Christianity which, in a later South African context, would be described as independent churches. As important were the attempts of those – in a West Indian context mainly of mixed descent – who took the claims of imperial ideology as proclaimed at emancipation and by the first post-emancipation governors at face value, but who were blocked in their aspirations by the retained power of the planter class.[12] And, in a different key, it was the ideology of respectability which turned Pakeha New Zealand and, to a lesser extent, white Australia into more faithful copies of Great Britain than the original ever was.[13]

This, then, is in summary the argument which this book attempts to present. As an aid to understanding, though, it is probably necessary that a certain basic narrative of Cape history be presented, as this provides the context against which the rest of this book is set.[14]

The Cape Colony was founded in 1652 by the Dutch East India Company (VOC) as a refreshment station for its ships on the long haul between the Netherlands and the East. Initially, it consisted of little more than a fort on the shores of Table Bay, where Cape Town would later arise. From the 1680s onwards, the Colony began to expand, first into the immediate hinterland of Cape Town, where wine and grain farms were established, and then across the mountain ranges of the South-West Cape. In the interior, cattle and sheep farms were begun at a considerable rate, so that by the end of the eighteenth century the boundaries of white settlement were to be found on the Orange and Fish Rivers.

This expansion did not take place in a human vacuum, nor could it be achieved without labour. The latter was arranged by the import of slaves from all coasts of the Indian Ocean, probably somewhat over 60,000 in the course of a century and a half.[15] At the same time, the indigenous inhabi-

---

[12] E.g. Thomas C. Holt, *The Problem of Freedom: Race, Labor, and Politics in Jamaica and Britain, 1832–1938*, Baltimore and London, Johns Hopkins University Press, 1992; Gad Heuman, *The Killing Time: The Morant Bay Rebellion in Jamaica*, London and Basingstoke, Macmillan, 1994. A full-scale comparison of the Morant Bay and Kat River rebellions would illuminate both episodes but is beyond the scope of this book.

[13] E.g, James Belich, *Making Peoples: A History of the New Zealanders from Polynesian Settlement to the End of the Nineteenth Century*, Harmondsworth, Allen Lane for the Penguin Press, 1996, esp. pp. 278ff.

[14] For an extended discussion of this, and much more, see Richard Elphick and Hermann Giliomee (eds.), *The Shaping of South African Society, 1652–1840*, 2nd edn, Cape Town, Maskew Miller Longman, 1989; also Timothy Keegan, *Colonial South Africa and the Origins of the Racial Order*, Cape Town and Johannesburg, David Philip, 1996.

[15] Robert C.-H. Shell, *Children of Bondage: A Social History of the Slave Society at the Cape of Good Hope*, Hanover, NH and London, Wesleyan University Press, 1994, 40.

tants of the Cape, the Khoisan,[16] pastoralists and hunter-gatherers who had lived at low population densities throughout the region, were deprived of their lands and pasturage and reduced to labourers for the whites, in a position little different from, and often in fact worse than, that of the slaves. This did not go on without a struggle, and until the early nineteenth century there were continual low intensity wars between colonists and Khoisan, and right at the end of the eighteenth century a full-scale rebellion in the Eastern Cape, primarily driven by those who had been labourers on the farms. At the same time the incorporation of the Khoisan, both culturally and genetically, proceeded apace. This resulted in the creation of a group of people known as Bastards, the offspring of European or slave men and Khoisan women,[17] or at least those of Khoisan descent who adopted European mores.

By the late eighteenth century, the advance of European settlement was temporarily halted as the farmers reached the ecological boundary which had marked the western edge of African agro-pastoralism. The Xhosa and Thembu chiefdoms of what is now the Ciskei in the Eastern Cape proved a much more formidable military barrier than the Khoisan had ever done. Further expansion had to be northward, towards and across the Orange River. This was slow at first, but in the 1830s it led to the rapid expansion of white settlement into the Free State the Transvaal and Natal, most dramatically in the Great Trek of Afrikaners to the north and east.

At the same time, the Cape experienced a change of imperial master. From 1795 (with a short recession to the Dutch Batavian Republic from 1803 to 1806), the Colony was ruled by the British. With the Cape's inclusion in the British Empire, economic growth could proceed, if at an erratic and somewhat slow pace. Initially British settlement was not large, but in 1820 some 4,000 people were assisted in emigrating to South Africa. Most of them were settled in Albany district in the Eastern Cape. As there was also a steady influx of Britons into the Western Cape, notably into Cape Town, which remained the major city of the Colony and the centre of both government and social life, the British came to form a substantial minority of the white population and to dominate political and social life, particularly as the army, with the Governor at its head, was always a major presence. The British army, indeed, from 1811 onwards, was able to achieve a narrow military supremacy over the Xhosa, and in a succession of wars the

[16] This is a portmanteau word, deriving from an early twentieth-century collation of the Khoi, or Khoe, words for men (often used as Khoikhoi 'men of men') and San, the cattleless poor, who were outsiders to Khoi society, frequently spoke different languages and were known to the Europeans as 'bosjesmannen' or 'Bushmen'.
[17] Since the children of a slave woman remained a slave, no matter who their father may have been, and since there were few unions between Khoikhoi men and European women, 'Bastards' were of these parentages.

Eastern frontier of the Colony was driven forward, and the Xhosa expelled from much of their land.

A few years before the first British conquest of the Cape, there arrived the first missionaries, who began the steady process of converting and 'civilising' the Khoisan, the slaves and the Xhosa. Initially, the missionaries were members of the Moravian Brotherhood, of German and Dutch extraction, but later British non-conformists were the most important, certainly as regards their public profile and their explicitly formulated ideas as to what constituted Christian society and behaviour. In this they could draw upon the political resources of the Evangelical Revival in Britain, which was at the forefront of the campaigning to end the abuses of British colonial societies throughout the world. Thus it was that in 1807 the slave trade to South Africa was outlawed; in 1828, by Ordinance 50, the civil rights of the Khoikhoi and other free persons of colour were recognised; and in 1834 slavery itself was abolished, although it took another four years of so-called Apprenticeship before the slaves achieved *de facto* freedom.

Despite the transition to British rule, the inhabitants of the Colony, white and coloured, had little formal say over its government. In part this was because the Colonial Office in London did not wish to divest itself of power in favour of slave-holders or, after 1838, those who were thought still to hold the opinions deriving from the era of slavery. Eventually, though, the autocracy of the colonial rulers was recognised to be equally dangerous, and in 1854 a Parliament was instituted in Cape Town, with a franchise based not on race but on wealth. Indeed the threshold for voting was set relatively low. Nevertheless, those of at least partial European descent, whether English- or Dutch-speaking, continued to hold the monopoly over political office.[18] This, and the hesitant expansion of the economy, would continue until, in 1870, the discovery of diamonds in the semi-desert to the north of the Orange River would initiate a massive change in the nature of colonial society in South Africa.

---

[18] On why this statement is more hedged than might seem appropriate, see below, pp. 173–4.

2   Under the VOC

Clothing and display

In 1755, the Government of the Cape was faced with a problem. They had received the new regulations to control the display of pomp which had been issued in Batavia, and which in theory were also applicable in all the factories of the VOC. However, in certain particulars these regulations were not suitable for the circumstances in South Africa, and therefore the Council of Policy issued a *plakkaat* which modified, to some extent, the orders which had been issued for the rest of the Dutch Empire in the East. In so doing they demonstrated very clearly how they conceived the order of society in the Cape to be arranged, in theory if not always in fact.[1]

The High Government in Batavia had itself issued these regulations for a definite ideological purpose. As they wrote in the preamble to this ordinance, despite numerous ordinances to the contrary 'the splendour and pomp (*pracht en praal*) among various Company servants and burghers . . . reached such a peak of scandal' that the *Heren XVII* were forced to order the Government in Batavia to take measures against this. This was necessary

to prevent the ruin of many servants and citizens who, with little or no reflection or ruled by an intolerable puffed up pride, forget themselves and do everything almost to exceed the first ministers of the Dutch Company – in whose territory and rule distinction, according to station (*character*), and subordination are the major pillars on which rests the prosperity of the said Company and that of its servants, burgers and inhabitants – or at least to be equal to them in all externals, so that those few goods which they owned before being possessed by this cancerous and emaciating sickness are lost to them and they are brought by the passage of time into the most miserable circumstances, where they become the objects of derision and finally, withdrawing from the world's gaze, they pass such little time as is left to them.

---

[1] These *plakkaten* are to be found in J. A. van der Chijs (ed.), *Nederlandsch-Indisch Plakkaatboek 1602–1811*, 16 vols., Batavia and The Hague, Landsdrukkerij and M. Nijhoff, 1885–97, VI, 773–95, *plakkaat* of 30 Dec. 1754 and S. D. Naudé (ed.), *Kaapse Plakkaatboek*, III, Cape Town, Cape Times, 1949, 12–15, *plakkaat* of 15 July 1755.

In these circumstances, the unabated lust for display was conducive to a mentality which led 'such persons to lose respect for their betters, and above all those who, though in a higher and more prominent station than they, are not possessed of greater means and so must bear the insupportable from such wastrel Company servants, burgers and other inhabitants'. This denial of the principles of hierarchy might even lead to 'the disadvantage of both the Company, and of its true servants and burghers'. Therefore the Governor and his council decided to issue the *plakkaat* which then followed.[2]

The first section of the ordinance was concerned with the display which was allowed on the carriages and horses of the various ranks of Batavian society. In the first instance, only the Governor-General and the members of the Council of India (a body which included the Governor of the Cape) were allowed to decorate their carriages with gold and silver, and only those with the rank of Upper Merchant (in the Cape only the chief law officer, known as the *Fiscaal*, and the *secunde*) were permitted to decorate their carriages with their arms, or other personal emblem. The same rules applied to their wives' sedan chairs and to the small carriages in which children were transported about the town, although in these cases it was the status of the husband or father which was determinant. In Batavia it was further ordained that only the highest ranks were allowed to inspan more than two horses in their carriages and to employ Europeans to guide their horses, but at the Cape it was decided that this would be impracticable, given the nature of the roads and the necessity of bringing agricultural products to market. However, if Europeans were to be used for such tasks, they were not to be allowed to wear any form of livery whatsoever. In addition, individuals of lesser ranks had to give way to the Governor and members of the Council when they met them on the road.

The clothing of both men and women was subject to equally firm rules. Only the members of the High Government and the President of the Court of Justice (at the Cape, therefore, only the Governor), together with their wives and children, were allowed to wear clothing embroidered with gold or silver thread, while only those one step lower in the hierarchy were allowed to wear gold or silver buttons.[3] In addition, only Upper Merchants were allowed to wear velvet clothes, and only Lower Merchants and their

---

[2] Van der Chijs, *Nederlandsch-Indisch Plakkaatboek*, VI, 773–4.

[3] This is to a certain extent remarkable, since such buttons were a generally used method of storing wealth, even among common sailors. See Robert Ross, *Cape of Torments: Slavery and Resistance in South Africa*, London, Routledge & Kegan Paul, 1982, 59; Jan de Vries, *The Dutch Rural Economy in the Golden Age*, New Haven and London, Yale University Press, 1974, 218.

equals were allowed to wear gold or silver shoe buckles. The display of jewels by the women was limited by their value, as only those whose husbands were of high rank were allowed to wear jewellery worth above 1,000 Rix-dollars.

These regulations did not of course eliminate all competition between the women of Batavia to display the best finery. Even within the limits set by the Company it was possible to score points in the continual conflict for prestige. Frequently, indeed, comfort was subordinated to display, or some form of compromise was reached, so that, for instance, a man going on a visit would remove his long frock coat, sword and wig as soon as the initial greetings had been made, only to replace them in order to take his leave with suitable pomp.[4] Equally European fashions were much admired, and a woman newly arrived from Europe would be expected to appear in the latest finery at her first ball, and be inspected like a model on a catwalk.[5] Similarly, in Cape Town the latest European fashions were very closely followed, so that, for instance, the presence of large French garrisons during the 1780s led to the widespread adoption of French fashions, and gave Cape Town the temporary (and never repeated) appellation of 'Little Paris'.[6]

Some time later these last regulations had to be sharpened at the Cape, since it was noted that emancipated slave women were 'not only wearing clothes that were the equal of respectable burger women, but were many times exceeding them'. As a result, emancipated slave women were forbidden to wear 'coloured silk clothes, hooped skirts, fine lace or any other adornments on their caps or on their waved hair, nor ear-studs, whether of precious or false stones'. They were thus exclusively to wear chintz or striped linen. The only exception was that those of good character were permitted black silk dresses for marriages, when they were witnesses at a baptism or when for some other reason they went to church.[7]

Since slaves were one of the major articles of consumption in both Batavia and the Cape, it is not surprising that they too were used to demonstrate wealth, and therefore that the VOC came to regulate their clothing and numbers too. Thus only the wives and widows of members of the High Government were allowed to parade through the streets followed by a train of three slave women, and only women of such status were allowed to have their slaves wear gold and silver jewellery (though not even they were allowed to put diamonds or pearls into their slaves' hair). All

[4] F. de Haan, *Oud Batavia*, 2nd edn, 2 vols., Bandung, Nix, 1935, I, 537.
[5] De Haan, *Oud Batavia*, I, 544.
[6] M. Whiting Spilhaus, *South Africa in the Making*, Cape Town, Juta, 1966, 110.
[7] Naudé, *Kaapse Plakkaatboek*, III, 62, 12 Nov. 1765

Figure 1 Captain Hendrik Storm, with son, daughter and servants
(*Stellenbosch Museum*)

other women were only allowed two or, for the really lowly, one slave woman behind them. Similarly, only the highest in Batavia might dress their slave men in livery trimmed with braid or with aiguillettes. Those somewhat lower in the hierarchy were allowed to put their slaves (or at least three of them) in a simple livery. Thus the painting of Captain Hendrik Storm, commander of the Cape garrison, with his daughter, young son and slaves shows how the underlings wore the same basic clothing as their master, with the distinction of rank preserved (Figure 1).[8] Those men who held the rank of merchant or below could merely dress their slaves in red or blue linen, which might be striped as was desired, except that coachmen were allowed to wear a simple coat and hat, presumably as protection against the weather. By the same logic, slaves at the Cape could be dressed in woollen cloth, but it had to be 'totally plain, without any cuffs or collars of another colour'.

These rules as to the clothing of slaves suffered from one of the inherent contradictions in the institution of slavery itself. A slave could not be simply equated with a carriage or a frock coat. He or she was at once an object in

[8] This picture was painted around 1760.

the struggle for status and a participant in that same struggle. A slave might demonstrate his or her owner's importance, but it was still necessary that it was seen that he or she was a slave. The status of slavery itself had to be sufficiently marked. This too was done by forbidding slaves to wear certain articles of clothing, although apparently not by formal ordinance.[9] As the Swedish botanist and traveller C. P. Thunberg remarked, slaves 'as a token of their servitude, always go barefoot and without a hat', and he further noted that whenever a slave was emancipated the first thing he or she did was to purchase footwear and an extravagant hat.[10] Before then, slaves would indeed wear a cloth wound round their head as a turban, but the adoption of the concave conical straw hat so typical of Cape Town's Muslims in the early nineteenth century seems to have been more recent.[11] Slave clothing remained distinctive into the early nineteenth century. When the Cape Regiment was raised in 1806 from among the Colony's Khoi, their uniform was designed by their commander, Colonel John Graham, as 'Green and I flatter myself very neat; black facings and white lace, service trousers nearly the same colour as jacket'. However, to the dismay of the commander and the fury of his men, when the cloth for the uniforms finally arrived, some fourteen months later, it was found to be for a blue jacket, with scarlet facings, to be worn with a round hat with white tapes and plume. This outfit, Graham wrote, seemed to have been chosen purposely 'to disgust the men. It is the same they had with Dutch, whom they detest, and the same which the generality of the slaves wear in this colony.' Moreover, the War Office in London failed to send shoes to the Colony, apparently because 'an idea prevails in England that the Hottentots do not wear shoes'. Eventually, though, green and black uniforms were

---

[9] The matter is somewhat complicated. According to the 'Statement of the Laws of the Colony of the Cape of Good Hope regarding slavery', which was compiled by the *Fiscaal*, D. Denyssen for the use of the British in 1813, the only part of the *pracht en praal* regulations which were still applied was 'the prohibition of slaves wearing shoes and stockings' and even that was by then 'but little attended to'. *RCC*, IX, 159. However, at least in the published version of these regulations this does not appear, and indeed it is stated that the slave coachmen of important men might wear shoes and stockings. In the seventeenth century it had been laid down that only those slaves who spoke and understood good Dutch were allowed to wear a hat. *Nederlandsch-Indisch Plakkaatboek*, I, 459. Perhaps, despite his legal training, Denyssen confused an absolute custom with a dictate of the law.

[10] C. P. Thunberg, *Travels at the Cape of Good Hope, 1772–1775*, edited by V. S. Forbes, Cape Town, Van Riebeeck Society, 1986, 26, 35,

[11] Thunberg, *Travels*, 26. For an example of the turban, see the drawing by J. Rach in the *Atlas van Stolk*, Rotterdam, reproduced on the dust jacket of Ross, *Cape of Torments* and in A. F. Hattersley, *An Illustrated Social History of South Africa*, 2nd edn, Cape Town, Balkema, 1973, between pp. 62 and 63; see further, Robert C.-H. Shell, *De Meillon's People of Colour: Some Notes on their Dress and Occupations, with Special Reference to Cape Views and Customs: Water-colours by H. C. de Meillon in the Brenthurst Collection*, Johannesburg, Brenthurst Press, 1978.

introduced, more suitable for the Regiment's role as sharpshooters, and a mark of distinction from the Colony's slaves.[12]

These various signs for the identification of slaves were, in fact, insufficient. Shoes and hats could be acquired, if necessary by theft, and not everyone who was entitled to wear them actually did. As Graham pointed out, there was even the impression among the whites that Khoi never should wear shoes. As a result, slaves were on occasion able to pass themselves off as 'Bastard-Hottentots'. In this way they could desert their masters and travel relatively freely around the Colony, without being apprehended. In 1774, the Landdrost and *Heemraden* of Swellendam wrote to the Governor complaining of the practice and suggesting that a pass system be introduced for the 'Bastard-Hottentots'. This was indeed introduced, which had the added advantage, so the Council of Policy thought, that the 'Bastard-Hottentots' themselves could be better controlled. However, it does not seem as though the system worked at all effectively, since six years later the Stellenbosch authorities were to complain of precisely the same problem.[13]

Hierarchy, age and gender

It is perhaps necessary to enquire why the rulers of the Cape placed such an emphasis on such matters of dress and display. It may not be enough to describe the outward show of status as an inevitable part of human society. Rather it is possible to see it as emanating, at least in part, from the structure of eighteenth-century Dutch society, whether in the Netherlands or overseas. The governing class of the Netherlands, particularly in the province of Holland, was relatively open, allowing those who had accumulated wealth through mercantile or manufacturing activities to work their way into the *patriciaat*. Unlike, for instance, contemporary England, those who wished to become members of the towns' governing bodies, which was the essential first step to acceptance in the elite, did not have to be landowners. Indeed few of their colleagues were. Rather they derived their incomes,

---

[12] Cited in Ben Maclennan, *A Proper Degree of Terror: John Graham and the Cape's Eastern Frontier*, Johannesburg, Ravan, 1986, 29–30. Graham did not know that the shipment sent from London agreed fairly exactly with what had been requested for the Khoi regiment by General J. H. Craig in 1796, who believed that the recruits could make their own shoes, and that they would receive two cotton shirts, which were easily procured in Cape Town. See Craig to Dundas, 26 Oct. 1796, *RCC*, I, 474.

[13] Landdrost and *Heemraden*, Swellendam, to Governor Van Plettenberg, 25 Oct. 1774, printed in Donald Moodie (ed.), *The Record: Or a Series of Official Papers Relative to the Condition and Treatment of the Native Tribes of South Africa*, Cape Town, 1838–41, reprinted Amsterdam and Cape Town, Balkema, 1960, III, 34; *Resolutien van de Raad van Politie*, 6 Dec. 1774, ARA VOC 4278; Nigel Worden, *Slavery in Dutch South Africa*, Cambridge, Cambridge University Press, 1985, 127.

in large part, from the interest on the capital they had invested in government stocks and so forth. Nevertheless, whereas an established family might suffer a temporary decline in fortunes without this leading to immediate expulsion from the elite, newcomers were required to demonstrate their financial standing by maintaining a lifestyle appropriate to the position they wished to claim. Indeed all members of the *patriciaat* were required by social norms to live in a manner which accorded with their status. Thus, although this status could not be bought, it could be acquired by the use of money for public display.[14] The attitudes that this engendered were transported to the colonies. Both the officials and the burghers of Batavia were renowned for their personal display, as, perhaps even more, were their wives.[15] At a more modest level, so were those at the Cape. While there were few Cape families which were able to convert their wealth at the Cape into a position within the Netherlands governing elite,[16] the basic norms of metropolitan Dutch society, requiring those who possessed substantial fortune or high position to act as befitted their status, were nevertheless followed there, perhaps even to an exaggerated degree in comparison to the Netherlands.

Perhaps because the public world of the Cape was so exclusively male, the distinctions of rank were stressed particularly by the elite women of the Colony. O. F. Mentzel, the most informative writer on the Cape during the eighteenth century (though he was writing from memory some forty years after his unwitting departure from the Colony),[17] describes how an elaborate code of precedence dominated all relationships, and was itself prior to mere friendship. He gives an example of the contortions to which this could lead:

A and B were, as girls, the closest friends – more than sisters to each other. Both were daughters of under-merchants, but A had social precedence over B because her father was senior in rank to B's father. Both married under-merchants but B's husband was senior in standing to A's. All at once B's presence became hateful to A. Their long friendship was at an end. A avoided B whenever she could; she would not go to any function where B was expected. Nothing that B had done was

---

[14] J. J. de Jong, *Met goed fatsoen: De elite in een Hollandse stad, Gouda, 1700–1780*, Amsterdam, De Bataafse Leeuw, 1985; L. Kooijmans, *Onder regenten: De elite in een Hollandse stad, Leiden, 1700–1780*, Amsterdam, De Bataafse Leeuw, 1985; M. Prak, *Gezeten burgers: De elite in een Hollandse stad, Hoorn, 1700–1780*, Amsterdam, De Bataafse Leeuw, 1985; Simon Schama, *The Embarrassment of Riches: An Interpretation of Dutch Culture in the Golden Age*, London, W. Collins, 1987, esp. ch. 5.

[15] De Haan, *Oud Batavia*, esp. II, 119–49.

[16] The most significant, and perhaps the only one, of these was the Swellengrebel family. See G. J. Schutte (ed.), *Briefwisseling van Hendrik Swellengrebel jr oor Kaapse sake, 1778–1792*, Cape Town, Van Riebeeck Society, 1982, 3–4.

[17] In 1741, he went to say goodbye to a friend who was on a ship bound for Europe, fell asleep on board and awoke to find that the ship had already set sail.

responsible for this change in A's attitude. The fact was that by marriage their social status had changed. B now had precedence over A because of her husband's rank, and A could not become reconciled to the change. Most ladies hold that A's conduct was right and proper; that there was no other way; to me it all seems very petty.[18]

In addition, the etiquette of visiting and so forth was very sharply defined by the status which the women derived from the male heads of their families. While there was thus a female world parallel to the public world of men, women could not break out of it, except those who had been widowed. Then they were seen as the independent heads of their households.[19]

The distinctions were indeed much more rigorously observed by the women among themselves than in mixed company, for instance at Cape Town dances, although Mentzel stresses that a merchant's son would be more likely to dance with a townsman's daughter than a burgher's son with the daughter of a high official.[20] This may have resulted from the fact that the dancing couples would have been unmarried, since, certainly for the women, it was marriage which fixed the status they would then occupy. Until then, there was always the possibility that they might come to assume a status significantly higher or lower than the one they then enjoyed. Childhood, or at least adolescence, was allowed somewhat more licence than was granted to those who by their marriage had passed beyond that state.[21] Against this, however, it should be stressed that the formal presentation of children, as for instance when their portraits were taken, did not differ from that of their parents, at least until the last decades of the eighteenth century. Hendrick Storm's nine-year-old son is portrayed in exactly the same way as his father, although whether he would have been so dressed in ordinary life is another matter.[22]

Shame and punishment

To return to the public sphere, the first task of the ritual activities performed by the high officials of the Dutch East India Company was to demonstrate the power and the majesty of the VOC itself over the Colony that it had created. This was most regularly and most effectively done by the public executions ordered by the Cape Government. One example may

---

[18] O. F. Mentzel, *A Geographical and Topographical Description of the Cape of Good Hope*, trans. H. J. Mandelbrote, 3 vols., Cape Town, Van Riebeeck Society, 1921, 1924, 1944, II, 107. The work was originally published in Glogau in 1785.
[19] The *opgaaf* rolls, or annual tax lists, confirm this classification.
[20] Mentzel, *Description*, II, 105.   [21] *Ibid.*
[22] Daphne H. Strutt, *Fashion in South Africa, 1652–1900*, Cape Town and Rotterdam, Balkema, 1975, 137–8. How they dressed in less formal moments is of course another matter altogether, and their dress should certainly not be thought of as demonstrating that the concept of childhood had not been developed. See below, p. 87.

serve for many. On 2 July 1767, Alexander van Banda, who had murdered one of his fellow slaves, Magdalena van de Caab, apparently because he was jealous of her sexual awakening – he had been responsible for her upbringing – was sentenced by the Court of Justice

to be brought to the place usually used for the execution of criminal sentences and there delivered over to the executioner, to be tied to a cross and then to have his limbs broken, from the bottom up [in other words, beginning with the legs], without the *coup de grace*, and to remain there until the spirit shall have departed. His body will then be transported to the outer gallows field and then again tied to a wheel (*rad*), with the murder weapon above his head, as prey to the winds and the birds of the heavens.[23]

There are certain additional matters of importance in connection with this and other criminal sentences. First the full sentence, which included a full description of Alexander's offence and the note that the Cape Government was acting in accordance with the powers granted to it by the States General of the United Netherlands, was sent to the Governor, Rijk Tulbagh, to receive his *Fiat Executie*. Secondly, it was read out to the assembled Cape population (and for that matter to Alexander) from the balcony of the Castle. Thirdly, the execution ground was alongside the only road into Cape Town, between the Castle and the sea (approximately where the railway now runs). Those who entered the town from the countryside would therefore be confronted with the rotting bodies of executed criminals. While I obviously do not know how long a corpse would remain before it disintegrated, such executions were sufficiently frequent for it to be unlikely that the gallows would ever be entirely empty. On the other hand, the corpses of those who had committed crimes outside of Cape Town were often displayed near the scene of their actions. Thus the Cape Town suburb now known as Mowbray was originally called *Drie koppen* (Three heads) after such an exhibition, while after his abortive rebellion in 1739 various parts of Etienne Barbier's body were strung up at several locations in the Roodezand Kloof and elsewhere.[24] In 1767, not in any way an exceptional year, nine individuals were put to death and displayed, and one other who had died in custody was also strung up, since it was considered that, had she lived, she would have suffered the same fate. In addition, one man was drowned in the sea for sodomy and a woman was burnt at the stake for arson.

The lingering and exceedingly painful death imposed on Alexander van Banda may seem peculiarly barbarous to our sensibilities, as if capital

---

[23] VOC 10967, case 14.
[24] C. Pama, *Wagon Road to Wynberg*, Cape Town, Tafelberg, 1979; George McC. Theal (ed.), *Belangrijke Historische Dokumenten verzameld in de Kaap Kolonie en elders*, 3 vols., Cape Town and London, 1896–1911, I, 2, 12.

punishment itself were not barbarous enough. It was, however, in line with what was done at the time in the Dutch Republic,[25] and was indeed not the worst that the Cape Court of Justice could impose.[26] Moreover, the barbarity at the Cape had a clear social purpose. The members of the Court of Justice expressed this clearly when, in 1796, immediately after the first British take-over of the Cape, the new rulers expressed their displeasure at the extended capital punishments carried out there. The Court in its answer claimed, perhaps somewhat disingenuously, that the principles of punishment were the same irrespective of the status of the criminal in question. However, they did admit that 'with regard to slaves, . . . the equality of punishment ceases when they commit offenses against Europeans or free persons, particularly their Masters'. They derived this principle from the Roman law:

> Slaves were considered by the Romans as Creatures who from their enured bodies & their rude and uncultivated habits of thinking were much more difficult to correct and to deter from doing evil, than others, who from better education & better habits measure the degree of punishment by their internal feelings rather than by bodily pain: and this reasoning may be justly applied to our modern slaves, many of whom are descended from wild and rude Nations, who hardly consider the privation of life as a punishment unless accompanied by such cruel circumstances as greatly aggravate their bodily sufferings.

Without the excessively painful punishments, they argued, there would be no way 'to prevent the Slaves from disturbing the tranquility of the Family'.[27] Terror had to be used to control the slave population, and it had to be seen by them to be doing so.

The same principles of display also operated for the various other punishments applied at the Cape. It was not merely the physical pain that gave public floggings and brandings such efficacy as they may have possessed. Rather, the very fact of an individual having been on the scaffold was enormously shameful for him or her.[28] This was the reason why the criminal sentencers made a distinction between floggings carried out in or out of the

---

25 Peter Spierenburg, *The Spectacle of Suffering: Executions and the Evolution of Repression; from a Preindustrial Metropolis to the European Experience*, Cambridge, Cambridge University Press, 1984, 66–74. This section in general relies to a considerable extent on Spierenburg's book for its inspiration.

26 On this in general, see Robert Ross, 'The Rule of Law at the Cape of Good Hope in the Eighteenth Century', *Journal of Imperial and Commonwealth History*, 9(1), 1980, 5–16.

27 Craig to President and Members of the Court of Justice, 7 Jan. 1796, *RCC*, I, 298–300; Court of Justice to Craig, 14 Jan. 1796, *ibid.*, 302–9. This last statement would seem to call into question those arguments which claim that the slaves were seen as a genuine if inferior part of the family, let alone those which claim that the slaves saw themselves as such. See Shell, *Children of Bondage*, esp. ch. 7; cf. Robert Ross, 'Paternalism, Patriarchy and Afrikaans', *SAHJ*, 32, 1995, 34–47.

28 Spierenburg, *Spectacle of Suffering*, 66–9, 87–9.

public eye. This was also why, on occasion, they considered it right to have a man or woman stand on the scaffold with a noose round the neck, or have him or her kneel while the executioner waved a sword over his or her head. The shame of the public display of infamy was punishment in itself.

In one of the symbolic inversions which was enacted at the Cape, the servants of the *Fiscaal*, or official prosecutor and head of police, were themselves criminals, banished to the Cape from Batavia. They themselves were thus symbolically unclean, which could act as an extra deterrent or punishment for those with whom they came into contact. This came to the surface in the incident which sparked off the Patriot agitation at the Cape in 1779. The *Fiscaal* sent his servants, known as the 'kaffers', to arrest a certain Carel Buitendagh, a thoroughly disreputable burgher who had caused considerable difficulties on the northern frontier.[29] That he was taken by the kaffers was an extra insult, for, as the *Fiscaal* W. C. Boers later stated, 'it is true . . ., the kaffers one has to make use of are evil, yes very evil and the very dregs of humanity. They have almost all been on the scaffold themselves (*geschavotteerd*), and thus the least familiarity or connection with them is not very honorable.'[30]

The rituals of state

The greatest event of the year for the demonstration of the authority of the VOC at the Cape was the arrival of the return fleet from Batavia, under the command of a high official of the VOC who was, as it was then known, repatriating to the Netherlands. In principle, this fleet sailed as a single unit, with the Admiral's ship in the centre of a diamond formation, although naturally storms could disrupt the definite order.[31] When this fleet arrived in Table Bay, the harbour master was to inform the Governor of this happy event. Two members of the Council of Policy, with its secretary, would then proceed on board to escort the Admiral on land. When he set foot on shore he was greeted with a twenty-one-gun salute (or less if he was a relatively minor official) from the Castle. On the jetty, he was met by the Governor and the other members of the Council, by the lesser officials and by those burghers who held office in the various official bodies, in their uniforms. The various burgher military bodies would be drawn up along the route to the Castle, with their colours flying, while within the Castle itself the

---

[29] Nigel G. Penn, 'Anarchy and Authority in the Koue Bokkeveld, 1739–1779', *Kleio*, 17, 1985, 24–43.

[30] *Missive van Bewindhebberen der Oost-Indische Compagnie geschreven den 13 October 1785, met copie van alle de stukken, brieven, resoluties &c. relatief tot het werk van de Caab*, 4 vols, The Hague, for the VOC, 1785 (better known as the *Kaapsche Geschillen*), III, 143.

[31] Mentzel, *Description*, I, 103–4.

Company's forces would also be arraigned. When the visiting Admiral entered the Castle's courtyard they fired three volleys in salute. If the Admiral was accompanied by his wife, the senior ladies of Cape Town would wait on her in the apartments provided for the visiting couple in the Castle, but they did not otherwise take part in the official ceremonial. For his stay in Cape Town, the Admiral would lodge with the Governor, and, if he were a returning Governor-General, would review the conduct of the Government and issue instructions for its better conduct.[32]

The other major celebration in the course of the year was of the birthday of the Prince of Orange, at least during those periods when a prince was installed as *stadhouder* of the various provinces of the Netherlands and Director-in-Chief of the VOC. On those occasions, the trumpeters opened the day from the ramparts of the Castle by playing the *Wilhelmus*, the celebration of William the Silent which became the anthem of the House of Orange, and later of the Kingdom of the Netherlands. Thereafter, the guns of the Imhoff battery gave a twenty-one-gun salute, which was answered by all the ships, both Dutch and foreign, in the roads of Table Bay.[33] In 1772, at any rate, the Governor, Joachim van Plettenberg, gave a banquet that evening at his residence in the Gardens to the members of the Government, the other leading Company servants, the captains and important passengers on the ships in the harbour, the 'most distinguished' of the burghers and 'the leading young people of both sexes'. This ended in a ball which lasted till deep in the night.[34] There is no mention that this was repeated in other years, but this may have been an oversight on the part of the Company diarist, as it was clearly a private banquet. On the other hand, in 1772, Van Plettenberg was still attempting to establish his position following the death of Rijk Tulbagh the year before, and indeed Pieter van Reede van Oudtshoorn would be sent out the next year to replace him.[35] In other words, the ball itself may have been designed to strengthen Van Plettenberg's position in the Cape, and its reporting to the Netherlands would strengthen his position with the Prince and the *Heren XVII*.

Much more irregular were the occasions when a new ruler was formally introduced to the population of the Colony. This could occur *in absentia*,

---

[32] H. C. V. Leibbrandt (ed.), *Precis of the Archives of the Cape of Good Hope*, 17 vols., Cape Town, Richards, 1896–1906, *Requesten*, I, 169; DR 18 Jan. 1772, VOC 4269; Anna Böeseken, 'Die Nederlandse Commissarisse en die 18de Eeuse samelewing aan die Kaap', *AYB*, 7, 1944.

[33] There were in general a considerable number of ships at anchor, since the birthday of Willem V, Prince of Orange for much of the late eighteenth century, chanced to fall in early March when the fleets were usually still in Cape Town.

[34] DR 8 Mar.1772, VOC 4269.

[35] In the event, Van Oudtshoorn died on the voyage to the Cape, and so Van Plettenberg was installed definitely as governor.

as was the case when the Prince of Orange, Willem V, attained his majority and took over the duties of his station in 1768,[36] or when a new Governor-General of the Netherlands Indies took office in Batavia,[37] but a new Governor of the Cape Colony was naturally presented in person.[38] On all these occasions the Council of Policy and other officials took an oath of allegiance in the Council chamber. Then the members of the Government went out onto the veranda of the Castle and made formal speeches to the Cape citizenry assembled in the courtyard, ending with the question whether they were prepared to accept the new ruler. This was answered with a great shout of 'Yes'. There then followed extensive feasting, which was spread over several days to ensure that the whole garrison was not drunk simultaneously.[39]

Two funerals, Elizabeth Swellengrebel and Rijk Tulbagh

The greatest display of both the pomp and the hierarchy of the VOC establishment at the Cape came at irregular intervals, namely at the occasion of the funeral of the Colony's Governor or his wife. A print of the formal procession which accompanied the body of Baron Pieter van Reede van Oudtshoorn to his grave has been preserved in the *Atlas van Stolk* in Rotterdam, and is illustrative of such occasions (Figure 2). Nevertheless, it is the funerals of Rijk Tulbagh in 1771 and of his wife Elizabeth Swellengrebel some eighteen years earlier which give the opportunities to analyse the ways in which these ceremonies were carried out.[40]

Rijk Tulbagh died on Sunday, 11 August 1771, aged seventy-two. He had been Governor of the Colony for twenty years, and was apparently much respected. From then until he was buried the following Saturday the bells tolled for three hours a day, and the flags flew at half mast. On the evening of the 12th his body was transported from his house to the Castle on the shoulders of twelve junior officials of the Company, surrounded by a multitude of torches and accompanied by the new head of the Cape Government, Joachim van Plettenberg, and by many others of the official hierarchy. There it lay, under constant guard of two grenadiers until the funeral itself.

On 17 August the ceremony, which had been arranged by the

---

[36] RCP 8 Jan. 1768, VOC 4254, f458.

[37] K. M. Jeffreys (ed.), *Kaapse Archiefstukken*, 7 vols., Cape Town and Pretoria, Cape Times and Staatsdrukker, 1926–38, IV: *1780*, 373f.   [38] E.g. DR 18 May 1774, VOC 4278.

[39] O. F. Mentzel, *Life at the Cape in the mid-Eighteenth Century, being the Biography of Rudolph Siegfried Allemann*, trans. by Margaret Greenlees, Cape Town, Van Riebeeck Society, 1919, 111.

[40] These descriptions are based on DR 13 Oct. 1753, VOC 4191 and DR 11 and 17 Aug. 1771, VOC 4266.

Figure 2 The funeral procession of Governor van Reede van
Oudtshoorn (*Atlas van Stolk, Rotterdam*)

Commander of the Militia and the Secretary of the Council of Policy, took place. The bells of both the Castle and the church tolled alternately for half an hour from seven in the morning until two in the afternoon when the procession began. As was the case with all major rituals at the Cape, it consisted entirely of men. The Castle guns began to fire a salute every minute. In the van marched the Burgher Infantry, with the band playing the dead march on its drums and trumpets. Then followed the Company's horse artillery, pulling the three light cannons which the Cape possessed, and then the rest of the garrison. All the soldiers wore black velvet bands round their hats, while the guns were decorated with the same stuff. Behind the military were displayed Tulbagh's personal and official insignia, namely his standard, his horses, his arms, his helmet, his commander's baton, a tabard decorated with his arms, his gloves and his unsheathed sword. The horses were led by the stablemen and the other ornaments carried by ranking Company officials. Ending the van of the procession were eight undertakers, no doubt dressed in their best black clothes.

The centre of the procession was of course the coffin. It was carried by twelve lower officials of the Company (bookkeepers and assistants), while another six marched alongside them to relieve them at regular intervals. In addition four Under-Merchants carried the corners of the mourning cloth, and the whole coffin was guarded by a sergeant, a corporal and twelve grenadiers. Behind the coffin followed Tulbagh's *bloedvrienden*[41] and his executors and then all the members of the Government who had no specific task in the procession. Naturally they were in precise order of precedence, beginning with the acting Governor and the members of the Council of Policy, and proceeding downwards through the clergymen, the members of the Court of Justice, the surgeons, the members and ex-members of the *Burgerraad* and the other official bodies, ending with the ex-deacons of the church, the sick-visitors and the heads of the Company's workshops. The final position in the train was taken up by 'certain burgers who do not belong to the burger militia'. Then, bringing up the rear, was the Company cavalry.

Clearly, this procession was a complete representation of the hierarchy of the Cape's officialdom, not merely in fact but also in theory. This can be seen, for instance, from the fact that in his description of the procession for Elizabeth Swellengrebel's funeral the official diarist mentioned that Rudolph Siegfried Alleman marched in two places in the train, in his dual capacities as head of the Company forces and member of the Council of Policy. As this was evidently beyond his powers, it is clear that the description given by the diarist, and thus by myself, was somewhat idealised, and

---

[41] Literally 'blood friends'. A detailed analysis of the meaning of this term follows below.

not a literal description. For the purposes of this book, of course, it is none the worse for that.

The procession proceeded out of the Castle and through to the Heerengracht, the main thoroughfare of the town (modern Adderley Street). From there it went left up the street and then turned left again into the square behind the church. Care had been taken that the space in the centre of the square had been left vacant, and the Company's forces then arraigned themselves around its sides, presenting arms until the body was taken into the church, where, accompanied by trumpets, it was lowered into the grave. The signal was then given for the firing of salute volleys, first by the field pieces and then by the assembled soldiery. At this moment the tolling of the bells and then firing of the minute guns ceased, although the volleys were answered by the Castle's guns. After this, the main battery of the Castle fired a nineteen-gun salute, and the other batteries discharged lesser numbers of shots. At the time, in August, there were no ships in Table Bay, otherwise they would have answered these salutes. The ceremony having been completed in 'perfect order and without the least confusion, notwithstanding the great mass of spectators', the procession paraded back to the Castle.

This order, it should be stressed, was not purely the result of the display that the Company hierarchy arranged to demonstrate the power of the Colony's rulers. Symbolic power was of great importance, but it was never enough to guarantee control over the potentially unruly town. Thus, on the day of the funeral, all the drinking shops were ordered to be closed until after the ceremony was over, the 'servants' of the Court of Justice and the *Fiscaal* were arranged along the route with half-pikes to control the masses should it be necessary and there were companies of the Burgher Militia who did not take part in the parade, but were rather ordered to patrol the streets to prevent disturbances by 'slaves and other evil people'.

The most salient category in the procession was, of course, the *bloed-vrienden*. In the case of Rijk Tulbagh's funeral, the diarist does not record who they were precisely, but eighteen years earlier, when his wife died, this information was given. On that occasion, forty-three men were mentioned, while the only woman was in the coffin. Of these men only fourteen were actually related, by blood or marriage, to Elizabeth. Their connection to her can be seen in Figure 3. For the other twenty-nine no immediate connection can be found, so that it can only be assumed that they were in some way or other members of the Tulbagh–Swellengrebel household, close friends or at any rate clients of the couple. For instance Rijk Tulbagh's future executor walked, in a lowly position, in this group. In addition, two of the men in this category were themselves called Rijk, not a common Dutch name, presumably to honour their fathers' patron.

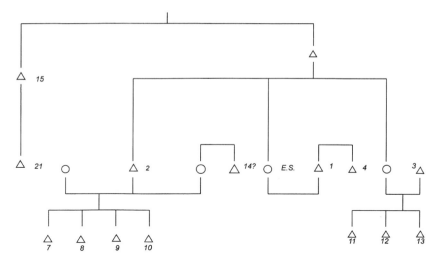

Figure 3 Diagram of the funeral procession of Elizabeth Swellengrebel

Key
Triangles represent men, circles women. The numbers refer to the
individual in question's place in the order of precedence; missing
numbers therefore refer to those in the procession without evident
kinship connection to Elizabeth Swellengrebel (E.S.). The women
represented in the diagram, other than E.S., are there to show
genealogical links, but did not walk in the procession.
  1 Rijk Tulbagh, Governor
  2 Hendrik Swellengrebel, ex-governor
  3 Frans Le Sueur, *Predikant* in Cape Town
  4 Johannes Tulbagh
  7 Johannes W. Swellengrebel
  8 Hendrik Swellengrebel Jnr
  9 Willem M. Swellengrebel
 10 Ertman B. Swellengrebel
 11 Jacobus Johannes Le Sueur
 12 Petrus Lodewyk Le Sueur
 13 Hendrik Le Sueur
 14 Lambert van Ruyven*
 15 Sergius Swellengrebel, *Secunde*
 21 Sergius Swellengrebel Jnr

 * Hendrik Swellengrebel only married Helena van Ruyven after his
    return to Holland a year later. The precise nature of Lambert's
    connection with the Swellengrebel/Tulbagh family cannot therefore be
    ascertained, but it would seem plausible that there was some connec-
    tion at least.
Source: C. C. de Villiers, *Geslagsregisters van die Ou Kaapse Families*,
edited by C. Pama, 3. vols., Cape Town and Amsterdam, Balkema, 1966.

Two other points are of very considerable interest. The first is that the order in which the men walked in this procession was determined by their relation to the dead woman, not by their status in the Colony. Thus Sergius Swellengrebel, who was Elizabeth's uncle, took his position after her nephews, even though he was the *secunde*, the number two in the whole Colony, and they were as yet of very minor importance. For all the stress on the hierarchy of the Colony that is manifest throughout the day's events, the family, widely defined to include dependants (though not slaves) and, perhaps, close personal friends, was at the centre of the proceedings. The kin and connections even of people who lived as much in the public domain as did a Governor and his wife were seen to be more important on such an occasion than their official colleagues.

Secondly, and most confusingly, the list of *bloedvrienden* included a number of men who were certainly not actually present at the funeral. The second in the list, Elizabeth's brother and ex-Governor of the Colony Hendrik Swellengrebel, for instance, had sailed to Europe as Admiral of the homebound fleet two years earlier, and several others could not be found in any list as being at the Cape in 1753. Perhaps some form of substitute was in their place, but this seems unlikely.[42]

The life-cycle rituals of the burghers

The great state funerals of the Colony's Governors were reproduced, *mutatis mutandis*, lower down the social scale. Mentzel describes how 'funerals are simple or elaborate according to the wealth or the importance of the deceased', but that the distinction lay not in the degree of ceremonial, which was always relatively sparse, but rather in 'the greater number of mutes and bearers, in a greater throng of mourners and in more expensive funeral furnishings' which would be seen for the burial of the rich. Even the poorest of the free did not go to the earth without ceremony. When the fourteen-year-old Cornelis Walboom died in 1725, the Deaconry of the Cape Town church paid 29 florins for a coffin, a barrel of wine, 150 cakes, three loaves of bread grated to breadcrumbs (presumably to be made into some sort of pudding), pipes and tobacco for his funeral.[43] As with the great processions for the Governor or his wife, women did not attend the funeral.[44] As in Holland, the position of the grave – in the church or in the

---

[42] There is a contrast here with the description of Tulbagh's funeral, when it was explicitly stated that the Landdrost and *Heemraden* of Swellendam, who should have taken up their positions in the parade, had been unable to reach Cape Town in time to do so.

[43] Maria M. Marais, 'Armesorg aan die Kaap onder die Kompanjie, 1652–1795', *AYB*, 6, 1943, 20.

[44] Mentzel, *Description*, II, 123; for another description, see Robert Percival, *An Account of the Cape of Good Hope*, London, C. Andr. Baldwin, 1804, 275.

graveyard, near the pulpit or not – was of great importance, and the church consistories could charge differential rates for this sort of privilege.[45] The importance attached to the display of rank at funerals can also be seen from the remarkable provision that the number of mourners who might follow a slave's coffin to the grave was dependent on the status of his or her owner.[46]

These were of course regulations and practices which related to Cape Town and the nearby countryside.[47] In the more thinly settled districts, far from a church or a centre of population, funerals were much more private affairs, though still a matter for care and concern. At the end of the century, John Barrow wrote of the farmers around Plettenberg Bay:

> To almost every home was attached, generally in a grove of trees, a small inclosure with ornamented walls, serving as the family burying-ground. The decorations usually bestowed on those mansions of the dead appeared to have much more engaged the attention than those of the living. In the internment of the dead, the Dutch have no kind of service or ceremony.[48]

Since in a Calvinist theology the ceremony of burial could have no effect on the ultimate destination of the deceased's soul, there was no reason to go to any greater lengths. The religious content of the funeral was merely to remind the living of their mortality and thus encourage their spiritual reformation. At the same time, it could be used to remember the dead man or woman, and to stress the deceased's status, and thus that of his or her relatives.

Marriages, too, were of course occasions for the display of status. As we have seen, they marked the end of juvenile status. Moreover, the choice of a partner was of consummate importance. At one end of the scale, it was virtually impossible for the Governor's daughters to find a suitable mate, and in general they were forced to return to Europe to find someone to whom they could be married 'without disparagement'.[49] At the other end of the social scale, a knecht found it very difficult to marry into the ranks of the established farmers. In 1729, for instance, Claas van Mook, who was living and working on the farm of Hendrik Neef near Riebeek-Kasteel in the Swartland, asked his employer (who he incidently addressed as 'Vader [father] Neef') for the hand of his stepdaughter Catharine Knoetsen. Neef's reply was most eloquent of the social order: 'No, not to you, but if you had

---

45 Leibbrandt, *Requesten*, I, 354; RCP 13 Nov. 1764, VOC 4239, on the institution of a new graveyard in Cape Town. cf. T. van Swigchem, T. Brouwer and W. C. A. van Oss, *Een huis voor het woord: Het protestantse kerkinterieur in Nederland tot 1900*, The Hague, Staatsuitgeverij, 1984, 7; H. W. Saaltink, 'Om de plaats van het graf', *Holland*, 19 (1987).

46 Naude, *Kaapse Plakkaatboek*, III, 6. This *plakkaat* was regularly repeated, but seems not always to have been observed; D. Denyssen, 'Statement of the Laws of the Colony of the Cape of Good Hope regarding Slavery', *RCC*, IX, 159.

47 See Mentzel, *Description*, III, 117, for a description of the country funerals.

48 John Barrow, *Travels into the Interior of Southern Africa*, 2 vols., London, Cadell and Davies, 1801–4, I, 342–3.   49 Mentzel, *Description*, II, 116.

been a farmer's son, I would have said Yes.' ('Neen . . . aan jou niet, maar dat je een boeren seun was, dan wel.') The result was a fight in which Neef was killed, and for which Claas van Mook was eventually hung.[50]

Once a suitable partner had been found the ceremony was performed with considerable luxury. The sumptuary laws issued in Batavia laid down how extensive the bridal meal might be, who was allowed to erect bridal arches outside the bride's house, what clothes the bride and groom might wear and how many slave women, in what costumes, might accompany the bride, all according to the status of the groom or the bride's father.[51] This did not prevent very considerable festivities. Thus, in 1795, Cornelius de Jong, *Schout-bij-nacht* (Vice-Admiral) of the Dutch navy, married Maria Magdalena Le Sueur, eldest daughter of the ex-landdrost of Stellenbosch. Their importance was such that the Commissioners of the matrimonial court, whose duty was to check that there was no impediment to marriage, themselves called at the house of the bride to perform the necessary formalities. At that moment, all sorts of snacks – 'tea, preserves, lemonade and cakes' – were served, and that evening a supper and ball, known as the 'Commissioners' meal', were held in honour of the bridal pair. On that occasion so many guests were invited that it became necessary to move from the house of the bride's father to the residence of the Governor in the Gardens. In all 160 people sat down to the meal, in their best finery in which 'as you know, the Cape women particularly excel'. After the requisite time for the reading of the banns announcing the marriage, the ceremony itself took place, not, as was usual, during the regular service in church, but at another time, since 'this prevents the great and unpleasant flood of curious and frequently rude spectators who always cause difficulties at such occasions'. This had naturally to be paid for. They then drove by coach to Le Sueur's country residence at Rondebosch. There another party was held for fifty guests, who danced till late in the night.[52]

It may well be that the wish to avoid the crush of a wedding during a Sunday service was a symptom of some increased level of privatisation at the Cape by the last years of the Company's rule. Mentzel's description of the events some forty years earlier does not suggest this as a possibility, but rather stresses the public nature of the ceremony, with 'stroysel' of gold leaf and tin foil being strewn before and around the bride as she entered the

---

[50] *Case against Claas van Mook*, 21 Mar. 1729, VOC 4112. There were of course many knechten who managed to marry into the farming community, these sorts of prejudices notwithstanding. However, they were almost certainly a small minority of the knechten, and in a number of cases, including the most famous, their wives were widows, rather than *boere dochters*.

[51] Van der Chijs, *Nederlandsch-Indisch Plakkaatboek*, VI, 787–8, 790–2.

[52] Cornelius de Jong, *Reizen naar de Kaap de Goede Hoope, Ierland en Norwegen in de Jaren 1791 tot 1797*, 3 vols., Haarlem, François Bohn, 1802–3, III, 79–81.

church, and enormous care being taken over the decoration of the house and the dress of the various parties.[53] No doubt, though, Cornelius de Jong and Maria Le Sueur would have been accompanied by a best man and bridesmaids, and all care would have been taken with their attire and the adornment of the places where the festivities were held. Probably, too, De Jong and 'she in whose possession my whole happiness is now held'[54] would have been ceremonially led to their marriage bed, and left to begin their married life there.

In the countryside, weddings were necessarily rather simpler than in Cape Town itself, although there can be no doubt that the festivities were just as extended – and enjoyable – as in Cape Town.[55] Those who lived in the agricultural districts of the South-West Cape, close to the Commissioners of the matrimonial court and to the churches, which until 1787 were all within a hundred miles of Cape Town, would have found no difficulty in fulfilling the requirements of the state for matrimony, but even those who lived in the depths of the Colony, and who had to journey for up to six weeks to reach Cape Town, did not shirk from the process.

Of all the ceremonies, baptism was the least surrounded by pomp and display. As Mentzel describes it, the child's father and a close friend to act as sponsor went to the pulpit rail with the child (who was generally carried by a slave) after the conclusion of the sermon at a Sunday service. The clergyman then read the service of baptism, with the godfather making the responses, and proceeded to christen the child in the font. Apparently no further festivities were generally held on such occasions.[56]

Even though the ceremony of baptism was not particularly marked, it was, with marriage, of paramount importance within the structure of Cape society, far more indeed than the much more evident funerals. A burial, after all, signals the end of a person's life, and thus, as at the Cape, is not necessarily an affirmation of the continuity of the social world. In contrast, marriage was the necessary condition for the procreation of legitimate members of society, and baptism was the affirmation that a baby was to belong to that select group.

As always, the importance of such rituals can be best seen by examining those incidents at which social classification was uncertain or contested, not those where there was no doubt as to an individual's standing. The crucial case occurred in the last decade of Company rule. In 1787, the Council of Policy decided, at the request of the Burgher Military Council, to institute a new militia company in Cape Town. Until then there had been

---

[53] Mentzel, *Description*, II, 117–20.   [54] De Jong, *Reizen*, III, 81.
[55] E.g. Mentzel, *Description*, III, 116–17; H. Lichtenstein, *Travels in Southern Africa in the Years 1803, 1804, 1805 and 1806*, trans. by A. Plumtre, 2nd edn, 2 vols., Cape Town, Van Riebeeck Society, 1928–30, II, 99.   [56] Mentzel, *Description*, III, 122

a single distinction between the burghers and the emancipated slaves, who, as we shall see, were mustered into the Fire Service. Now, it was considered necessary to form a new company, known as the Free Corps, which would perform the same duties as the burghers but would be for those 'who, though not born in slavery, have not been born in wedlock, and for that reason cannot be enrolled among the burghers doing service; also that they cannot very well be employed with those at the Fire Engines and Public Works, who have been born in slavery'.[57] Thus, what was considered of significance for this social category was their birth, in freedom but not within a legitimate marriage. It was the religious and official ceremonies which were thought to be sufficient to create the necessary distinctions within society.

These criteria were, in the event, inadequate. A few years later, Johannes Smook, a thoroughly respectable burgher who had even been promoted to Corporal of his own Corps on the very day that the new Free Corps had been instituted,[58] challenged the rulings that were being made in these matters. His own sons, who had been born in lawful wedlock, were refused entry to the Burgher Cavalry, but were rather enrolled in the Free Corps. The Burgher Military Council thus had to reinterpret its own statements and equate those born out of wedlock with

such other inhabitants whose parents have not been born in a state of freedom. It is . . . evident that the real intention of the burgher Military Court was that such residents whose father or mother had been born in a state of slavery should belong to and do service in the Free Corps, in order thus to be dissociated from the burghers, as otherwise the establishment of such a Corps would not have been necessary.[59]

In other words, two criteria which were considered entirely coincident were found not to be so, and the stigma of slave descent was thought to be more important than that of Christian marriage.

Many of the same considerations surrounded the matter of baptism. In 1775, the Swedish naturalist Anders Sparrman was in the region of modern Caledon, where

I saw two brothers . . ., the issue of a Christian man and of a bastard[60] negress of the second or third generation. One of the sons, at this time about thirty years of age, seemed not to be slighted in the company of the Christian farmers, though, at

---

[57] Leibbrandt, *Requesten*, I, 170–1.

[58] Leibbrandt, *Requesten*, I, 171. Smook had been one of the butchers who contracted to supply the VOC with meat for the period 1779–84, in partnership with two of the Van Reenen brothers. This also demonstrates that he was one of the leading members of Cape Town's burgher elite. See Gerard Wagenaar, 'Johannes Gysbertus van Reenen – Sy aandeel in die Kaapse geskiedenis tot 1806', MA thesis, University of Pretoria, 1976, 39–40.

[59] Leibbrandt, *Requesten*, I, 222.

[60] It should be noted that in Dutch, and thus presumably in Sparrman's use of Swedish, 'bastard' means 'mongrel' rather than, or in addition to, 'illegitimate'.

that time, he had not been baptized. The other, who was the elder brother, in order to get married and become a farmer, as he then was, had been obliged to beg, and probably even bribe, to become baptized.

Sparrman could not conceive why the clergymen of the Cape were so reluctant to administer this sacrament, certainly in contrast with the Catholics who had forced it on the heathen 'with fire and sword'. However, he gave a hint of the reason when he wrote, further, that:

> It is true, a great many of the whites have so much pride, as to hinder, as far as lies in their power, the blacks or their offspring from mixing with their blood; but it appears to me that Christian humility ought to operate so far with the clergy, as to prevent them from being ashamed to see their black fellow-creature walking cheek by jowl with them on the road to heaven.[61]

It would clearly be too much to hope that the clergy would go against the accepted social rules of the society in which they worked. What was at issue here were the principles of classification within the Cape Colony. A major distinction was evidently made between the 'Christians' – those who had been baptised – and the 'heathens', who had not been. It is true that this was overridden by the even more fundamental distinction between the slaves and the free. Thus, it was possible to baptise slaves without jeopardising their slave status, even though this was not done with great regularity except by the VOC itself for those of its own slaves who were born at the Cape.[62] Among the free, baptism was a crucial sign of status. This was what gave privileges and acceptance into the mainstream of rural society and it was thus a closely guarded privilege. Those who could claim it did so. There are few instances of parents presenting children for baptism who were at that moment more than a year old, and these were usually born out of wedlock and christened after they were legitimated by their parents' marriage.[63]

The stress placed on baptism can also be seen from the attitude of the religious and secular authorities to the first Moravian missionary in South Africa, Georg Schmidt, who came to the Colony in 1737. He encountered

---

[61] Anders Sparrman, *A Voyage to the Cape of Good Hope, towards the Antarctic Polar Circle, round the World and to the Country of the Hottentots and the Caffers from the Year 1772–1776*, edited by V. S. Forbes, trans. J. and I. Rudner, 2 vols., Cape Town, Van Riebeeck Society, 1975–6, I, 264.

[62] Richard Elphick and Robert Shell, 'Intergroup Relations: Khoikhoi, Settlers, Slaves and Free Blacks, 1652–1795', in Elphick and Giliomee, *Shaping*, 188–9. The listing of Company slaves in ARA VOC 4347 makes it clear that all children born in the Company's slave lodge were baptised.

[63] Despite occasional comments by travellers of delayed baptism and despite the great distance of the frontier boers from the nearest church (which could be as much as 500 miles before the foundation of Graaff-Reinet in 1787), a study of Afrikaner genealogies shows that the number of multiple baptisms was in fact less than could have been predicted purely on the incidence of twin births. See Robert Ross, 'The "White" Population of South Africa in the Eighteenth Century', *Population Studies*, 29, 1975, 210–22.

little opposition to his work until, after four years, he began to baptise the Khoi whom he had gathered around him. At this moment, both the Reformed *predikanten* and the VOC Government turned against him, and forced him to abandon his work. They may have had good theological reasons for this, since Schmidt's ordination was highly dubious and they mistrusted the Moravian brotherhood itself. They also wished to preserve the monopoly of the Reformed faith at the Cape and were at that moment in conflict with the Colony's Lutherans on this very issue. Nevertheless, it is very hard not to believe that the social meaning of baptism played no part in their deliberations, even though it was not made explicit.[64]

By the end of the century, though, the rite of baptism was beginning to lose its social significance. With the establishment of a church at Graaff-Reinet in the frontier region in 1787, a subtle shift in the attitude of the Reformed Church authorities towards proselytisation and the founding of the first permanent missions in the colony in the following decade, a new social group, known as the 'baptised bastards' came into existence. As the term suggests, they were people of at least partial Khoi descent who had gained entry to the church. On the basis of the latter criterion they began to claim various rights from which they had previously been excluded, occasionally in vigorous fashion.[65] As a result, in the early part of the nineteenth century, baptism ceased to be a sure social sign. As will be shown later in this book, other signs would have to be found to delineate the cleavages within Cape society.

The Bastards, the Free Blacks and the Fire Service

Within the social structure of the Colony, there were two main groups which might be considered as taxonomically anomalous, neither slave nor free, neither burgher nor Khoi. These were the 'Bastards' and the Free Blacks. The Bastards, whether baptised or not, were very largely to be found on the geographical fringes of the Cape Colony, and in time many of them moved right beyond its borders to establish what became known as the Griqua captaincies north of the Orange River.[66] There they did their

---

[64] H. C. Bredekamp and J. L. Hattingh (eds.), *Das Tagebuch und die Briefe von Georg Schmidt: Dem ersten Missionar in Südafrika*, Bellville, Wes-Kaaplandse Instituut vir Historiese Navorsing, 1981; Bernhard Krüger, *The Pear Tree Blossoms: A History of the Moravian Mission Stations in South Africa, 1737–1869*, Genadendal, Genadendal Printing Works, 1966, 31–9.

[65] Hermann Giliomee, 'The Eastern Frontier, 1770–1812', in Elphick and Giliomee, *Shaping*, 456–8.

[66] The name 'Griqua' came into existence when an English missionary considered that the term 'Bastaard' would not go down well in his home country, and asked the Bastard community in Klaarwater (modern Griquatown) what alternative name they wished to choose. 'Griqua' is a mishearing on his part of the old Khoi tribal name 'Guriqua'.

best to reclaim a position within the colonial hierarchy, behaving as far as possible in the ways in which they had seen the frontier farmers doing.[67] Many others were not so lucky, and those with slave fathers and Khoi mothers in particular were pressed into the service of the farmers, on a level little if any better than that of the slaves themselves.[68]

The Free Blacks ('Vrije zwarten'), in contrast, lived almost entirely in the Western Cape, and very largely in Cape Town itself, where they worked at a variety of occupations, with many fishermen and small retail traders amongst their number. The taxonomic principle by which this group was defined was not what might be expected on the basis of a knowledge of later South African history. Khoi and Xhosa were not described as 'zwarten', but as 'Hottentotten' and 'Kaffers', terms which were admittedly to become even more derogatory.[69] Rather, a Free Black was either an emancipated slave or an ex-convict, one of those men banished to the Cape from Batavia in punishment for some crime.[70] As a result, the Chinese in Cape Town, most of whom were in this latter category, were considered to be among the Free Blacks, which would have been anomalous if skin colour had been the principle of distinction employed. Moreover, as is made clear by the case of Johannes Smook's children, described above, Free Black status was not passed on from parents to their children, at least not via the female line, although the stigma of slave descent was maintained, if perhaps only for one generation. Passing up into burgher society was certainly possible. At the end of the century, Samuel Hudson wrote that, though manumission was rare,[71] when it was granted chances for social mobility existed.

several persons in Cape Town of great wealth and respectability have been formerly slaves or descended from them. One Generation does away the Stain and though it may be remembered by some Ill-natured persons they are generally received by the Inhabitants according to their present situation in life. If wealthy, by the first in the settlement.[72]

---

[67] Martin Legassick, 'The Northern Frontier to c. 1840: The Rise and Decline of the Griqua People', in Elphick and Giliomee, *Shaping*, 373, 376–84.

[68] Richard Elphick and V. C. Malherbe, 'The Khoisan to 1828', in Elphick and Giliomee, *Shaping*, 28.

[69] Interestingly, a man from New Guinea, whose physiognomy presumably was not dissimilar to that of the Xhosa, was named 'Martinus Kaffer'. Case of 7 Aug. 1704, ARA VOC 4051.

[70] On the west coast of Africa, the Dutch made an analogous distinction between the 'negers', who were slaves, and the 'zwarten', who were free Africans. See Johannes Menne Postma, *The Dutch in the Atlantic Slave Trade, 1600–1815*, Cambridge, Cambridge University Press, 1990, 228.

[71] Elphick and Shell, 'Intergroup Relations', 135–45. See also below, ch. 7, for a discussion of manumission and emancipation.

[72] Samuel Eusebius Hudson, 'Slaves', edited by Robert Shell, *Kronos, Journal of Cape History*, 9, 1984, 64.

There are indeed a very few such cases known from the history of the Cape in the eighteenth century.[73]

From 1722, the Free Blacks of Cape Town were organised into a militia company, as indeed were the burghers. The main difference was that, whereas the burghers bore arms and performed various ceremonial duties, the Free Blacks' task was expressly to fight fires and to prevent the looting of ships wrecked on the beach.[74] The reason for this specific task must be seen not so much in the functional requirement for the extinction of fires, great as this was in a city where the houses were roofed with thatch and which is notorious for the strength of its winds. When a major fire broke out, in fact everyone came out to fight it.[75] Rather, it must be seen against the background of the fear which the slave-owners had of their slaves. Not without reason, they were seen as arsonists, and also as the looters of wrecks *par excellence.*[76] It was thus a thoroughly explicable form of symbolic inversion that it was the manumitted slaves who had to justify their freedom, as it were, by combatting the efforts of their former fellows in bondage.

The stereotyping of slaves

The hierarchical ordering of the Cape Colony was continued in the perceptions that were held of the slaves by those above them. There was indeed no general stereotype of the slaves as such, except in the most generalised possible terms. Rather the slaves were distinguished according to their land of origin, and characteristics attributed to them on that basis. The Europeans who wrote on the Cape were fairly consistent in their stereotyping of slaves by land of origin.[77] The basic distinctions were made between slaves of

---

[73] E.g. Margaret Cairns, 'Geringer and Bok; a Genealogical Jig-saw', *Familia*, 13, (1976); J. L. Hattingh, *Die Eerste Vryswartes van Stellenbosch, 1679 -1720*, Bellville, Wes-Kaaplandse Instituut vir Historiese Navorsing, 1981; H. F. Heese, *Groep sonder Grense (die rol en status van die gemengde bevolking aan die Kaape 1652–1795)*, Bellville, Wes-Kaaplandse Instituut vir Historiese Navorsing, 1984; Hermann Giliomee and Richard Elphick, 'The Origins and Entrenchment of European Dominance at the Cape, 1652–c. 1820', in Elphick and Giliomee, *Shaping*, 551.

[74] South Africa, Archives Commission, *Kaapse Plakkaatboek, 1652–1806*, 6 vols., Cape Town, Cape Times, 1944–51, II, 93.

[75] E.g. Mentzel, *Life at the Cape*, 100–1; Ross, *Cape of Torments*, 54.

[76] *Kaapse Plakkaatboek*, II, 90.

[77] E.g. Robert C.-H. Shell, 'S. E. Hudson's "Slaves" ', *Kronos: Journal of Cape History*, 9, 1984, 46–8; *Gleanings in Africa* (London, James Cundee, 1806), 58–9; Percival, *Account of Cape of Good Hope*, 296–8; Mentzel, *Description*, II, 129–31, III, 109; Sparrman, *Voyage*, II, 152, 258; W. W. Bird, *State of the Cape of Good Hope in 1822*, London, John Murray, 1823, 72–3; W. J. Burchell, *Travels in the Interior of South Africa*, edited by I. Schapera, 2 vols., London, Batchworth Press, 1953, I, 27–8; A. Gordon-Brown (ed.), *James Ewart's Journal*, Cape Town, Struik, 1970; Robert Semple, *Walks and Sketches at the Cape of Good Hope, 1805*, 2nd edn, Cape Town and Amsterdam, Balkema, 1968, 47–9; Barrow, *Travels*, I, 45, II, 108–9.

Indonesian, of Indian and of African and Malagasy origin, although by no means all authors employed the same taxonomy. Perhaps the most extensive description of the attitudes of the whites is that given by Robert Semple during the First British Occupation. He wrote of a Cape Town woodcutter that:

His black complexion, his curly hair, his thick lips, and his tattooed forehead, announce him from the coast of Mozambique, his strong make shows him capable of fatigue, and in his inoffensive and humbled countenance, you may read that he often submitted to blows and unmerited reproaches without for a moment thinking of revenge; he performs the task which is set him without objections and without inquiry.

On hearing the music of one of his compatriots, though, 'pleasure steals into his soul . . . [he] gives himself up to the wildest and most inconsiderate joy, and, occupied only with the present, thinks neither of the hours of bitterness which are past, nor of those which are yet to come'.

In contrast, a Malay[78] was

the king of slaves. As he approaches, mark his long, coal black hair which hangs half down his back, his yellow complexion, his glancing and jealous eye, which looks askance upon slavery. He knows well that from his class are formed the housepainters, the musicians, the ingenious workmen of the Cape. He is proud of this distinction and glories in the name of Malay.

When reproached by his master, so Semple believed, the Malay would hoard up the insult in his heart until it burst out. Then

he intoxicates himself with opium and the madness of revenge, he rushes upon his unguarded master with his kris or crooked Malay dagger, and stabs him once, twice, ten times. The unfortunate wife and children are not safe, if they cross his way, he sallies into the street, and running madly along, sacrifices all that he meets, till overpowered by numbers he is brought to suffer the punishment of his crime.[79]

Intermediate between these two was the slave who hailed from the Malabar coast.

He is in all respects the best of the household slaves. Without the inactivity or dulness [sic] of the Mozambiquer, or the penetrative genius of the Malay, he forms an excellent medium between the two – More intelligent, more industrious and more active than the former; more docile and more affectionate than the latter, he unites steadiness with vivacity, and capability of instruction to winning manners.[80]

---

[78] In these English works of the turn of the eighteenth century, the term 'Malay' probably refers only to these slaves' origin, and has not yet acquired the religious connotation that it now has in South Africa. On this, see below, ch. 7.

[79] Running amok, as here described by Semple, was indeed not unknown at the Cape. See, e.g., Edna Bradlow, 'Mental Illness or a Form of Resistance: The Case of Soera Brotto', *Kleio*, 23, 1991.   [80] Semple, *Walks and Sketches*, 47–9.

This favourable stereotype of the Malabaris may of course have been influenced by the fact that by the late eighteenth century there were very few Indian slaves at the Cape any more. Indonesians and, increasingly, Africans and Malagasies formed the great majority of those not born at the Cape.[81] In general, the Mozambicans (and indeed the Malagasies) were seen as stupid and only fit for menial labour, while the Malay slaves were seen as skilled but dangerous. Within this latter category, distinctions were also made. Joachim von Dessin wrote to his agent in Batavia requesting that slaves of a good 'caste' be sent him, although he was equally concerned with the skills they possessed.[82] The inhabitants of some islands in the archipelago were given specific attributes. Thus the Bugis men from South Sulawesi were thought of as demonstrating to excess the qualities which made Indonesian slaves in general so feared and mistrusted. They were very strict in their demands for justice and particularly prone, when slighted (or disciplined by women), to exact revenge by murdering their master's family and running amok. The women, in extension of this view, were considered to be exceptionally faithful and fine lovers, who also demanded faithfulness from their partners. They were thought able to punish any transgressions in this regard by magically causing the offender's penis to shrink, thus presumably inflicting impotence.[83]

Surprisingly missing from many of these accounts is a clear distinction between those slaves who had been born in the Colony and those who had been imported. Slaves of Indonesian descent were thought to maintain their characteristics even though native to the Cape. Against this, however, it was reported by Mentzel, one of the best observers at the Cape, that the offspring of European men and slave women were particularly prized as 'better mannered and better educated than imported slaves'.[84]

Even though the falsehood of such stereotypes as descriptions of whole

---

[81] Shell, *Children of Bondage*, ch. 2.

[82] J. L. M. Franken, ''n Kaapse huishoue in de 18de eeu uit von Dessin se briefboek en memoriaal', *AYB*, 3, 1940, 17. Von Dessin used the word 'caste' in his Dutch letter. For an exposition of its changing meaning see J. Pitt-Rivers, 'On the Word "Caste" ', in T. O. Beidelman (ed.), *The Translation of Culture: Essays to E.E. Evans-Pritchard*, London, Tavistock, 1971, 231–56.

[83] Sparrman, *Voyage*, II, 258; Mentzel, *Description*, III, 109; J. S. Stavorinus,, *Voyages to the East Indies*, trans. S. H. Wilcocke, 3 vols., London, G. G. & J. Robinson, 1798, II, 398. See also Sirtjo Koolhof and Robert Ross, 'Upas, September and the Bugis at the Cape of Good Hope: The Context of a Slave's Letter', *SARI: A Journal of Malay Studies*, forthcoming. In this regard it is instructive to relate the list given to Sparrman by a Hanoverian farm bailiff of 'the constant order of precedence which ought to be observed among the fair sex in Africa: . . . First the *Madagascar* women, who are the blackest and best; next to these the *Malabars*, then the *Bugunese* or *Malays*, after these the Hottentots, and last and worst of all, the white Dutch women.' Sparrman, *Voyage*, I, 101 (original emphasis).

[84] Mentzel, *Description*, II, 130.

classes of people must have been regularly demonstrated to the slave-owners, they nonetheless influenced their actions in a number of ways. The logic of scientific falsification is after all rarely used in normal social life. There were different price structures for slaves of different origins.[85] Slaves of African and Malagasy origin may have been overrepresented among the menial labourers of the Colony, although the distinction was by no means absolute and there were many Indonesians and Cape-born slaves in the fields.[86] The experience that these slaves had before arriving at the Cape may, however, have effected such distinctions, which were necessarily those of probabilities rather than absolutes. More telling were the actions of the Government in response to what were seen as slave outrages. The murder of a high official by a gang of Bugis and Sumatran slaves was enough for them to prohibit the importation of new Indonesians.[87] In this case the actions of a small number of men led to a measure relating to all those of their place of origin. No greater evidence for the depth of awareness of ethnic differences could be found.

The question then arises as to how far ethnic awareness played a role of any importance among the slaves themselves. As might be expected, given the heterogeneity of the slaves, both ethnically and in their experience at the Cape, the evidence is contradictory. Asian and African languages continued to be spoken at the Cape into the nineteenth century.[88] The musical traditions of the slaves' homelands were still maintained – or at least there were clear differences between them as performed in Cape Town.[89] There were occasions when slaves gloried in the qualities of their nation in Indonesia, but these were comparatively rare.[90] The large groups of slaves which occasionally gathered in resistance to the established order were usually, but not always, of many different lands of origin, and generally, but again not always, this did not lead to friction.[91] It would at any rate seem that the divisions in the slave mass seen by the masters and their associates were not of such salient importance to the slaves themselves.

[85] Shell, *Children of Bondage*, 51.   [86] *Ibid.*; Worden, *Slavery in Dutch South Africa*, 93.

[87] Ross, *Cape of Torments*, 1; Van der Chijs, *Nederlandsch-Indisch Plakkaatboek*, VIII, 291–2.

[88] Burchell, *Travels*, I, 32; Marius F. Valkhoff, *Studies in Portuguese and Creole, with Special Reference to South Africa*, Johannesburg, Witwatersrand University Press, 1966, 231; Achmat Davids, 'The Afrikaans of the Cape Muslims from 1815 to 1915: A Socio-linguistic Study', MA thesis, University of Natal, 1991; Elizabeth Helen Ludlow, 'The Work of the London Missionary Society in Cape Town, 1812–1841', BA hons. thesis, UCT, 1981, 10, 35, 39: it is however doubtful whether the services in Malagasy to which she refers were attended by ex-slaves or by those who, like the missionary in question, were refugees from anti-Christian persecution.

[89] Lichtenstein, *Travels*, II, 425.

[90] E.g. case 22, *against Baatjoe van Mandhaar*, 21 Oct. 1757, VOC 4209; case 5, *against Augustus van Mandhaar*, 3 Feb. 1759, VOC 1759. Mandhaar is a region on the island of Sulawesi.   [91] This is based on Ross, *Cape of Torments*, esp. chs. 4 and 5.

Hierarchy and the limits of hegemony

The degree to which the slaves were able to transcend the ethnic divisions between them which were recognised by the master class raises a major problem for the understanding of hierarchy in eighteenth-century South Africa, namely the extent to which the unequal order was accepted by those who suffered under it. It is a problem which is difficult to address, because of the deficiencies of the evidence, as was seen by one of the sharpest critical intelligences ever to observe a system of slavery, even if only briefly. Charles Darwin's career as a naturalist was almost aborted when, during the *Beagle*'s visit to Brazil, Captain Fitzroy, a Tory martinet, related how the slaves he had met all claimed to be contented in their bondage. Darwin's reply, that no other answer was conceivable from slaves in the presence of their owners, nearly led to him being turned off the ship, but was of course thoroughly perspicacious.[92] No statement by a slave accepting his or her slavery made to a slave-owner, or to someone who could be presumed to be allied to the owners, can be accepted at face value, nor, *a fortiori*, can any made by a slave-holder about the opinions of the slaves.[93]

It is in part for this reason – and in part because they give otherwise unobtainable insights into many aspects of daily life – that historians have turned to the voluminous records accumulated in the course of criminal proceedings.[94] These have demonstrated that there were a number of slaves who took drastic, indeed almost suicidal, action against their oppressors, and many others who deserted their owners and took to living in the hills of the Western Cape, when they could not escape the Colony altogether, or travelled into the Cape interior, or to Europe or Asia on board a ship. They also show that the slaves acted very largely as individuals. Until the early nineteenth century there is no sign of a community in the Western Cape, except to the extent that Islamic teachers were beginning to build underground networks which would come to the surface with the establishment of the first mosques immediately after the turn of the century.[95] Put the

---

[92] Adrian Desmond and James Moore, *Darwin*, London, Michael Joseph, 1991, 120.

[93] There is a useful analogy to be drawn with the position of domestic servants in modern South Africa, as reported by Jacklyn Cock. In *Maids and Madams: A Study in the Politics of Exploitation*, Johannesburg, Ravan, 1980, she reports that a substantial minority of the employers considered their employees to be members of their family, but not a single one of the employees felt likewise. See pp. 87, 132.

[94] Ross, *Cape of Torments*; Worden, *Slavery in Dutch South Africa*; Nigel Worden, 'Violence, Crime and Slavery on Cape Farmsteads in the Eighteenth Century', *Kronos: Journal of Cape History*, 5, 1982, 43–60.

[95] Adil Bradlow, 'Imperialism, State Formation and Establishment of a Muslim Community at the Cape of Good Hope, 1770–1840: A Study in Urban Resistance', MA thesis, UCT, 1988.

other way, this would seem to suggest that slave discontent was not yet expressed in a consistent idiom, let alone one which was given by the master class.

Study of the criminal records, however, cannot be expected to provide information as to the slave population of the Colony as a whole. Clearly, only a small minority of the slaves ever figured in them as leading characters, or even as witnesses, and those who did were, almost by definition, those who were less well adapted to the white-run society. The argument could be made that there was a small proportion of slaves who were not prepared to accept their own place in the hierarchical order of society, rebelled against it and so became 'criminals', and a large majority who were peaceable, law-abiding, submissive subjects. Formally speaking, there is no way to test the validity of this argument, but in practice it seems absurd. Rather it is much more sensible to employ Occam's razor and assume that the inchoate resistance of those slaves who are visible to the gaze of the historian is an indication of a far more widely spread, although less violent, inchoate resistance within the slave population as a whole.

In general terms, then, while the relations of the Cape Colony's rulers to their immediate underlings may have been characterised by a fair degree of acceptance, those between them and their slaves certainly were not.[96] The rules of deference which the Company elite imposed were followed – how could they not be? – but there is no evidence to suggest that they were internalised and every reason to believe that they were not. The various languages – physical, material and verbal – by which the slaves were required to demonstrate their subordination, may be thought of as an attempt by the Cape's rulers to achieve their hegemony, but in such a situation even the outward show of deference should be seen as the success of their rule, as something enforced, not accepted.

---

[96] The distinction I am making here is derived from that employed by Gramsci between 'rule' and 'hegemony'. In this I am following Raymond Williams, *Marxism and Literature*, Oxford, Oxford University Press, 1987, 108–9.

3   English and Dutch

In the winter of 1795, a British expedition under General Sir James Craig and Admiral Elphinstone sailed into False Bay and landed at Simonstown. It carried with it orders from the Prince of Orange, as hereditary director of the Dutch East India Company, to the commanders of the Dutch establishments overseas, that they should surrender to the British until such time as the conclusion of peace should restore the independence of the Republic of the Netherlands. The Prince had of course been driven out of the Netherlands by the invasion of the French, who were themselves welcomed by the numerous 'Patriot' opponents of the House of Orange and of the old order in general.[1]

For almost two months the negotiations between the British and the VOC officials in Cape Town continued. Eventually, the Dutch decided, somewhat half-heartedly, to expel what they had come to conceive of as foreign invaders. They came to this decision too late, however, as the British received timely reinforcements which allowed them swiftly to overrun the main defensive lines of the VOC, at Muizenberg, and to establish their rule in Cape Town. The commander of the Dutch forces, Robert Gordon, himself a protégé of the Prince, was so torn between his various loyalties, and so ashamed of the performance of the troops under his command, that he committed suicide. A contributory factor in his decision was that, in the event, the British did not rule in the name of the Prince of Orange, but rather in that of His Britannic Majesty King George III. But for a single short interlude of three years a decade later, the Cape was to remain in British hands for more than a century.

During the negotiations, which preceded the Battle of Muizenberg, General Craig wrote to the Company administration informing them of the options before them, as he saw it. If they did not accept British suzerainty, then they would be faced with

---

[1] Hermann Giliomee, *Die Kaap tydens die Eerste Britse Bewind, 1795–1803*, Cape Town and Pretoria, HAUM, 1975, 44; on the Patriot movement and the Netherlands in the French revolutionary wars, see above all Simon Schama, *Patriots and Liberators: Revolution in the Netherlands, 1780–1813*, New York, Alfred A. Knopf, 1977.

a Government on French principles of Jacobinism, . . . Liberty, Equality and Fraternity, possibly under the protection of a French force – with the dissemination of the too captivating idea of universal freedom and the rights of man among your Slaves (the universal practice of the French, by which they have already laid waste the finest islands of the West Indies), forcing the unfortunate Inhabitants of the Settlement from the peaceable enjoyment of their homes and families in the Country to meet the guillotine on your market place. You have to encounter the total want of money, necessaries & succours from the mother country, the failure of your markets and the entire annihilation of the little commerce which you now enjoy.[2]

What Craig and Elphinstone were propounding was an argument which had become commonplace among the officer corps of the British military to which they, and indeed all the British Governors of the Cape Colony until 1854 (bar two), belonged. It was their justification for fighting the war against the French in which they were engaged. But it was of wider import. The late eighteenth century saw, it has been argued, the emergence of a clear British nationalism, for the first time, and Anti-Gallicanism was perhaps the main theme and source for what would later be known as English chauvinism.[3]

Of course, it was not just against the French that the British vented their feelings of superiority. While it would have been tactless for Craig and Elphinstone to attack the Dutch, with whom they were after all negotiating, in general the British flattered those who had been their enemies in the seventeenth century even less than they did those who they were to fight until 1815. When Dutch power and prosperity was at its height, the Netherlands were the envy of Europe, castigated for their meanness, avarice and obesity.[4] When their relative fortune waned, the Dutch were seen as but a shadow of their former glory. An anonymous author who had apparently been attached to the British embassy in the Hague was exemplary in his judgement. He wrote:

Thus *virtue*, the main spring of commonwealth, no longer subsisted among the Dutch; the public was poor; the great riches of individuals destroyed the equality necessary to a free state; their avarice, still greater than their wealth, extinguished public spirit, its necessary principle; their trade was decreasing, their manufactures diminished; their navigation on the decline; their public finances in ruin, and their

[2] Elphinstone and Craig to Sluyskens and the Raad van Politie, 29 June 1795, *RCC*, I, 95–6.
[3] Gerald Newman, 'Anti-French Propaganda and British Liberal Nationalism in the Early Nineteenth Century: Suggestions toward a General Interpretation', *Victorian Studies*, 18, 1975, and *The Rise of English Nationalism: A Cultural History, 1740–1830*, London, Weidenfeld & Nicolson, 1987; Linda Colley, 'Whose Nation? Class and National Consciousness in Britain 1750 -1830', *Past and Present*, 113 (1986); and, *Britons: forging the nation, 1707–1837*, New Haven and London, Yale University Press, 1992; Hugh Cunningham, 'The Language of Patriotism, 1750–1914', *History Workshop Journal*, 12 (1981).   [4] Schama, *Embarrassment of Riches*, 257f.

fisheries expiring; and their navy, their barrier, their military strength, their great commercial companies, their government, their administration, their consequence, their whole republic, were in the last stages of degradation, debasement and decay.[5]

These sentiments were echoed by the first Englishmen to rule the Cape of Good Hope. Robert Percival, a Captain in the British army who was dismayed at the Dutch so often fighting on the wrong side, wrote of them that:

Dead to all sense of public interest, and to every generous sentiment of the soul, the thirst of gain and individual aggrandisement has extinguished from amongst them the spirit of patriotism, the love of glory, the feelings of humanity and even the sense of shame. A total want of principle prevails in Holland. Every other sentiment is absorbed in the desire of riches, which the stupid possessors want taste to convert to any pleasurable use or real enjoyment; but which are superior in the eyes of a Dutchman to all the talents of the mind and all the virtues of the heart. Avarice is the only passion, and wealth the only merit in the United Provinces.[6]

The English at the Cape in the years of the First British Occupation did not merely think badly of the metropolitan Dutch. They also held strongly negative opinions about the white inhabitants of the Colony they had just conquered. These are most clearly exemplified in the writings of John Barrow, a remarkable man who worked his way up on the basis of his intelligence from very humble beginnings to become Second Secretary of the Admiralty, a knight of the realm and the patron of many Arctic expeditions, including the one which gave his name to the most northerly point of Alaska.[7] At the Cape, as a protégé of the Governor, Earl Macartney, his dislike of the Cape Dutch was not sufficient to prevent him marrying one, but his love of his wife not such as to preclude him from abusing her countrymen.[8] His descriptions became stereotypical for much of the early nineteenth century. The inhabitants of Cape Town were seen as lazy, pampered by their slaves and living only for their pleasures and their table. Their only occupation was attending the auctions and gambling on what we would now call the commodity market.[9] He had relatively little to say on the rich wine and wheat farmers of the South-West Cape, but his descrip-

---

[5] *Introduction to the History of the Dutch Republic for the Last Ten Years, reckoning from the Year 1777*, London, M. C. Miller, 1788. This work has been said to have been by Sir James Harris, the British ambassador in the Hague for much of the 1780s, but, according to the distinguished Dutch historian Robert Fruin, such an attribution is mistaken. See the notes in his copy of the work, held in the Leiden University Library, class mark 1499 D 36[1]. Harris, who apparently held similar views, was later enobled as the Earl of Malmesbury. His daughter, Lady Francis Harris, married Sir Lowry Cole, who was to become Governor of the Cape and name the town in the Swartland in honour of his father-in-law.

[6] Percival, *Account of Cape of Good Hope*, 233.

[7] Christopher Lloyd, *Mr Barrow of the Admiralty*, London, Collins, 1970.

[8] In fairness, it should be pointed out that Anna Maria Truter, the lady in question, was a member of one of the great official families at the Cape, and would have seen herself as set apart from the mass of the burgher population.   [9] Barrow, *Travels*, II, 104–5.

tions of the Graaff-Reinet frontier boers became classic, whether or not they should be believed. Their main motif is fat, whether on the boers' table, belly or floor. In this land of grease, in which all forms of cultured entertainment were lacking, indolence once again prevailed, sustained by systematic brutality towards the Khoi labourers.[10]

Behind these denigrations of all foreigners lay a phenomenon of enormous significance for the history of South Africa since 1795, namely the emergence of an English nationalism. This was the prime nationalism of South Africa, against which all the subsequent ones, whether Afrikaner or African, reacted, either directly or at a remove. Despite this, it has scarcely been studied, mainly because the English have been so successful in imposing it on South African society. They themselves, those who have assimilated to the English and those who have reacted against it, have all taken it for granted, have assumed that it is part of the natural order of things that English ways are the best. Nevertheless, like so much which is thought to be part of the structure of the universe, it was invented at a specific time by specific people. Through much of the first half of the nineteenth century, and indeed later, Englishness was the major symbol used to determine what was right and acceptable in the political life of the Cape Colony.

In the years of the First British Occupation, between 1795 and 1803, the superiority of English institutions and ways was not stressed, although Barrow did have occasion to write, somewhat complacently, that 'no real cause . . . of complaint could possibly be alleged against the English government'.[11] He also believed that the Cape economy would be stimulated by 'the spirit of improvement that has always actuated the minds of the English in all their possessions abroad'.[12] In general the authors who had had experience of the Cape during this period were primarily concerned to denigrate the existing white population of the Colony, thereby implicitly arguing that British rule would be more beneficial to all concerned, and to stress the strategic and commercial importance of the Cape to Britain in its struggle with the French. Only after the second conquest of the Cape, in 1806, and particularly after it had become clear that British rule was to be permanent did this theme come to be widely enunciated.

As is so often the case, the complaints that were to become commonplace were first enunciated by a wild eccentric, Lawrence Halloran. He had acquired a post as Anglican chaplain to the army on the basis of a forged ordination certificate supposedly issued by the Bishop of Meath, and on occasion signed himself O'Halloran to make his Irish ancestry seem more

---

[10] Barrow, *Travels*, I, 76–81.   [11] Barrow, *Travels*, I, 51.
[12] Barrow, *Travels*, II, 435–6; cf. James Sturgis, 'Anglicisation at the Cape of Good Hope in the Early Nineteenth Century', *Journal of Imperial and Commonwealth History*, 11, 1982, 9.

plausible. Eventually he was exposed as a result of the close connections between the Governor, the Earl of Caledon, who was a large Ulster landowner, and the Anglican episcopate of Ireland. This imposture came to light because of a conflict between Halloran and the commander of the troops at the Cape, Lieutenant-General Grey. Grey had had one Captain Ryan, who was engaged to marry Halloran's daughter, court-martialled for fighting a duel. Halloran sprung to Ryan's defence, which lead to Grey transferring him from Cape Town to Simonstown. This was particularly unfortunate, since Halloran's mistress was living there, unbeknown to his wife, who was in Cape Town, but probably not to Grey. Halloran's response was to issue libellous doggerel against Grey, for which he was arrested and banned from the Colony.[13] In an attempt to justify himself, Halloran then set about pillorying the judiciary and Dutch ecclesiastical establishment, which he clearly and unwarrantedly considered responsible for his downfall. He considered that the 'Africo-Batavian' colonists were generally sympathetic to the French and that Caledon was far too indulgent towards them. He wrote: 'The English Inhabitants are still more disgusted and dissatisfied; . . . as they are in every instance, exposed to Individual Imposition and Insult; and subjected to the operation of Arbitrary Laws, administer'd in the most summary way, while all judicial proceedings are determined by a Junto of Seven *Dutchmen*, called a Court of Justice.'[14] The English were equally discriminated against by the laws of marriage, which forced them to go before the Dutch matrimonial court and have their banns published in Dutch before a Dutch congregation, and by the administration of burial in Cape Town. The only cemetery, apart from that for the slaves, which was 'literally a "Golgotha"', was under the control of the Dutch sexton, who charged exhorbitant fees. Things had even gone so far that the sentence of banishment was not enforced on a man who had refused to allow the playing of 'God Save the King' in a Cape Town theatre because it was 'offensive to the Dutch'.[15] The remedy was the introduction of an English system of law and an Anglican church.

What Halloran had proposed became the official policy of British colonial governments in the succeeding years, albeit not as a consequence of his protests. While the Napoleonic wars were still in progress, this was conceived of as a prudent measure, as the 'introduction of every British principle and practice, besides an allowable confidence in their excellence, forms precisely

---

[13] It can be found in *RCC* VII, 341f; on Halloran's career in general see Kelvin Grose, 'Dr. Halloran's Secret Life at the Cape', *QBSAL*, 41, 1987, 145–58.
[14] Political article enclosed in Halloran to the Earl of Liverpool, 25. Sept. 1810, *RCC*, VII, 381.
[15] Halloran's digest of cases in Halloran to the Earl of Liverpool, 8 May 1811, *RCC*, VIII, 69.

so many steps towards the attainment of belief in inseparable connection'.[16] Later, after the recession of the Cape to the Dutch had ceased to be a possibility, 'to Anglicise the colony' became a fixed item of British policy.[17]

In the course of the 1820s a series of measures were introduced to give substance to this policy. Essentially, they consisted of three main initiatives, namely the attempt to bring the colonial system of law into agreement with that of Great Britain; the designation of English as the only official language of the Colony, which naturally had consequences in the field of education; and the encouragement of emigration by Britons to the Cape of Good Hope.

Given the later history of conflict between the English and Afrikaner nationalism, it is perhaps surprising that the opposition to these policies was virtually non-existent. If it was to come, the only real source would have been among the elite of officials and rich farmers in Cape Town and the South-West Cape, but it was not forthcoming. Obviously there were conflicts within white Cape society, for instance over slavery, and there was a correlation between the position that an individual might take and the language which he (hardly ever she) spoke at home. This was to be expected in a society where few of the slave-owning farmers, but many of the merchants and professionals, were English-speaking immigrants. Nevertheless, the correlation was not at all perfect. The most racist and most articulate of slavery's defenders was a recent British immigrant by the name of R. P. Jones.[18] Moreover all public political debate was in English.[19] A clash between the English and the Dutch was not a feature of Cape life in the first few decades of British rule. Even the Great Trek was not an ethnic conflict. It was not for nothing that Piet Retief published his manifesto in English in the *Graham's Town Journal*.[20] Equally, opposition to the Trek was widespread among the Cape Dutch, for instance among church leaders,[21] or in Dutch papers such as *De Zuid-Afrikaan*.[22] Ethnicity was not introduced

---

[16] Cradock to Alexander, 6 Dec. 1811, *RCC*, VII, 206.

[17] Wilmot Horton, Parliamentary Under-Secretary at the Colonial Office, in the House of Commons debates (*Hansard*) 16, c. 310, 1826, cited in Sturgis, 'Anglicisation', 6; in what follows I have relied to a considerable extent on this article, though not unreservedly.

[18] R. L. Watson, *The Slave Question: Liberty and Property in South Africa*, Hanover, N.H. and London, University Press of New England, 1990, 106–8, 130–2.

[19] Of the documents included in André du Toit and Hermann Giliomee, *Afrikaner Political Thought: Analysis and Documents*, I, *1780–1850*, Cape Town and Johannesburg, David Philip, 1983, which were written after 1806 and published contemporaneously, only five needed to be translated into English, and, of these five, there is a contemporary English translation of two, and one was from the Latin of a Leiden Ph.D. thesis.

[20] It is republished, for instance, in C. F. J. Muller, *Die Britse Owerheid em Die Groot Trek*, Johannesburg, Simondium, 1963, facing p. 87.

[21] A. Dreyer, *Die Kaapse Kerk en die Groot Trek*, Cape Town, Van de Sandt de Villiers, 1929, 6–8.

[22] H. C. Botha, 'Die rol van Christoffel J. Brand in Suid-Afrika, 1820–1854', *AYB*, 40, 1977, ch. 6.

into the political discourse of the Colony until the 1840s, and then, as we shall see, it was primarily an English introduction.

The reasons for this acquiescence were threefold. First, the Cape Dutch elite of officials, clergymen and so forth found that their jobs were in general held safe by the British. They could easily work their way into a position of trust, acting as a cartilage between the Governor and his suite, on the one hand, and the mass of colonists on the other. Men like Sir John Truter, President of the Court of Justice, and Daniel Denyssen, the *Fiscaal*, were the leaders of Cape Dutch society and automatic recruits to the councils of Cape Town's leading schools, for instance. Though they maintained a certain emotional attachment to Dutch as a medium of culture, they and all around them were loyal to the British Government and did very well out of the British presence. Indeed, it was not until the late 1820s that a pro-gramme of reform began to change the relationship between government service and personal remuneration which had been so characteristic of eighteenth-century Europe, including both the Netherlands and its colonial outposts.[23]

Secondly, the British Governors, most notably Lord Charles Somerset, were able to establish cordial, if still hierarchical, relationships with the Western Cape farmers, thus doing much to soften any pain which the official policies of the Government might have caused. It is tempting to see the social activities of Lord Charles as deliberate attempts to this end, but that would be to credit him and his entourage with a low cunning that they did not possess.[24] Somerset was a high Tory aristocrat, the second son of the Duke of Beaufort. He had risen on the back of influence and a pleasing manner to be the commander of the Brighton garrison despite apparently never seeing action, even though he was a serving officer throughout the Revolutionary and Napoleonic wars. His administration at the Cape, which was notable for its numerous controversies, at times resembles the more racy type of comic opera – he was on one occasion libelled for having a

---

[23] J. B. Peires, 'The British and the Cape, 1814–1834', in Elphick and Giliomee, *Shaping*, 491–3. Peires's most serious allegation is that the Cape Council of Policy divided the con-tents of the Batavian Military Treasury between themselves at the 1806 British conquest and, to cover their tracks, sold the main witness, a slave of Truter's named Marie, to Graaff-Reinet; I consider this story to be at best non-proven, as admittedly would be the case if it were successful. Some plausibility might be given to such stories by Truter's own family history. His grandfather, head gardener to the VOC, was the only man who in the eight-eenth century managed to go bankrupt twice, and his father had also gone bankrupt. The later Sir John may well have been particularly concerned to establish his own fortune. CA CJ 2926/125, CJ 2933/217, CJ 2934/229.

[24] For an analogous instance, see the comments of T. C. Colchester, an ex-colonial civil servant in Kenya, on historians imputing too much consistency to the actions of his former colleagues, cited in Bruce Berman, *Control and Crisis in Colonial Kenya: The Dialectic of Domination*, London, James Currey, 1990, xv.

homosexual affair with Dr James Barry, assistant surgeon to the military at the Cape, who was later discovered to have been a female transvestite. Nevertheless, his popularity among many sections of Cape society was great. His extravagant rebuilding of government buildings called down the wrath of the Treasury in London, but did allow him to distribute lavish hospitality.[25] His patronage of horse-racing and the Cape hunt for black-backed jackal undoubtedly persuaded the rich Cape farmers, whose inclinations mirrored his own, that any qualms they might have had as to the rightness of British rule were unfounded.[26] But it was not only the farmers who thought so. When he was about to leave the Colony, he was given a farewell dinner at the Commercial Exchange, after which the Colony's chief merchants unhitched the horses from Lord Charles's carriage and drew it across the Parade to the Castle themselves.[27] If for no other reason, they could be thankful for his efforts to spare the Cape from the worst effects of the changes in British customs duties on the import of Cape wine. He had, for instance, chaired the inaugural meeting of the Cape Wine Trade Committee.[28] After his departure, *De Zuid-Afrikaan* could look back on his rule as a golden age in the relations between the Government and the Cape colonists.[29]

Thirdly, a clear, if never fully explicit, decision was taken by the potential formulators of Cape Dutch ethnicity not to employ such an identity politically. In recent years it has been regularly argued that nations and ethnicities are at least in part intellectual creations. For whatever reason, they are imagined or invented – the terminology differs, but the message is much the same – by intellectuals, often lawyers, schoolteachers, clergymen and so forth.[30] Later Afrikaner nationalism is indeed one of the classic examples of this process. In the later nineteenth and earlier twentieth centuries, there were those engaged in 'building the nation with words', as Isabel Hofmeyr put it.[31] However, such an activity was not a necessary, not an unthinking instinctive

---

[25] Ronald Lewcock, *Early Nineteenth Century Architecture in South Africa: A Study in the Interaction of Two Cultures, 1795–1837*, Cape Town, Balkema, 1963, 112–27.

[26] Hattersley, *Social History*, 115–16; A. K. Millar, *Plantagenet in South Africa: Lord Charles Somerset*, Cape Town, London and New York, Oxford University Press, 1965, 64–5, 186.

[27] Millar, *Plantagenet in South Africa*, 230.

[28] D. J. van Zyl, *Kaapse Wyn en Brandewyn, 1795–1860*, Cape Town and Pretoria, Hollandsch Afrikaansche Uitgevers Maatschappij, 1974, 62.

[29] 20 Jan. 1832 and 24 Oct. 1834, cited in J. du P. Scholtz, *Die Afrikaner en sy taal, 1806–1875*, Cape Town, Nasionale Pers, 1939, 19–20.

[30] For Southern African examples, see Leroy Vail (ed.), *The Creation of Tribalism in Southern Africa*, London, Berkeley and Los Angeles, James Currey, University of California Press, 1989, esp. Vail's introduction, 'Ethnicity in Southern African History', 5, 10–15.

[31] Isabel Hofmeyr, 'Building a Nation from Words: Afrikaans Language, Literature and Ethnic Identity', in Shula Marks and Stanley Trapido, *The Politics of Race, Class and Nationalism in Twentieth Century South Africa*, London and New York, Longman, 1987, 95–124.

response to the opportunity for ethnic creation. In the first half of the nineteenth century, there were good strategic reasons not to take such a step.

The preconditions were there. The burghers had long made a distinction between themselves and their slave and Khoisan underlings. Furthermore, during the 1820s and 1830s, it seemed as though white politics in the Cape Colony was crystallising out along the lines of the linguistic divide. The interlocking conflicts about slavery, the treatment of Khoikhoi labourers and the activities of the missions seemed to be resolving themselves into a clash between the Dutch and the British. The conflict between the *South African Commercial Advertiser* (*SACA*) and *De Zuid-Afrikaan* came to symbolise this, as the former railed against the 'despotism of 50 Koeberg boers' and the latter against 'Philippijnsche humbug'.[32] The Governor described the Dutch farmers as being 'under the entire dominion of a numerous political party of their countrymen in Cape Town who, by means of a newspaper belonging to them called the "Zuid-Afrikaan", have contrived . . . to change the feelings of the great mass of the Dutch inhabitants towards the British Government'.[33] Petitions for the establishment of a Representative Assembly for the Cape Colony were refused by London, not just because the existence of such an assembly would make protection of the rights of slaves, Khoikhoi and Free Blacks more difficult, but also because it was feared that it would lead to a direct confrontation between the English- and the Dutch-speaking inhabitants of the Colony.[34]

At the same time, the intellectual expressions of Cape Dutch ethnicity were being developed. Most notable of these was the *Nederduitsch Zuid-Afrikaansch Tijdschrift* (*NZAT*). This was founded in 1824 in tandem with the English language *South African Journal*, but whereas the latter soon ran foul of British Government censorship, the former continued, edited by Abraham Faure, who was also minister of the *Groote Kerk* in Cape Town. At first sight the *NZAT* seems innocuous enough, as it contains mainly pious exhortations and a certain amount of verse. However, it also published historical works, notably an edition of Jan van Riebeeck's diary.[35] These were edited, almost certainly, by P. B. Borcherds, son of the dominee of Stellenbosch and a rising official who would become magistrate of Cape Town.[36] The popularity of history left something to be desired.

---

[32] On this, see Botha, 'Brand', 31, and *John Fairbairn in South Africa*, Cape Town, Historical Publication Society, 1984, 172–3.

[33] Cole to Goderich, 19 June 1832, cited in Botha, 'Brand', 31.

[34] See debate in House of Commons, 24 May 1830, *Hansard*, 1007.

[35] These appear in every number of the *NZAT* from 1(2), 1824 until 17(1), 1840.

[36] D. B. Bosman and H. B. Thom (eds.), *Daghregister gehouden by den Oppercoompman Jan Anthonisz van Riebeeck*, 3 vols., Cape Town, Balkema, 1952–7, I, xxvi; two other possible candidates for the editor (who was described only as the 'Wel-Ed. Hr. B.') are given, but are less likely, as Borcherds was already active in the early records of the Colony, collecting material for the Commissioners of Eastern Inquiry.

When the 'Maatschappij ter uitbreiding van Beschaving en Letterkunde' (Society of the Extension of Civilisation and Literature) announced an essay competition on the subject of 'The history of the Cape Colony up till the beginning of Simon van der Stel's administration', it received no entrants.[37] Nevertheless, men like Daniel Denyssen, who had by then retired as chief law officer of the Colony, largely because of his indifferent command of English,[38] and P. B. Borcherds regularly stressed the importance of the Colony's history in, for instance, their lectures to the 'Maatschappij', which the *NZAT* published.[39] In part, these lectures were interventions in the very vigorous debate on the history of the Colony, whose main protagonists were Dr John Philip and Donald Moodie. This debate was vitriolic, because, like most such, it was an argument about contemporary politics conducted by proxy.[40] It did, however, allow, almost without contestation, the creation of a history in which the Cape Dutch elite could share.

One of those engaged in this project, which might be seen as laying the basis for a Cape Dutch (not an Afrikaner) ethnicity, was Christoffel Joseph Brand. Son of a VOC official, and godson of Sir Joseph Banks, for whom his grandfather, the *posthouder* of Simonstown, collected plants, Brand was educated in Cape Town and in Leiden, where he took two degrees. His doctorate in law was gained for a thesis entitled *De Jure Coloniarum*.[41] In this he argued that colonies should possess their own legislature, and related this explicitly to the situation at the Cape of Good Hope. Were it not that a thesis in the decent obscurity of an ancient language would have little impact on Cape public opinion, Brand might well have been charged with incitement to revolt, so at least it was claimed later, probably with exaggeration.[42] Returning to Cape Town in 1821, he practised as a lawyer and later applied to be appointed as a judge. His political involvement, perhaps his training in the Netherlands rather than Great Britain, and later his bankruptcy, precluded this. He did, however, see the prescriptions of his thesis put into practice, and in 1854 he became the first speaker of the Cape House

---

[37] D. Denyssen, 'Voorlezing in de Algemene Vergadering der Maatschappy ter Uitbreiding van Beschaving en Letterkunde', *NZAT*, 12, 1835, 30.

[38] *RCC* XXVII, 63–4; XVII, 493–5.

[39] Denyssen, 'Voorlezing'; P. B. Borcherds, 'Over het belang der Geschiedenis als de beste bron van algemeen onderwys', *NZAT*, 16 (1839). There are a number of other articles on similar themes in the *NZAT* for 1836–8 (14–16).

[40] Andrew Bank, 'The Great Debate and the Origins of South African Historiography', *JAH*, 38(2), 1997, 261–83, which extends Robert Ross, 'Donald Moodie and the Origins of South African Historiography', in Robert Ross, *Beyond the Pale: Essays on the History of Colonial South Africa*, Hanover, N.H. and London, Wesleyan University for the University Press of New England, 1993, 192–212.

[41] As all Dutch theses are, this was published, in this case by L. Herdingh and Sons, Leiden, 1820. For extracts, in English, see Du Toit and Giliomee, *Afrikaner Political Thought*, 206–8, 273–5.   [42] Botha, 'Brand', 13.

of Assembly. His son, Johannes Hendrik, was for many years the President of the Orange Free State, although he had not crossed the Orange before his election to that office.

In 1824, Brand was one of those associated with the foundation of the *NZAT*, and he continued to combine journalism with his advocacy. In 1837, as editor of the short-lived journal, *The Mediator* – the title is significant – he wrote that 'England has taken from the old colonists of the Cape everything that was dear to them: their country, their laws, their customs, their slaves, their money, yes even their mother tongue.' At the same time, though, he stressed that the colonists of Dutch descent 'had done everything to prove that they wanted to be British; while their conquerors had continually worked to remind them that they were Hollanders'.[43]

This was the line that Brand, and indeed others of his circle, notably W. F. Hertzog,[44] took between 1834 and the establishment of the Cape Parliament twenty years later. The stress was not on their Dutch descent but on their status as subjects of a British colony. Their long-term goal was the establishment of a Representative Assembly at the Cape, as Brand had indeed desired ever since he wrote his thesis. No doubt they had worked out that in such an assembly the Cape Dutch would be in a very strong position, as indeed they were.[45] However, in order to do so, they stressed a colonial-wide, not a specifically Dutch-speaking, identity. Brand and his erstwhile (and to some extent future) adversary, John Fairbairn, the editor of the *SACA*, worked together in the political moves which led to the establishment of Parliament.[46] When, in 1850, Robert Godlonton was appointed as a representative of the Eastern Province English settlers, to be the fifth non-official member of the Legislative Council although he had come only eleventh in the informal elections to this body, Brand's reaction was sharp:

I hope the public will remember that not one word about Dutch or English has been uttered by us, and I regret that the Attorney-General . . . should have wandered from [his resolution] to indulge in observations about a separation between the two classes . . . The Attorney-General complained, in bitter language, of the British possessions and the British people of Albany not being represented, as though he considered them the only true British portion of the colony . . . Your Excellency – I am a British adopted subject, and it is against the British constitution . . .

---

[43] *The Mediator*, 10 Oct. 1837, cited in Botha, 'Brand', 41–2. Although Brand's editorial was undoubtedly published bilingually, I do not have the English original, and have translated this myself.   [44] J. C. Visagie, 'Willem Fredrik Hertzog, 1792–1847', *AYB*, 37, 1974.

[45] T. R. H. Davenport, *The Afrikaner Bond: The History of a South African Political Party, 1880–1911*, Cape Town, Oxford University Press, 1966.

[46] They had not always been only adversaries. In the 1820s, Brand had on occasion acted as Fairbairn's advocate in his law suits with the Cape Government.

At this point, the Governor, Sir Harry Smith, broke into his speech.[47] Nevertheless, the argument is clear. Anglicisation could be accepted in public life, because it could form the basis of a Cape colonial identity, set off against narrow Englishness. It was a position which was to be held until almost the end of the century by the Cape Afrikaner elite, who whenever appropriate stressed their loyalty to the British Empire, and could indeed find common cause with ideas of a wider white South African nationality which were propagated in the years between the South African war and Union.[48]

Part of the reason for this was that Cape Dutch identity was in no way fixed, nor did it include all those who would later consider themselves Afrikaners. Other identities which stressed distinction from, not inclusion with, other Cape Dutch were temporarily possible. In the 1820s, recognition of their Huguenot descent came to the fore among the wine farmers of the Berg River valley. Very possibly the French consul in Cape Town, M. Delettre, who may of course himself have been a Protestant, did something to awaken this feeling. Certainly he compiled a list of the French families who had settled at the Cape in the late eighteenth century. When the first French Protestant missionaries, who had come to the Cape because of the presence there of Huguenot descendants, arrived in Paarl, they carried with them a letter to their fellow nationals and religionists, which was written in Dutch by the President of the Missionary Society in Paris, a Dutch sailor who had become an Admiral in Napoleon's navy. They were greeted as long-lost brethren. The date of the last sermon preached in French in the church at Paarl was still remembered.[49] Evidently, those of Huguenot descent needed a way of differentiating themselves from the rougher trekboers of the interior. As Frenchmen and women, even if they did not speak any French, they were at least civilised.

Law

The British, on conquering the Cape, confirmed that the legal system then in force would be maintained. On one level this happened. The legal charters of 1828 and 1834 both stressed that the basis of law would remain

---

[47] BPP 1362, 1851, 64, cited in Botha, 'Brand', 92.
[48] Mordechai Tamarkin, *Cecil Rhodes and the Cape Afrikaners: The Imperial Colossus and the Colonial Parish Pump*, London, Frank Cass, 1995, 50–74; Saul Dubow, 'Colonial Nationalism, the Milner Kindergarten and the Rise of "South Africanism", 1902–1910', *History Workshop Journal*, 43, 1997, and Shula Marks and Stanley Trapido, ' "A White Man's Country"? The Construction of the South African State and the Making of White South African "Nationalisms", 1902–1914', (as yet unpublished), both papers originally presented to the Institute of Commonwealth Studies, London, 1996.
[49] *JME*, 5, 1830, 97–111, 133–4.

unchanged. The South African legal system is thus still based on that of the eighteenth-century Netherlands, and thus ultimately on the law of Rome, in particular as codified under Justinian. Since this body of law was codified out of authority in the Netherlands during the early nineteenth century, South African law has become a coelacanth, a living fossil surviving as a result of peculiar historical circumstances long after its relatives have become extinct.[50] This degree of continuity was not recognised at the time. As has been noted, Christoffel Brand commented that the British had taken their laws from the Dutch. He deplored this, but there were many who would applaud.

To some extent, the distinction between the two views was the result of the work of Brand and many others like him who worked to maintain the purity and allow the development of what came to be known as Roman-Dutch law. Such individuals were not only the Leiden-trained lawyers of Dutch descent. There were also British judges who did so, notably William Menzies, who as a Scot was sympathetic to a legal system closely akin to that of his own country. They managed to develop the law on the basis of Roman and Pre-Revolutionary Dutch examples in some fields. In others, notably commercial and insurance law, Cape law came to adopt and adapt that of England. The strength of the British merchant community in Cape Town and probably the degree to which the British had developed mechanisms to cope with rapidly changing commercial practice made this both inevitable and attractive.

In at least one area of the law, the conflict between the Cape's laws and those of England became sharp, namely with regard to marriage and inheritance. Now, any two sets of arrangements will differ to the advantage of some party and the disadvantage of another, although in most cases, provided precautions are taken at a suitable time, it is possible to avoid some of the more stringent provisions of the law. What is of course important is that all parties know to which laws they are subject. British settlers might suffer most uncomfortable shocks on discovering that the Cape law applied to them, and in 1822 a badly drafted ordinance was issued to the effect that the property of husbands and wives who had married in Europe was to be distributed according to the laws of the country in which they married. Further than this in the recognition of the English laws of marriage and inheritance the Cape lawyers would not go. There were occasional calls for the introduction of the English system, notably in 1848 after the Swedish brewer and merchant Jacob Letterstedt had suffered temporary and highly public financial inconvenience following the death

---

[50] This metaphor is apt, not just because the first modern coelacanth was captured in South African waters, but also because a second specimen, incorrectly believed to belong to a different genus, was named after South African Prime Minister D. F. Malan.

of his first wife.[51] Cape lawyers, with the Attorney-General William Porter, an Ulsterman, in the van, pointed out just how sexist English law in this matter was. Though they did not use such anachronistic language, they were of course correct, certainly before the passing of the Married Women's Property Act in 1882. When in 1865 a Select Committee of the Cape Parliament was appointed to investigate the inheritance laws, the same men, above all Christoffel Brand and William Porter, made one witness look ridiculous when he claimed that English laws were *ipso facto* best. Rather, their final report noted: 'We are aware that it is saying little for the colonial law to say that it is immeasurably superior to the law of England.'[52]

If the body of law changed only slowly, and rarely if ever as a result of deliberate Anglicisation, this is above all of interest to lawyers and legal historians.[53] In terms of the awareness of British power, and its symbolisation, what mattered was the administration of justice. Whereas around Cape Town and Stellenbosch judicial arrangements had long been arbitrating social relations,[54] the institution of the Circuit Courts in 1813 was seen as the first true imposition of the colonial state's power in much of the Colony's interior.[55] The half-yearly progress of judge and council round the Colony became mythical within the legal profession. They saw themselves, in both comic and heroic vein, as bringing justice to the farthest points of the Colony. They were the representatives of the King (after 1837, of course, the Queen), to the extent that in 1842 Judge Menzies annexed a portion of territory stretching from the Orange River to well north of Pretoria – an annexation which was promptly disavowed by the Governor. The arrival of the circuit in town was greeted by massive celebrations and dinners, and the first circuit to the Transkei, late in the century, apparently was accompanied by triumphal arches, fireworks and patriotic addresses. The judge was British rule incarnate, and the justice he dispensed was what British rule was about – at least in the eyes of the judges.[56]

---

[51] Since Letterstedt had been married in community of property, on the death of his wife half their joint property had to be disbursed to her heirs, at least if she had died intestate. Even if she had made a will, a considerable sum (the 'legitimate portion') had to be paid out by her husband.

[52] *Report on the Law of Inheritance for the Western Districts*, CPP G15, 1965, viii, 32–9; see also E. B. Watermeyer and William Porter, *Community of Property and the Law of Inheritance at the Cape of Good Hope*, Cape Town, Saul Solomon, 1859.

[53] Martin Chanock, 'Writing South African Legal History: A Prospectus', *JAH*, 30(2), 1989, 265–88.

[54] Wayne Dooling, *Law and Community in a Slave Society: Stellenbosch District, South Africa c. 1760–1820*, Centre for African Studies, UCT, Communication No. 23, 1992; Ross, 'Rule of Law', 5–16.   [55] Peires, 'British and the Cape', 496–9.

[56] Albie Sachs, *Justice in South Africa*, London, Heinemann for Sussex University Press, 1973, 41–6.

Justice was dispensed by the judge who, after the new legal charter of 1828, was appointed from among members of the British bars, and thus was only towards the end of the century likely to have been born in the Cape Colony. Questions of fact, though, were decided by a jury. On the one hand, this was seen as bringing back some of the local participation in the administration of justice which had been lost by the abolition of the boards of *Heemraden* by the charter. On the other hand, juries were thought to be the essence of British justice. There had been agitation for their introduction as the only way in which Britons could be fairly judged,[57] an unwarranted and chauvinistic slur on the capacities of the Dutch legal system as it had developed. In the event, after the question as to whether jurors had to be able to understand English had been solved,[58] the jury system tended to entrench white supremacy in the Colony. 'Coloureds' were enrolled on juries regularly in Cape Town, and occasionally elsewhere. When the Kat River settlers found that they were not being enrolled as jurors, the liberal Attorney-General, William Porter, replied that this was because they lived more than six hours on horseback from the circuit town, Grahamstown in this case, and not because of any racial disqualification.[59] Nevertheless, there were a number of notorious cases, notably the Koegas atrocities of 1878, in which juries acquitted white men who had killed blacks, largely on the basis of racial solidarity, and advocates had no scruples at playing on the juries' feelings of racial solidarity, often to the displeasure of the judge.[60] On the one hand, there is nothing strange in this. All legal systems are biased in favour of the strong. On the other hand, despite everything, the courts could be, and were, used to challenge miscarriages of justice and the abuse of power by rulers, and the judges saw themselves as protecting that privilege of the ruled.[61] To the extent that this is what is meant by British justice, it was an unmitigated

---

[57] E.g. Report of J. T. Bigge to Earl Bathurst upon Courts of Justice, 6 Sept. 1826. *RCC*, XXVIII, 24–5; Sturgis, 'Anglicisation', 22–4.

[58] Initially this was a prerequisite for jury service, which precluded far too many of the Dutch-speaking population; after 1834 non-proficiency in English was grounds for a challenge, which would be applied depending on the circumstances of the case. See Sturgis, 'Anglicisation', 24.

[59] Sachs, *Justice*, 60–1; J. L. McCracken, *New Light at the Cape of Good Hope: William Porter, the Father of Cape Liberalism*, Belfast, Ulster Historical Publications, 1993, 104–5.

[60] Sachs, *Justice*, 60–1.

[61] Sachs, *Justice*, 60–1; *Upington v. Solomon and Dormer*, 1879, reported in Eben. J. Buchanan, *Cases decided in the Supreme Court of the Cape of Good Hope during the Year 1879*, Cape Town, Port Elizabeth and Johannesburg, J. C. Juta, 1894, 240ff.; Neville Hogan, 'The Posthumous Vindication of Zacharias Gqishela: Reflections on the Politics of Dependence at the Cape in the Nineteenth Century', in Shula Marks and Anthony Atmore (eds.), *Economy and Society in Pre-industrial South Africa*, London, Longman, 1980, 275–92.

good, and one that has survived into the present, to South Africa's lasting benefit.[62]

Language

Matters of language policy were set in motion by the Deputy Colonial Secretary, Henry Ellis, in a series of memoranda addressed to Henry Goulburn, the Parliamentary Under-Secretary at the Colonial Office. As usual, there was also a hidden agenda behind these memoranda. Ellis wanted to displace his immediate superior, Colonel C. Bird, who had married a Dutch Cape woman, by suggesting that he was too closely involved with the Dutch colonial elite.[63] The local system of administration, Ellis suggested, had been 'Hollandize[d]' by intermarriage between the colonial officials and the local colonists, so that to produce 'an alteration so natural and so necessary' would require a 'very decided opinion' on the part of the 'home' government. What was needed, above all, was the proclamation of English as the language of government. The Dutch in and around Cape Town were already largely bilingual so they would have no grounds for complaint. This was almost certainly an exaggeration, as indeed Ellis himself demonstrated by his comment that the members of the Court of Justice were themselves 'if not wholly unacquainted with the English language', at the very least unable to deliver complicated judgements in it. The result was that the English, particularly the merchants, were suffering considerable inconvenience from the fact that their disputes were being tried before such a court. There had as yet been no significant complaints from the mercantile community, but that was beside the point.[64]

Ellis's memorandum, it is generally agreed,[65] formed the trigger for the Proclamation issued on 5 July 1822 by Governor Lord Charles Somerset on the direct orders of Earl Bathurst, the Colonial Secretary.[66] Somerset had been working for some time to provide bilingual, Scots, ministers for the Colony's Dutch Reformed churches and to ensure a sufficient supply of English teachers for its schools. By now there were enough, he claimed, for the following step to be taken, namely the progressive phasing in of English as the only permitted language in the Colony's courts and public offices.

[62] Stephen Ellman, *In a Time of Trouble: Law and Liberty in South Africa's State of Emergency*, Oxford, Clarendon Press, 1992; Richard L. Abel, *Politics by Other Means: Law in the Struggle against Apartheid*, New York and London, Routledge, 1995.
[63] Sturgis, 'Anglicisation', 18; Ellis ironically ruined his chances by the irregularity of his own marital status, or rather lack of it, as he was living openly with his mistress in Cape Town.
[64] Ellis to Goulburn, 1 Dec. 1821, *RCC*, XIV, 183–7.
[65] In addition to Sturgis, 'Anglicisation', see Scholtz, *Die Afrikaner en sy taal*, 14–16.
[66] For the text, see *RCC*, XIV, 452–3.

This would definitely occur from 1 January 1827. In the event, it took a year longer before such a total transformation could be effected, but from 1828 court proceedings were held exclusively in English, which frequently necessitated a cumbersome use of translators and interpreters. For a while it was uncertain whether jurors, too, had to be able to understand English, but the matter was finally cleared up by a Proclamation in 1835, to the effect that jurors had to be able to communicate with each other, and that if two or more were unable to do so, those who were ignorant of English would not be empanelled.[67]

There was little protest against these measures. Shortly after the issuing of the Proclamation, the Synod of the Dutch Reformed Church met for the first time. There was clearly a certain amount of unease about the requirements to use English, which was crystallised in the report on the Synod which the Political Commissioner, Sir John Truter, wrote to Lord Charles Somerset.[68] On the one hand the members of the Synod, in other words the Colony's Dutch Reformed clergy, unanimously recognised the utility of promoting the use of English, and agreed to do what they could to achieve this. On the other, they were quite reasonably convinced that, since Dutch was almost universally the 'domestic language', 'religious instruction cannot be given otherwise than in the Dutch Language, except at the expense of Religion itself'. There was, Truter had noted, an 'apprehension . . . among the public that their children will not be allowed to receive any further instruction in Dutch, and that the language is to be totally proscribed'. Though the state could oblige its officials to know English, and could thus promote an interest among its subjects to do likewise, it could not, or at least should not, extend such an obligation into the sphere of religion. In his reply, Somerset acknowledged the force of these observations, though he repeated his stress on the need for children to learn English, as the only means by which they might acquire government employment.[69]

Within the Colony's schools, the same ambivalence prevailed. On the one hand, the old monolingual Dutch teachers soon went out of business. As early as 1824, P. J. Truter, another member of the large family of officials, wrote in a report that 'in the country districts where English schools are

---

67 Scholtz, *Die Afrikaner en sy taal*, 59; Keith S. Hunt, *Sir Lowry Cole, Governor of Mauritius 1823–1828, Governor of the Cape of Good Hope 1828–1833: A Study in Colonial Administration*, Durban, Butterworths, 1974, 158–9.

68 Truter to Somerset, 30 Jan. 1825, in A. Dreyer (ed.), *Boustowwe vir die Geskiedenis van die Nederduits-Gereformeerde Kerke in Suid-Afrika*, III: *1804–1836*, Cape Town, Nasionale Pers, 1936, 265–7; the Political Commissioners were appointed by the Government to ensure that the discussions and resolutions were acceptable: Truter himself was the leading Cape lawyer and a member of the DRC.

69 Somerset to Truter, 7 July 1825 in Dreyer, *Boustowwe*, 270.

established, the Dutch schools had fallen into decay and entirely ceased to exist'.[70] Against this, monolingual English schools did little better. The comments of the *SACA*, made in 1832, on this matter are very apposite, and deserve to be cited at length:

A principal object in establishing the Schools was the diffusion of the English language, but in order to effect this on a great scale it was necessary that both languages, the Dutch and English, should be taught in them indifferently, according to the wishes of the guardians of the pupils. It was not reasonable to expect that parents would send their children to Schools from which their own language, that of their country and their kindred, was rigidly excluded. It was, alas, impracticable for a teacher, ignorant of the Dutch language, to convey knowledge to a child who knew no other. The consequence was that these District or Free Schools [Government sponsored] were very poorly attended, except in one or two places, where the teacher admitted the Dutch language into his system, taught the elements of general knowledge in Dutch to certain Classes, and made *Translation* from one language into the other a part of the daily business of the School. Such Schools became very popular, and no objection was ever made by parents or guardians of Dutch pupils to their acquiring in this manner an early acquaintance with the English tongue.[71]

As is to be expected, parents had a far better idea of what made educational sense than politicians. Private schools, in which there were no such restrictions, flourished greatly.

This reaction to the possibilities of education on the part of the Cape Dutch elite only needs explanation in the light of later Afrikaner nationalism. The material advantages of bilingualism were many, and the emotional reservations towards it few. As Sir John Herschel commented, when asked to construct a suitable curriculum for the Cape Town school *Tot nut van 't Algemeen*, where many of the Cape's leading figures had been and were to be educated: 'Probably no Parent would be found so culpably negligent of his Child's future comfort and advancement as to allow him to attain the age of 13 . . . entirely ignorant of English.'[72] Following his advice, the school, which had been monolingual in Dutch, changed to become bilingual, and no doubt the prospects of its pupils correspondingly improved.

It was not just a matter of material advantage. There was also the profoundly ambivalent relationship of the Cape Dutch elite towards the language which they spoke. Eventually, of course, what the South Africans call 'High Dutch' and what its European speakers called 'Low Dutch'[73] was

[70] Published in *Report of a Commission appointed to inquire into and report upon the Government Educational System of the Colony*, CPP G16, 1863, 45–50, cited in Scholtz, *Die Afrikaner en sy taal*, 33.   [71] *SACA*, 5 Sept. 1832.

[72] W. T. Ferguson and R. F. M. Immelman, *Sir John Herschel and Education at the Cape, 1834–1840*, Cape Town, Oxford University Press, 1961, 45.

[73] *Nederduitsch*, literally 'Low German', more often replaced by *Nederlands*, or 'Low country language'.

replaced in South Africa by its somewhat creolised derivative now known as Afrikaans. Now, the social history of Afrikaans is not merely a highly contentious issue, as might be expected given the symbolic load which the language has acquired in the course of the twentieth century, it is also one which is set about with grave difficulties, largely because of the problems inherent in recovering the spoken language of the past. Essentially, the language of the illiterate can only be heard when they are caricatured, for instance on the stage, while the texts produced by the literate contain the grammar they learnt at school, which accords to greater or lesser degree with what they actually spoke.[74] What seems incontestable is that those at the bottom of the social ladder spoke in ways that deviated strongly from standard (*Algemeen beschaafd*) Dutch, more indeed than modern standard Afrikaans does from modern Dutch, and that deviation decreased the higher the speaker's status.[75] The Cape Dutch elite, like elites the world over, were effectively bilingual. A Dutch officer held at the Cape in 1806 noted that they learnt 'Bastard Dutch' from their slave nurses, but as adults, and in appropriate circumstances, they could switch into what was thought of as 'correct' Dutch.[76]

The clearest evidence from the first half of the nineteenth century comes from two linguistically aware Dutchman. The first was J. G. Swaving, who worked as an interpreter in the Cape Town courts in the 1820s. He wrote that he had to learn

a language entirely new to me, namely that form of mongrel Dutch which is spoken in this country by the farmers and slaves and also by the Hottentots and all sorts of free heathen tribes, and which is not entirely strange to even the more civilised (*beschaafden*) of the Christian and leading classes, with the exception of those who had been born or educated in the Netherlands.

Swaving commented further that it was much less strange to his ears than the so-called Dutch Creole spoken in the Guyanas, where he had previously lived, but since Sranan, the language in question, is actually an English-based creole this is not altogether surprising.[77]

The second, much more extensive set of observations were made by

---

[74] The texts at the Cape which come closest to escaping this dilemma are those Islamic devotional works which were composed in Arabic script and thus give a fairly accurate phonetic record of their authors' actual speech. However, since these texts were necessarily written by Muslims, they are only marginally relevant to the issues addressed here.

[75] A useful introduction to this problem can be found in Achmat Davids, 'The "Coloured" Image of Afrikaans in Nineteenth Century Cape Town', *Kronos: Journal of Cape History*, 17, 1990, 36–47.

[76] H. C. Nahuys van Burgst, *Adventures at the Cape of Good Hope in 1806*, Cape Town, South African Library, 1993, 37.

[77] J. G. Swaving, *J. G. Swavings zonderlinge ontmoetingen en wonderbaarlijke lotswisselingen na zijne vlugt uit Delft*, Dordrecht, Blussé and Van Braam, 1830, 302–3.

A. N. E. Changuion, professor of Dutch at the South African Athenaeum, one of Cape Town's leading elite schools. He published them in a short book entitled *De Nederduitsche Taal in Zuid-Afrika hersteld* [The Dutch Language in South Africa Restored], which was primarily a school grammar, published in Cape Town in 1844. When Changuion had arrived in the Cape, he had believed that it was possible to stem the evil being done to the language. Now he thought of Cape Dutch 'as a doctor views an incurable patient, whose pernicious symptoms can be somewhat alleviated and whose certain death can be postponed for a while, but whose full recovery can no longer be hoped for'. Changuion then published a list of expressions which he heard with some regularity in the speech of the Dutch of Cape Town – he had hardly ever been into the countryside – in the hope that it could be used to purify a language which was suffering from increased indifference among its speakers, 'a natural consequence of a failure of nationality'. Nor was what he had recorded a full description of colloquial Cape speech, because that would not have helped the desired restoration and because 'that language *in its pure form* [Changuion's italics] is only spoken by Hottentots and other riff-raff (*gepeupel*)'.

Changuion expected that his writings would be greeted with the comment that 'this is not the way we speak at the Cape', in other words that the Cape elite did not employ such a deviant form of Dutch.[78] This was indeed the criticism he received, written by J. Suasso da Lima in the true tones of nineteenth-century polemic. For Suasso, Changuion's examples only proved that he had consorted with the lowest classes of Cape society, and was never a guest in polite society (*den burgerkring*). He had slandered the *Kapenaar* by making him appear to speak in the language of the 'most uncivilised Hottentot and meanest Negro'.[79] Rather the speech of the Cape Dutch elite, according to Suasso da Lima, differed scarcely if at all from that of Haarlem, traditionally the city in the Netherlands where the purest Dutch is spoken.

Who was correct, as a socio-linguistic recorder, is impossible to say, though Suasso da Lima's protestations of purity are so extreme that he would appear to be attempting to cover up defilement. What matters in this context is not just that, as Achmat Davids has argued, what was to become Afrikaans was seen in the early nineteenth century to be the language of the lower orders of society, literally a vernacular in the original Latin sense of

[78] A. N. E. Changuion, *De Nederduitsche Taal in Zuid-Afrika hersteld: Zijnde eene handleiding tot de kennis dier taal naar de plaatselijke behoefte van het land gewijzigd*, 2nd edn, Rotterdam, J. van der Vliet, 1848; the quotations are taken from the 'Voorrede', iii and 'Proeve van Kaapsch Taaleigen', iv and v.
[79] J. Suasso de Lima, *De Taal der Kapenaren, tegen de schandelijke aanranding derzelver van Professor Changuion, verdedigd*, Cape Town, J. Suasso de Lima, 1844, 6, 11.

'the tongue of slaves born in the house'.[80] Equally, all those who were brought up speaking Dutch were aware of the danger that they might pollute their tongues with the barbarisms of the linguistic environment in which they moved. While this attitude towards the emerging Cape dialect was universal, which seems to have been the case until deep into the nineteenth century, a Cape Dutch challenge to the hegemony of English, and Englishness, was improbable.

Later, Dutch was to have its revenge. South African dialects of creolised Dutch, initially those of the Western Cape but later those that were spoken in the Eastern Cape and the northern republics, were raised to the status of a separate language by Afrikaner nationalists. However, as Afrikaans became respectable, it steadily became much more like Dutch. In part in a vain attempt to stem the creeping Anglicisation of 'Die Taal', the standardisers of the language pushed for the incorporation of Dutch vocabulary into Afrikaans, and, when they had a choice, they opted for a syntax that most resembled that of the Netherlands. Ironically, as it was given the status of a separate language, Afrikaans, though retaining its characteristic markers of difference, came to diverge less from standard Dutch than did any of the dialects from which it was created, and which continue to exist alongside the standard version.[81]

1820 settlers and English nationalism

In 1820, about 4,000 settlers arrived from Britain in the Eastern Cape, as the beneficiaries of a major scheme of assisted migration. They were greeted on the shores of Algoa Bay by Henry Ellis. He made a speech in which, as Thomas Philipps recalled in one of his letters, he

alluded to us Emigrants in the most feeling animated manner, and I regret being unable to give even an outline, indeed I felt too much to enable me to retain more than the impression. In speaking of Britain he adverted in very pretty terms to her being the Saviour and Protector of our quarter of the Globe, peopling and stamping with her language another quarter and still with all her exertions, full even to repletion with goodness and greatness, had now sent her Sons and Daughters to cultivate the arts of civilised life amidst the long neglected natives of the third Quarter.[82]

The British Government had sent the settlers to the Eastern Cape both as a palliative against unemployment in depressed, post-Waterloo Britain and

---

[80] Davids, 'The "Coloured" Image of Afrikaans'; A. M. Hugo, *The Cape Vernacular*, Cape Town, UCT, 1970.
[81] Fritz Ponelis, *The Development of Afrikaans*, Frankfurt-on-Main, Pieter Lang, 1993.
[82] Arthur Keppel-Jones (ed.), *Philipps, 1820 Settler*, Pietermaritzburg, Shuter & Shooter, 1960, 48.

as a bulwark against Xhosa attacks in South Africa. In the event, neither end was achieved. The British labour market could in no way be alleviated by 4,000 emigrants and the settlers did more to provoke wars with the Xhosa than to prevent them. Rather, the settlement introduced an aggressively British pressure group into the Cape Colony, so that from then till well after mid-century there was an illegitimate conflation of ideas of Englishness with the interests of the Eastern Cape settlers, particularly those settled in Grahamstown.

Englishness was of course a contested concept. The early history of the settlement was marked by sharp conflicts between those known at the time as the 'serviles' and those known as the 'radicals', appellations chosen because of their relation to the Government of Lord Charles Somerset. The clash derived from the social positions the various settlers had held in Great Britain, and which they wished to retain, or better, in South Africa. On the one hand, the 'radicals' were those who came to South Africa as the proprietors of parties, bringing with them a number of indentured servants. They generally came from gentry families in Britain, and hoped to recreate a society of deference, with themselves at the top, at the Cape. In general they found it difficult to do this, as the indentured servants found more lucrative employment as soon as their terms of servitude were over, or even before. Moreover, the truly aristocratic Somerset – who could claim that if a certain liaison in the fifteenth century had been legitimised he would have been the brother to the legitimate King of England – was offended by the pretensions of petty gentry claiming to be aristocrats. On the other hand, the 'serviles' were those of humbler, generally artisan, background who were out to better their status and economic position in South Africa, and saw quickly that the best way to do this was by collaborating closely with the Government.[83]

In time, the great majority of the 1820 settlers came to realise that connection with the Government was the way to prosperity. The relationship might be unequal. One Governor, probably Sir George Napier, is said to have replied to an address of welcome and advice in Port Elizabeth that 'he was very much obliged to them, but flattered himself that he could govern the colony without their assistance, and wished them a very abrupt good morning'. His aide-de-camp was heard to wonder 'what tinkers and dealers in soap could know about government, and that sort of thing'.[84] Nevertheless, several of the Governors, notably Sir Benjamin D'Urban and Sir Harry Smith – who himself came from much the same background as

[83] M. D. Nash, *Bailie's Party of 1820 Settlers: A Collective Experience in Emigration*, Cape Town, Balkema, 1982, 59–79.
[84] Alfred W. Cole, *The Cape and the Kafirs: Or Notes of Five Years' Residence in South Africa*, London, Richard Bentley, 1852, 65.

the settlers – came to rely on the English settlers for political support, in the first instance because their non-conciliatory policies towards the Xhosa were those the settlers themselves promulgated.

During the second quarter of the nineteenth century, the 1820 settlers began to articulate their own interests in ways which are highly comparable to those which, later and elsewhere in the sub-continent, led to the creation of ethnicities.[85] A number of individuals who in the broad sense of the word can be described as intellectuals were creating a clear sense of common settler identity, as a weapon for the achievement of definite and hardly hidden political goals. The great majority of the settlers were proponents of a hard line towards the Xhosa and the Eastern Cape Khoikhoi. They considered the Xhosa solely responsible for the wars which broke out in 1834, 1846 and 1850 and could see no conceivable justification for the rescinding of the annexation of the Ciskei by ministers in London – which moreover deprived them of the opportunity to claim farms in the area so given back. All the same they profited even more than the rest of the Colony from the expenses incurred by the British Government in protecting them.[86] Missionary work as such they applauded. Many were staunch Methodists, and the Wesleyan Church in the Eastern Cape made no separation between its mission work and its regular services to white congregations. On the other hand, the political activities of some missionaries, above all John Philip and James Read, were anathema to them. They also believed that the Cape Colony should be split, although it was a matter of dispute whether the capital of the Eastern Province should be in Grahamstown or Uitenhage, near Port Elizabeth. In doing so they believed, almost certainly erroneously, that they themselves would have a majority of the white population in the new province. But, before such a moment arose, they had no compunction in taking jobs in the Cape Government, and often used their official positions to turn their ideas into reality.

There were many prominent settlers who espoused such views and propagated them wherever possible.[87] The most prominent among such men was Robert Godlonton, largely because he held the most strategic position as editor of the *Graham's Town Journal*. In England he had been a simple

---

[85] Cf. Vail, *The Creation of Tribalism*, for a number of relevant case studies.

[86] J. B. Peires, *The House of Phalo: A History of the Xhosa People in the Days of their Independence*, Johannesburg, Ravan, 1981, 123–4; Robert Ross 'The Relative Importance of Exports and the Internal Market for the Agriculture of the Cape Colony, 1770–1855', in G. Liesegang, H. Pasch and A. Jones (eds.), *Figuring African Trade: Proceedings of the Symposium on the Quantification and Structure of the Import and Export and Long Distance Trade of Africa in the Nineteenth Century*, Berlin, Kolner Beitrage zur Afrikanistiek, 1985, 248–60.

[87] E.g. John Mitford Bowker – see his *Speeches, Letters, and Selections for Important Papers*, Grahamstown, Godlonton and Richards, 1864 – or various members of the Biddulph and Southey families.

printer. By the time of his death he had been a member of the legislature for many years, and owned several farms and houses. His most important companion in these matters was J. C. Chase, a member of the London Livery Company of Founders, who, in South Africa, travelled widely in the interior before settling, first as a magistrate and then as a landowner near Port Elizabeth, having 'by sharpness and a lucky marriage' to the heiress of the town's richest merchant, the Dutchman Frederik Korsten, 'risen above his former grade in society'.[88] Godlonton and Chase differed from time to time, notably on the issue of the location of the Eastern Cape's capital.[89] They were united, though, in glorifying the Eastern Province and the role of the British within this. Thus Godlonton could assert that 'the British race was selected by God himself to colonize Kaffraria'.[90] Chase, marginally more soberly, could see the society of Eastern Cape 'leavened by the spirit of Anglo-Saxon enterprise, and by English sentiment'.[91] In so doing they were attempting to capture the idea of Englishness for their political ends, and in Godlonton's case very largely for his own Methodism.[92]

In 1844, settler identity was celebrated for the first time in a really large festival, to mark the twenty-fourth anniversary of the landing in April 1820. It is not quite clear why the festival was held a year early, as it were, although it does seem that they were marking the silver jubilee of leaving Britain on the date on which they arrived in the Eastern Cape, and leading settlers had begun agitating for an annual 'Settler day' from 1843. Be that as it may, the celebrations on 10 April, particularly in Grahamstown, were lavish. They began with a service of thanksgiving in St George's Anglican church, in which the address was given by the Rev. William Shaw, as the only minister who had accompanied the settlers and was still in Albany. Then the company proceeded to Oatlands, the farm – or really estate – of Colonel Henry Somerset, one of the army officers who had welcomed the settlers to Albany and who had remained. There, after an adapted version of *God Save*

[88] Sidha M. Mitra, *The Life and Letters of Sir John Hall*, London, Longman, 1911, 132, cited in Edna Bradlow, 'The Culture of a Colonial Elite: The Cape of Good Hope in the 1850s', *Victorian Studies*, 29, 1986, 387.
[89] Basil A. Le Cordeur, *The Politics of Eastern Cape Separatism, 1820–1854*, Cape Town, Oxford University Press, 1981, 148–9.
[90] Address to a public meeting at Bathurst, 21 Aug. 1847, in Cape of Good Hope, *Documents Relative to the Question of a Separate Government for the Eastern Districts of the Cape Colony*, Grahamstown, Godlonton & White, 1847, 96, cited in Tony Kirk, 'Self-Government and Self-Defence in South Africa: The Inter-relations between British and Cape Politics, 1846–1854', D.Phil. thesis, Oxford, 1972, 76–7.
[91] *Eastern Province Herald*, 15 Oct.1867, cited in M. J. McGinn, 'J. C. Chase – 1820 Settler and Servant of the Colony', MA thesis, Rhodes University, Grahamstown, 1975, 150.
[92] On these movements, see especially Alan Lester, 'The Margins of Order: Strategies of Segregation on the Eastern Cape Frontier, 1806–c. 1850', *JSAS*, 23(4), 1997, 635–54, and '"Otherness" and the Frontiers of Empire: The Eastern Cape Colony, 1806–c. 1850', *Journal of Historical Geography*, 24, 1998, 2–19.

the Queen,[93] and while various army bands, including that of the (coloured) Cape Mounted Rifles, played on, white Grahamstown picnicked, outside or in marquees provided by the army. All then returned to Grahamstown where, in a large store which had conveniently just been finished, places had been laid for a banquet for 250 people. This banquet, though, turned into a contest. According to Robert Godlonton, many more than the 250 for whom there were places turned up, so that several of the true settlers could not be seated. The gathering turned acrimonious and sour, and many of the speeches, given by William Shaw again and Colonel Henry Somerset, among others, could not be heard, but this only went to demonstrate the attractiveness of the cause being celebrated.[94] Not for nothing was a copy of the celebratory booklet despatched to Queen Victoria, who most graciously ordered it to be placed in the Palace Library.[95]

All the same, Godlonton was fudging matters. The main disturber of the gathering was Thomas Stubbs, as much an 1820 settler as Godlonton, but of a very different stamp. Not someone who would ever have acquired the nickname 'Moral Tom',[96] he earned his living as a saddler and tanner, and his fame as a commander of irregular cavalry in wars against the Xhosa. In England his family had had – at least he remembered them as having had – more wealth than they achieved in South Africa, in part because Thomas's father had been killed in an affray with the Xhosa in 1823. He took exception to the triumphalist view of settler history being propagated at the meeting. Of Shaw's sermon he wrote: 'it was all upon the golden side – there was nothing of the distresses the settlers had undergone'. His anger burst out while Somerset was speaking, because he felt that the Government had not done enough for the settlers, but his ire was not directed so much at Somerset as against those settlers whom he believed had profiteered in the wars. By the time he had finished 'exposing a great deal more humbugging by the government' and those associated with it, respectable Grahamstown had disappeared, and several of the toasts on the programme could not be given. Stubbs emerged as the victor on the field, spending the rest of the evening in hearty conversation, and no doubt carousing, with those who remained, including Colonel Somerset, who became his good friend.[97] But

---

[93] One of the additional verses ran: 'And lift on Albany,/ Our rising colony,/ Thy smiling face./ God of our father-land,/ Extend thy gracious hand/ To us, an humble band/ Of Britain's race.'

[94] This description is taken from Robert Godlonton, *Memorials of the British Settlers of South Africa*, Grahamstown, Robert Godlonton, 1844.

[95] This is recorded in John Ayliff, *Memorials of the British Settlers of South Africa*, Grahamstown, Robert Godlonton, 1845, 8.

[96] Godlonton was known, rather hostilely, as 'Moral Bob'.

[97] W. A. Maxwell and R. T. McGeogh (eds.), *The Reminiscences of Thomas Stubbs*, Cape Town, Balkema for Rhodes University, Grahamstown, 1978, 136–8.

Godlonton controlled the press and the interpretation of events provided for those who were not present. The disruption of a dinner and an attack on the dubious economic activities of Grahamstown's Methodist clique could not halt the celebration of an English ethnicity, one indeed in which Thomas Stubbs shared.

Similar, if less extravagant, meetings were held in Port Elizabeth, Salem and Bathurst. In this last case, the account which Godlonton published stressed that at the meal the company 'consisted *alone* of the British settlers of 1820 and their immediate descendants', so that no irregularities occurred.

The language that was used in these celebrations was self-congratulatory and smug, although it remained just on the acceptable side of self-adulation. The anthem used to open the church service in Grahamstown began 'To bless thy chosen race,/ in mercy, Lord, incline', but does not, in its entirety, suggest that the British, or indeed the 1820 settlers, are the chosen people, but rather those destined for salvation. The Grahamstown hymnodist was balancing sentiment against theological correctness. Similarly, William Shaw's address was to the text: 'Only fear the Lord and serve him in truth with all your hearts; for CONSIDER HOW GREAT THINGS HE HATH DONE FOR YOU.'[98] He has to be apologetic that the 1820 settlers did not come to South Africa to escape religious persecution, but rather to better themselves in this world, but nevertheless he believes that God has shone on them and brought them to prosperity, in part because they have always shown 'Christian forbearance' in their relations with the Xhosa and Khoi. The comparison Shaw makes is with the Pilgrim Fathers in Massachusetts, and in this he is not alone.[99] The 1820 settlers saw themselves as the 'Yankees' of South Africa, as the economically dynamic group settling and bringing progress to the new country. Chase, in Port Elizabeth, did propose a toast to 'the memory of Johan van Riebeck [*sic*] and his gallant band . . . and health and prosperity to their descendants and followers, the present inhabitants of the Cape of Good Hope, Dutch, French and of all nations'. His speech, though, gave the impression that the English had come to take the country over from those who had been there earlier.

A year later, again on 10 April, the choir of the Wesleyan church in Grahamstown sang the following anthem, 'composed by the Rev. Thornley

---

[98] 1 Samuel 12:24. Small capital letters in original.

[99] A year later, at the subsequent meeting, the Rev. John Ayliff made the same comparisons. Ayliff, *Memorials*, 10. It is an idea which has lasted, together with settler self-importance, late into the twentieth century. See, e.g., I. Mitford-Barberton and Violet White, *Some Frontier Farmers: Biographical Sketches of 100 Eastern Province Families before 1840*, Cape Town and Pretoria, Human & Rousseau, 1968, 1–2, where the arrival of the 1820 settlers is considered to be 'quite the most important event in the history of South Africa'.

Smith, imitation of "Montgomery's Ode on the Emancipation of the Slaves"':

> Sound ye the trumpet! o'er land and o'er sea
>   Ye sons of Britannia, whose spirits are free
> From Albion – light beaming star of the nations, –
>   We came to these regions, our fathers ne'er trod,
> And here have we founded our new habitations,
>   A home for our children and temples for God.
>   Sound ye the trumpet! o'er land and o'er sea
>   Ye sons of Britannia, whose spirits are free.
>
> Praise ye Jehovah! and sing to his name,
>   O'er Afric's rude mountains his goodness proclaim!
> Fly on the winds to tell all the glad story,
>   The light of salvation now shines on this land;
> In songs of rejoicing, give Him all the glory,
>   Who graciously smiles on the works of our hand.
>   Praise to the God of our fathers! 'twas He –
>   Jehovah! who sent us O Afric! – to thee.

This is the language – though not *in* the language – of twentieth-century Afrikaner nationalism.

The British settlers came perilously close to seeing themselves as sent by God to civilise Africa. At the same time, they could claim their rights as Britons. Godlonton, speaking in Bathurst in 1844, attacked an unnamed 'liberal-whig' Governor's despotism – in fact Sir Rufane Donkin, the man in question, had merely demanded that the early settlers honour the contracts they had made. What he could claim, looking back, was that 'the authorities of the day were taught that British subjects in this colony were determined to maintain unimpaired that liberty of action, which is their unquestionable birthright'.[100]

April 1852

In April 1852, Sir Harry Smith, the Governor of the Cape of Good Hope, took ship for Britain, having been recalled by the Secretary of State for the Colonies in London. A month later, John Montagu, the Colonial Secretary in Cape Town, and thus effectively head of the administration, followed him, although he officially continued in office until his death the next year. They had been driven out of office for a variety of reasons. Smith's failure to bring the war with the Xhosa to a satisfactory conclusion was a major factor. In addition, though, their failure to control the politics of the Colony meant that their position was untenable. Their replacements, Sir

[100] Godlonton, *Memorials*, 106.

George Cathcart and in particular his Lieutenant-Governor, Charles Darling, dismantled the alliances they had built. They broke the close circle of kinship and friendship, tracking back to the settlers, which had dominated official life, and they made possible the establishment of the Cape Parliament, with its low franchise, two years later.[101]

During the conflicts which led up to the establishment of the Representative Assembly, Cape conservatives linked to Smith and Montagu and generally of settler background claimed that the struggle was between the English and the Dutch. Their opponents thought otherwise. They did not claim to be Dutch but, as Christoffel Brand described himself, 'British adopted subjects', when they were not British by birth. They were also the liberals and the propagators of colonial progress.[102] Later politics was to be very different.

April 1852 thus represented one of the sharp turning points in the political history of South Africa. It was also the 200th anniversary of the foundation of the Cape Colony by Jan van Riebeeck. The day in question, the 6th, was not declared a public holiday. A request to that effect was turned down in one of his last acts by Sir Harry Smith, presumably because he was afraid such a festivity would turn into a demonstration of opposition.[103] In this he was probably right. The *SACA* used the occasion to herald the coming of a 'second birth', a 'nobler baptism' with the achievement of political liberty. It did this in an editorial in which it stressed the inclusiveness of Cape political culture. In it, John Fairbairn wrote that the society of the Cape seemed 'varied and broken', with

every shade of color on the skin, several distinct tongues and languages, and two or three well-defined distinctions in Religion. But the points in which all agree, have proved sufficient to secure internal peace, and to make society act harmoniously as a whole. They all love the land as the land of their birth, of their fathers, and, as they hope it will be – the inheritance of their children. The languages of the two principal classes are adopted, one or other of them, and understood sufficiently for common intercourse, by the whole population. The belief that God has made of one blood all the nations that dwell together on the face of the earth is universal, and no difference on matters of religious faith or ceremony, is permitted for a moment to interfere with civil rights, or to lead one step towards persecution. They all loyally acknowledge the authority of a common Sovereign and they enjoy the protection of the same laws publicly administered to all without distinction of class, creed,

---

[101] Kirk, 'Self-Government and Self-Defence', 447–86; Stanley Trapido, 'The Origins of the Cape Franchise Qualifications of 1853', *JAH*, 5(1), 1964.

[102] Jean du Plessis, 'Colonial Progress and Countryside Conservatism: An Essay on the Legacy of Van der Lingen of Paarl, 1831–1875, MA thesis, Stellenbosch, 1988, ch. 2; André du Toit, 'The Cape Afrikaners' Failed Liberal Moment: 1850–1870', in Jeffrey Butler, Richard Elphick and David Welsh (eds.), *Democratic Liberalism in South Africa: Its History and Prospect*, Middletown, Conn., Wesleyan University Press, 1987, 35–64.

[103] *De Gereformeerde Kerkbode in Zuid-Afrika*, March 1852, 112.

color, language, or descent . . . Thus the things in which they differ are superficial, and by no means inconsistent with social unity. The things on which they are agreed are the everlasting foundations of social life – of nationality, of combined action, of peace, prosperity, strength and greatness.[104]

While the *SACA* stressed unity, *De Zuid-Afrikaan*, which at this stage was closely allied politically to its commercial rival, virtually ignored the matter, merely commending the sermon which the Rev. A. Faure had given in the *Groote Kerk* in Cape Town on the 6th.[105] A major opportunity for ethnic mobilisation was passed over.[106]

Faure's sermon was preached in Cape Town as part of the religious thanksgiving for the establishment of a Christian church in South Africa which the Government did sanction. It was a learned disquisition on the history of the Cape church, based on the archives of the church itself and on other documents, many of which Faure himself had had published in the *NZAT*. It thus contains forty-five pages of appendices backing up his various assertions, as against thirty-six pages of original text. It is not rebel-rousing, nor could such be expected from a man who had been run out of Natal some nine years earlier for proposing a toast to Queen Victoria – as the rightful sovereign of the region – at a Voortrekker dinner. Its only hint of controversy comes from Faure's claim that Islam had been introduced to the Cape because the Colony was being used as a penal settlement, but any analogies to the anti-convict agitation of the previous years are deeply hidden.[107]

Faure's was not the only sermon given on 6 April 1852. In Paarl, the formidable reactionary dominee, the Rev. G. W. A. van der Lingen, used the occasion for much more polemical ends. It would be 'scandalously unthankful' if the establishment of Christianity at the Cape were not to be celebrated, and 'the behaviour of the new colonists who refuse or fail to celebrate this occasion is most impolite and even insulting to the others'. Van der Lingen then proceeded to attack those who 'forget the language and customs of their ancestors, . . . [who] prefer to speak a foreign tongue, no matter how badly and ridiculously; have their children taught in a foreign language, without ever taking the trouble to have them learn thoroughly the language which God had given them'. And this language was the 'only pure descendant of the noblest of the European languages, namely West Gothic' – Van der Lingen would not have approved of the adoption of Afrikaans in

---

[104] *SACA*, 3 Apr. 1852.   [105] *De Zuid-Afrikaan*, 8 Apr.1852.

[106] Cf. the events of April 1952. For a description see Ciraj Rassool and Leslie Witz, 'The 1952 Jan Van Riebeeck Tercentenary Festival: Constructing and Contesting Public History in South Africa', *JAH*, 34(3), 1993, 447–69.

[107] Abraham Faure, *Redevoering bij het tweede Eeuw-feest ter herinnering aan de vestiging der Christelijke Kerk, in Zuid-Afrika, gehouden in de Groote Kerk, in de Kaapstad op dinsdag den 6 April, 1852*, Kaapstad, Van de Sandt de Villiers & Tier, 1852.

the place of what came in South Africa to be known as High Dutch. 'It has pleased God', Van der Lingen commented further, 'to place us under a foreign people', and although they ruled the Dutch softly and in a conciliatory way, there was no need to take over more than was necessary. 'I commend unto you', Van der Lingen concluded, 'to hold firm to the old, as the Rechabites did.'[108]

In 1852, Van der Lingen was an exception, at least among those of Dutch descent whose words have survived. Progress and political rights were still the goals of the Cape Dutch leaders, and these could only be achieved by eschewing ethnic mobilisation. This was left to the English of Grahamstown. But the possibility was still there.

---

[108] This reference is to Jeremiah 35. The whole sermon, which was not published, is to be found in CA NGKA P62/1/6/4.

4   The content of respectability

A courtship and a marriage

In 1859 John Findlay, the twenty-year-old son of a Scottish tobacconist and merchant in Cape Town, had gone to live in the mountains of the North-East Cape.[1] There he became a trader, working in the store on the farm Oranjefontein which John Austen maintained as an outstation of his own store in Lady Grey. The village of Lady Grey itself had been founded only two years earlier, as a *kerkdorp*, to allow the farmers of the area to attend church even when the road to Aliwal North was cut by the flooding of the Kraai River and the depredations of Thembu and Sotho in the neighbourhood.[2] Findlay very quickly gained the respect of those among whom he moved – at least of the whites.[3] Despite his youth, the Dutch Reformed Church Council asked him to become a Justice of the Peace, an honour he refused because he felt himself too young.

While he was still in Cape Town, he had a sweetheart, known only as Mary Ann, but this does not seem to have been very serious. At any event, such a relationship as there may have been did not survive the 900 kilometres and two months' journey that separated them and John Findlay's sister Margaret felt called upon to warn him

Never think of marrying a Dutch girl, and don't be kissing the Boers' daughters too much, or perhaps some Boer will be thinking more than to please . . .?, and perhaps

---

[1] The sources for this section are Joan Findlay (ed.), *The Findlay Letters*, Pretoria, Van Schaik, 1954, 85 and 133–65, and Karel Schoeman, *Olive Schreiner, 'n lewe in Suid-Afrika, 1855–1881*, Cape Town, Human & Rousseau, 1989, 55–7.

[2] S. Hofmeyr, 'Mijne reis door den Graaff-Reinetschen ring – herinneringen, gedachten en opmerkingen', *Elpis*, 2(4), 1858, cited in Schoeman, *Olive Schreiner*, 48.

[3] As is too often the case, the African farmers, then beginning their trajectory through peasantry, do not figure in this story. On the adjoining Herschel district, see Colin Bundy, *The Rise and Fall of the South African Peasantry*, London, Heinemann, 1979, 146–64, and William Beinart, '*Amafelandawonye* (the Die-hards): Popular Protest and Women's Movements in Herschel District in the 1920s', in William Beinart and Colin Bundy, *Hidden Struggles in Rural South Africa: Politics and Popular Movements in the Transkei and Eastern Cape, 1890–1930*, London, Berkeley, Los Angeles and Johannesburg, James Currey, University of California Press and Ravan, 1979, 222–69.

Miss S. will not be pleased about it either; for I know I would not like a young man who was too fond of kissing. You say there is no respect of persons among the Boers. Now I would like you to be agreeable, pleasant and obliging to all, but only make intimate friends of a few.[4]

As Margaret's letter intimated, there was little danger of his becoming intimate with a Boer girl, because John Findlay had already met Katherine Schreiner. She was the eldest daughter of the dreamy and emotional German missionary Gottlob Schreiner and his formidable wife Rebecca, and her siblings included the later novelist Olive, and two distinguished politicians, William and Theo. Katherine, usually known as Katie, was a year older than John, and shortly after they met the two became engaged.

Katie's parents had met, and married, in the short time that Gottlob was in London before going to South Africa as a missionary of the London Missionary Society (LMS). Rebecca's father was Samuel Lyndall, a notable preacher of 'Wesleyan-Calvinist' persuasion, who had founded his own church in Hoxton, in the east end of London. At their marriage, so family legend had it, the flowers were pulled from Rebecca's bonnet by the Rev. John Campbell, as unbecoming for someone who was now a missionary's wife. Thereafter they lived a difficult life, even by the standards of nineteenth-century missionaries. After a short apprenticeship in the Kat River Settlement, where Katherine was born, they moved north of the Orange River. The Schreiners worked first at the Griqua capital of Philippolis, where in common with most of their predecessors and successors they fell foul of the town's ecclesiastical politics.[5] Then, switching from the LMS to the Wesleyans, they lived on a number of stations among the Sotho of the Eastern Orange Free State. In 1855, though, when the independence of the Free State was rightly seen as threatening that of the African communities among whom the Schreiners lived, they moved back south, to the inhospitable valleys of the Wittebergen, later known as Herschel district.

Throughout this odyssey, which had by no means ended,[6] the Schreiners were sustained by his faith and by her determination to bring up her children as befitted a woman whose wedding bonnet had been so despoiled. She does not seem to have fully shared her husband's simple convictions in the value of his missionary work, which perhaps explains her conversion to Catholicism shortly after his death. Her children certainly remembered her as the dominant partner in the marriage, and as someone who was unable to find full employment for her talents. She read regularly, and quite widely, but only for twenty minutes a day, when the drudgery of the day was finished and before darkness fell. Olive once compared her to a grand piano

---

[4] *Findlay Letters*, 85.   [5] Ross, *Adam Kok's Griquas*, 45.
[6] Gottlob, not the easiest of colleagues, gave up the ministry, became a trader and finally went bankrupt.

'shut up, and left locked all its existence, not played on by anybody, and used as a common dining-table, being vaguely conscious all the time of the other uses to which it might have been put under other circumstances'.[7] She ruled her family with rigour. Katherine played the piano, but only sacred music. Olive remembered being given fifty strokes with a bunch of quince rods because she had said 'Ach, how nice it is outside', and had thus broken the family rule against speaking Dutch.[8] Rebecca would not let her status as a missionary's wife influence her judgement of what was good and what was evil, and thus she would not see the Africans in ways which, to her mind, they did not deserve. Rather, when living among the Mfengu of Healdtown, her greatest worry was 'the difficulty of keeping my children separate from the swarthy demon of the house'. 'How difficult it is', she wrote, 'living as we do among gross, sensual heathen, to preserve that delicacy of thought and feeling so indispensable for a right development of the female character.'[9] It was not an attitude which inspired love in her children, particularly the elder ones.

John Findlay's entry into this family was, as can be imagined, not easy. The suspicion exists that Katherine latched onto him in order to escape from 'thralldom'[10] to her mother. Given the restrictions of race, background and behaviour which the Schreiners imposed on themselves, he must have been just about the first eligible man she had met, and she was not going to lose the opportunity he presented. All the same, her parents opposed the match. At one level, why they did so is a matter for speculation, since they would not have admitted, even to themselves, that they were striking back at a rebellion against their authority, and of course, and with good reason, they may have been fearful for Katherine's future happiness. But there is another level at which their public motives are as interesting.

In the first instance, Gottlob and Rebecca informed John Findlay that their daughter was of age, and that, though they would regret the marriage, they left her perfectly at liberty to do as she felt fit. What rankled above all with Rebecca was the notion that Katie 'should have in any way encouraged your attentions. This is something so foreign to my idea of feminine propriety. This sort of feeling constantly restrains me from showing kindness to young men.'[11] As Katie recalled the matter after her marriage, looking back on a fraught time:

---

[7] Cited in Schoeman, *Olive Schreiner*, 54.

[8] C. S. Cronwright-Schreiner, *The Life of Olive Schreiner*, London, T. Fisher Unwin, 1924, cited in Schoeman, *Olive Schreiner*, 58.

[9] Cited in Schoeman, *Olive Schreiner*, 63–4; the latter quotation is from Rebecca Schreiner to John Findlay, 16 Mar. 1860, *Findlay Letters,* 137.

[10] Theo Schreiner to Kate Findlay, 3 Jan. 1861, *Findlay Letters*, 163.

[11] *Findlay Letters*, 134.

it was made out that I sought Mr F.'s affections, not he mine, and that I was in the habit of doing so which is a most unjust charge.

Cullum, Dennison, Robertson, Hudson, Rosher, the only young men with whom I even had the opportunity of becoming acquainted never had the slightest cause to think I ever encouraged any attentions on their part. Indeed so had I been brought up that if I happened to say anything to any of them, I immediately felt my parents' eye on me and coloured, as if convicted of an awful crime. For I had learnt to think that if I spoke in company I sinned.

Her parents had imposed a discipline in such matters which she found difficult to meet. As she wrote to John: 'You admire my spirit. I am sorry for it. Oh it is a blessed thing to learn to be silent when one's anger is awake.'[12]

The hostility which Rebecca and Gottlob showed towards John, whatever may have been its deeper psychological cause, was ostensibly occasioned by a distrust of his levity. He had been caught winking at Katherine in church and making some unseemly comments about Rebecca. Rebecca's fears were, as ever, that John would corrupt his future sisters-in-law. John was however able to defend himself against the main charge 'That I hold the female character in light esteem: Far from it Mrs S. I have seen and read too much of female excellence. I need not go farther than in my own family, than in my eldest. I can almost say I have there seen female character in its full development.'[13] It was as well that Rebecca never saw the letter Margaret Findlay had written warning John against kissing Boers' daughters.

For a time, the conflict became serious. Gottlob apparently excommunicated John, illegally. Eventually, though, he came round, and performed the quiet wedding ceremony between Katie and John, and in the coming years John Findlay provided his parents-in-law with much-needed financial assistance. It would be nice to record that the marriage between Katie and John was happy, but this was not the case. Even John's sister Margaret wrote complaining of 'that utter carelessness and indifference about his personal tidiness and appearance [which] seems to me to show a want of self-respect'. Katie saw his character switching from the kind to the murderous. She was embittered by 'the harshness and coarse jesting on the subject of love', of which her mother had early complained, and at times hoped for a divorce. Her mother wrote to enjoin her to put her faith in God's wisdom, despite her unhappiness. John and Katie had twelve children, eight of whom survived infancy. In 1869, the death of one baby, together with the threat of !Kora raids to the isolated northern Cape town of Fraserburg where they lived, finally broke her mind. Her last years were spent in an asylum in

---

[12] *Findlay Letters*, 148.   [13] *Findlay Letters*, 139.

Pietermaritzburg, where she was described by the head of the institution as 'sane insane' and by her daughter as having a 'haunting distrust of everyone, especially of those who are kindest and most loving to her'.[14]

The opening words of *Anna Karenin* notwithstanding,[15] there are parallels between the marriage of John Findlay and Katherine Schreiner and that of Charles Leo Cox and Maria Bouwer, celebrated in the Anglican church of Bloemfontein on 20 January 1853.[16] Less than four years later, Cox was convicted of murdering his wife and hanged in the same town. The case became a *cause célèbre*, leading to protests from the English settler community about the enormity of the (Boer) Orange Free State Government executing an Englishman. But murder lays bare the hopes, aspirations and disappointments of those unhappy enough to be involved in it as no other event can.

Charles Cox was born in London on 13 December 1815. As he himself declared, 'he was born and bred a gentleman'. His precise family connections are unclear, and in later life he never exploited them. There are indications, though, that one of his uncles was an illegitimate son of one of George III's brothers, and that he had come from the 'faster' portion of gentlemanly society, that immortalised by William Makepeace Thackeray. At any event he had a certain amount of capital, presumably inherited, and decided to invest it in the burgeoning wool production of the Eastern Cape. After studying the raising of merinos in Saxony, he arrived at the Cape in 1838, bringing with him a flock of 235 Saxon sheep, and acquired a farm on the Bushman River. Though not scandalous, his life there was not that of the upright settler Methodists of Grahamstown. He drank heavily, on occasion, and was not always in control of himself when drunk. He had at least one illegitimate child, by a coloured woman, and, while he was said to be attached to the infant, he did not take either his mistress or her offspring into his household, whatever provision he may have made for them. As he himself said, 'I have committed sins like other men, but I never committed a crime.'

Cox's sheep farm did not prosper, apparently because of the actions of a dishonest agent. After a time as a tenant of a farm near Grahamstown, in 1848 he moved to the neighbourhood of Bloemfontein. Under the auspices

[14] Schoeman, *Olive Schreiner*, 288, 481–3.
[15] 'All happy families are alike but an unhappy family is unhappy after its own fashion', L. N. Tolstoy, *Anna Karenin*, trans. Rosemary Edmonds, Harmondsworth, Penguin, 1954, 13.
[16] In this section I am virtually entirely dependent on Karel Schoeman, *Die dood van 'n Engelsman: Die Cox-moorde van 1856 en die vroeë jare van die Oranje-Vrystaat*, Cape Town, Pretoria and Johannesburg, Human & Rousseau, 1982, a work written with the attention to detail one would expect from a highly talented novelist.

of the Orange River Sovereignty, which had been proclaimed that year by Sir Harry Smith, a small British community was developing there, drawn by the prospects of extending the wool economy of the Eastern Cape north.[17] He settled on the farm of a friend, A. H. Bain, and began to rebuild his fortunes. There he met Maria Bouwer, more than twenty years his junior.

Maria's father, Willem Christiaan, had been born in Albany district only three years before his future son-in-law. In the late 1830s he made his way north from the Cape in the wake of the trekboers. The missionary traveller James Backhouse met him living in a mat house nine miles from Thaba Nchu, trading with the Boers, the Rolong and the Sotho.[18] He was going in the opposite direction, socially and economically, to Cox. In 1849, he was able to send his daughter to Mrs Eedes's girls boarding school in Grahamstown, which advertised itself as providing 'a solid Education, based on religious principles'. The subjects taught there were 'the French language, landscape drawing, drawing from nature, etching, flower painting, the piano forte and harp'.[19]

After their marriage, Charles and Maria settled first at the farm of Fairfield, five to six hours by horse from Bloemfontein. It was difficult for Maria to make the adjustment to living on a lonely farm, and the sweets and lemon syrup which Charles regularly provided for her were not enough to keep her happy. Their first child, Susanna, was born, not ten months after their marriage, at Maria's parents' house in Bloemfontein. Shortly after, perhaps as a result of a post-natal depression, their marriage began to show terrible strains. They moved back to Douglasfontein, a farm owned by Maria's father, very close to Bloemfontein. In 1855, a second daughter, Charlotte Antoinette (Hetty), was born. Despite, or perhaps because of this, the conflicts between them only became worse. As one of Charles's friends later described matters,

Perhaps the monotony of, or the sudden change to, so sober a way of living, created in her discontent, or else her contracted mode and expression of thoughts did not accord with Cox's more educated and refined mind. Certain it was, she early showed an aversion to him. He tried all in his power to elevate her mind [and brought from Bloemfontein] some elevating and instructive literature which he would read to her for her especial amusement. But such intellectual treats she did not care for, preferring to sit in the kitchen with her *tottie* maids and listening to their loose talk and coarse gossip. And when Cox remonstrated with her about such conduct and

[17] See Timothy Keegan, 'The Making of the Orange Free State, 1846–1854: Sub-imperialism, Primitive Accumulation and State Formation', *Journal of Imperial and Commonwealth History*, 17(1), 1988, 26–54.

[18] James Backhouse, *Narrative of a Visit to the Mauritius and South Africa*, London, Hamilton, Adams & Co., 1844, 417.   [19] Schoeman, *Die Dood van 'n Engelsman*, 26

seeming neglect of himself, she would retort by calling him '*de verdomde Englischman*', and vituperate against him personally and his country in general.[20]

With the Khoisan servants, she could at least speak the language with which she had been brought up, and from which Cox may have been excluded. Moreover, she probably thought he was being hypocritical. On 26 April, when he announced that he was taking some horses to safety during the tensions caused by the Free State commando against Witzie, she told him that: 'That is a nice excuse indeed to go and see your favourite Black woman at Bain's.' In the arguments that followed, Charles seems to have announced that he would be getting a divorce. Later that night, Maria, Susanna and Hetty were dead. Maria had been beaten to death, Susanna poisoned with strychnine and Hetty smothered.

Precisely what happened is unclear. Perhaps the most likely reconstruction, given by Karel Schoeman, is that in her depression Maria had killed her two daughters – strychnine was generally available on South African farms to be used against marauding jackals[21] – and then, perhaps repenting of her earlier decision to do away with herself, had come out of her room to be met by a drunken Charles who then smashed her about so violently that she died shortly afterwards. Be that as it may, in a politically charged trial, Charles Cox was convicted of having murdered all the other members of his family and, as we have seen, he was hanged.

Why did they get married in the first place? Such sexual attraction as may have existed between them is outside the range of the historian's vision. Even their appearance does not seem to have been described, except that Maria was described as 'a little woman', and seems to have presented a persona of frail girlhood. Sociologically, though, their coming together is more explicable. Charles saw this Grahamstown-educated, English-speaking young woman as an acceptable mate, indeed as the only acceptable mate in Bloemfontein, as 'Hobson's choice', as one of his companions later, ungallantly, described her. Marrying her would allow him to preserve, or perhaps, by using his father-in-law's money, to regain, his gentility. Maria, for her part, saw her marriage as a way of consolidating her rise from the *hartebeeshuisje* on the Modder River. Marriage into the English gentry was the expected return on the investment of time and money which she and her parents had put into her education in Grahamstown. She had learnt the accomplishments of a young lady. Now, she could enjoy the respect such an achievement commanded.

It is tempting to moralise, to suggest that marriage on such a basis could

[20] W. D. Savage, Letter to the *Eastern Star*, reprinted in Schoeman, *Die dood van 'n Engelsman*, 35.

[21] William Beinart, 'The Night of the Jackal: Sheep, Pastures and Predators in the Cape', *Past and Present*, 158, 1998, 193–4.

only end in disaster. This is not the case. Maria Bouwer had had her future husband checked out, and he seemed solid. A twenty-year age gap between husband and wife was not that unusual. Probably none of Mrs Eedes's other former pupils were beaten to death by their drunken husbands. When aspirations fail, they look ridiculous, and it is these that historians see. But those very aspirations, for gentility and respectability, were central to the history of nineteenth-century colonial South Africa. It is not only the poor, but also the would-be middle class, who have to be rescued from the 'condescension of posterity'.[22]

Gender and gentility

What, then, were these stories all about? In the first instance, obviously, they were about gender, about the various ways in which men and women saw themselves as such and saw their relations to the other sex. The greatest charge made against Katherine Schreiner by her parents was that she had strayed from the ways of 'feminine propriety', by encouraging, rather than demurely awaiting, John Findlay's attentions. Maria Bouwer, too, had learnt how to be 'a little woman', with all that that phrase entailed, in Grahamstown. It may well have been her failure to behave with the refinement that was expected of her that led to the break-up of her marriage and to her death. Or again, perhaps it was her realisation of the emptiness of Charles Cox's manhood that brought her world down around her.

Obviously, these ideas, of maleness, femaleness and the relationship between them, were historically configured by the protagonists in these events. That is to say, they were not individual constructions, but rather they took their particular form from the aspirations and expectations of the colonial world in which Katherine Schreiner, John Findlay, Maria Bouwer and Charles Cox moved. Indeed, they would not have relished such blunt terms as 'maleness' and 'femaleness'. 'Femininity' might have been possible, though 'masculinity' probably not. Rather, they saw their conduct in terms of the adjectives 'gentlemanly' and 'ladylike'.

In one sense, of course, these terms are in opposition to each other. A gentleman could do things which a lady could not, and a lady could be things which a gentleman could not and might have to do things which a gentleman would not be prepared to do. More importantly, though, these were a complementary pair. Together, they formed part of a wider set of rules for conduct, ideologies of behaviour and self-images. It would be vain to investigate how far ideas of gender determined the wider codes of

---

[22] The reference is of course to E. P. Thompson, *The Making of the English Working Class*, 2nd edn, Harmondsworth, Penguin, 1968, 13.

behaviour. Causality in such matters is more a question of belief, of axiom, than anything else. What is clear is that, in the Cape Colony and probably everywhere, they formed a sub-set of such codes. In nineteenth-century colonial South Africa, these went under the appellations of gentility or respectability. The distinction between the two was largely economic, not in terms of their content. Genteel behaviour required a higher income than did respectability.

The outward signs: housing

Respectability and gentility were manifested most clearly in material things. After all, the distinction between them was largely a question of income, although a gentleman, assured of and recognised in his status, might be permitted transgressions of behaviour which would condemn to the ranks of the disreputable someone who was struggling to be recognised as respectable. It was thus the outward signs that truly mattered.

This is as clear in matters of housing as anywhere. Shortly after his arrival in South Africa, Thomas Philipps, one of the most self-consciously genteel of the 1820 settlers, saw the open savanna of Albany district as if it were British parkland, 'and the road was so tastefully planted out that it was in vain persuading some of the Party that we were not approaching a Nobleman's residence'.[23] The landscape invited gentrification. Slowly the settlers and others began to provide it. As early as 1820 Arthur Barker drew the plan of his future house – never actually built – with a parlour and drawing room separated by the main hall, four bedrooms, a kitchen and a dairy in two wings surrounding a yard with a well and leading out to the farmyard behind. This contrasted painfully with the almost windowless one-roomed cottage, with a perilously sagging ridge, in which he actually lived.[24]

Barker did not manage to realise his ideal. Even his cottage burnt down, and he and his large family were left with no more than the clothes they stood up in, though he did manage to recoup some of his fortunes by making a number of trading trips. Furthermore, he antagonised the Governor, Lord Charles Somerset, which did nothing for his temporal prospects.[25] Others did manage to create something approaching their ideals, although it was a slow process. Thomas Pringle, at Eildon in the Baviaans River valley, lived first in a beehive hut which he built himself to a Xhosa pattern. Within five years, the hut had been relegated to serve as a kitchen and replaced by 'a commodious farm-cottage of stone and brick',

[23] Kepple-Jones, *Philipps*, 50   [24] Lewcock, *Early Nineteenth Century Architecture*, 142, 162.
[25] Lynne Bryer and Keith Hunt, *The 1820 Settlers*, Cape Town, Don Nelson, 1984, 55–6; Nash, *Bailie's Party*, 44.

thatched first with grass, later with wheat straw, and with the first chimney in the veldcornetcy. Originally it had only two rooms, but others were added in the course of time.[26] Brick and stone were as yet rare. By mid-1823, there were apparently 374 farmhouses in the Albany district, of which only fifteen were of brick and twenty-seven of stone – and many of the latter may have been converted from existing houses. The remainder, of Devonshire cob or wattle and daub, were cheap to build but expensive to maintain, and few have survived. A few were already roofed with fired earthenware tiles, made perhaps at the mission of Theopolis, but most were thatched.[27] The landscape had been Anglicised. In 1826, a Wesleyan missionary passing through Grahamstown on his way to the Transkei wrote in his journal that:

The houses, the farm-yards, the cross-barred gates, the inhabitants in manners, dress and appearance are thoroughly English, and while looking at every object I met, and the fields of oats and barley, and the gardens with abundance of vegetables of the same kind as are met with in my native country, it almost seemed a reverie to conclude that I was in Africa. It certainly is pleasing to think that from my circuit in the heart of Caffraria I can at any time ride on horseback in the short space of 5 days to Graham's Town and behold England in miniature.[28]

During the war of 1835, the Xhosa destroyed most of the farms the settlers had just built. As a result, when the houses were rebuilt, they were more akin to the frontier towers of late medieval Northumberland than to the Georgian country houses and farms of the south of England on which the settlers had hoped to model their society. But this was not the ideal. West of Grahamstown, on the road to Port Elizabeth, farmers grown rich early on sheep farming – and no doubt by profiting from army contracts – were able to permit themselves bow-fronted elegance. One army officer, Major Selwyn, was even able to build a mock-gothic castle in the Grahamstown suburbs, whose battlements were clearly for show, not to give cover to soldiers.[29] Selwyn and his fellow officers, the officials, the merchants and the artisans were also slowly building up Grahamstown. There, gradually, 'cramped cottage-like town houses', the stock-in-trade of Piet Retief and his fellow contractors, gave way to 'small free-standing stucco

[26] Lewcock, *Early Nineteenth Century Architecture*, 135, 150f., citing Thomas Pringle, *African Sketches*, London, Edward Moxon, 1834, titled illustration 339–42.

[27] Lewcock, *Early Nineteenth Century Architecture*, 140–3, 149; Journal of George Barker, 13 September 1823, in Marion Rose Currie, 'The History of Theopolis Mission, 1814–1851', MA thesis, Rhodes University, Grahamstown, 1983, II, 117; two of the four kilns at Theopolis were washed away in a great flood, and 100,000 bricks lost.

[28] Hildegard H. Fast (ed.), *The Journal and Selected Letters of Rev. William J. Shrewsbury, 1826–1835: First Missionary to the Transkei*, Johannesburg, Witwatersrand University Press for Rhodes University, Grahamstown, 1994, 27.

[29] The building later became the official residence of the Lieutenant-Governor of the Eastern Province, and now houses the anthropology department of Rhodes University.

villas'. As the century wore on, these villas too became larger and more imposing.[30]

Matters are evident in the settler country of the Eastern Cape because there the settlers were creating town- and farmscapes where none had previously existed, at least none that they would recognise as such. In the Western Cape, matters were somewhat different. Gentrification there entailed the upgrading of a landscape that was already under control, even if this might mean the building of a new house or the major alteration of one that already existed. This was beginning to happen from the 1760s on as the rich wine farmers of Stellenbosch district built the first of the great whitewashed and gabled houses that are its pride. Cape Dutch architecture, though, reached its zenith, at least in numerical terms, in the last decade of the eighteenth century, and, after a gap caused by a temporary drop in agrarian prosperity, the second decade of the nineteenth.[31] It was a form of architecture specific to the Cape, at least in the elaboration which it acquired. Indeed, a house built in Batavia in the late eighteenth century is now described as being in the Cape style. While the houses themselves are of relatively simple plan, essentially single-storey sheds run together in various combinations, their most distinctive feature, and true architectural glory, is their gables. There was, of course, a long tradition of ornate gables in the Dutch towns, of which the Cape examples are in some sense a continuation. However, while in the Netherlands, the decorated gables are generally an elaboration of a structurally essential feature of the building, in the Cape the front gables at any rate are fairly superfluous. They do surround a window, it is true, but they do not give the impression of having been built merely to provide lighting to the loft. Rather, they were the clearest possible display of the opulence, and thus of the status, of their owners.[32]

After the beginning of the nineteenth century, these architectural statements were saying something else as well. From this time, the houses can properly be described as 'Cape Dutch', not just as 'Cape'. In other words, Dutch and British architecture was, for a time, distinct. The Cape Dutch farmhouses became symbols displaying what was perhaps an ethnic affiliation, and certainly membership of a distinct social stratum, that of the prosperous rural gentry. The front-gabled house on the farms was set against the more classical, rectangular buildings put up by the Cape Town elite.

As always, things were not quite as simple as this might suggest. Even before the British occupation, and under the influence of the French architect Louis Thibault, classic models began to be followed. In the 1780s, Dirk

---

[30] Lewcock, *Early Nineteenth Century Architecture*, 232.   [31] Ross, *Beyond the Pale*, 27.
[32] E.g. Martin Hall, 'The Secret Lives of Houses: Women and Gables in the Eighteenth-Century Cape', *Social Dynamics*, 20, 1994.

Gysbert van Reenen, a member of the richest burgher family, had a house built on the slopes of Table Mountain to resemble the Palladian villas of the Veneto.[33] Other villas, in similarly classic styles, would follow in the Cape Town suburbs, notably those built by order of the British Governors, such as at Newlands. These were of course the most lavish of the Colony's houses. Simpler forms of architecture were employed by most of the towns-people who were building houses in the early nineteenth century, although the apogee of style entailed the building of a suburban villa with a large and 'picturesque' garden.[34] The houses they had constructed derived from British styles, as they had developed above all under the influence of the Adam brothers. If the Cape Dutch farmhouses can be described as plastered sheds, those of the British can be called brick boxes. In general they were well proportioned, increasingly embellished with cast-iron verandas, known in South Africa as 'stoeps', and provided with railings to accentuate the division between the house and the street. But, even when the bricks were whitewashed, as they often were in a wise concession to the climate, a clear distinction could be made between the English and the Dutch styles, as the missionary traveller Backhouse noted in Swellendam in 1838.[35] The increased stress on privacy which the English strove for meant that they built houses with halls and corridors, from which the rooms opened, rather than having a *voorkamer* opening directly to the street from which all other houses emanated. Benjamin Moodie, taking over a Dutch house at Grootvadersbosch near Swellendam, felt himself required to erect an interior partition to separate his living quarters from those of the servants and from the smells of the kitchen.[36]

Obviously, concern about the style of a house implied considerable sufficiency on the part of its owner. It was not a luxury that those lower down the economic scale could permit themselves. For this reason, it is not really possible to comment on the exteriors of the houses inhabited by the respectable poor and lower middle class, except for those who lived on the mission stations.[37] In any event, they generally lived in rented accommodation, and so, even in Bo'kaap, had relatively little say over the architecture of their houses. They were not indifferent to their circumstances, of course. In 1842, a petition against the imposition of a rate on Cape Town's fixed

---

[33] Lewcock, *Early Nineteenth Century Architecture*, 28–9. The house, Papenboom in Newlands, burnt down in the mid-nineteenth century.

[34] Graham Viney and Phillida Brooke Simons, *The Cape of Good Hope, 1806–1872: Aspects of the Life and Times of British Society in and around Cape Town*, Johannesburg, Brenthurst Press, 1994, ch. 8.   [35] Backhouse, *Narrative*, 105.

[36] Derek and Vivienne Japha, *The Landscape and Architecture of Montagu*, Cape Town, School of Architecture and Planning, UCT, 1992, 41–2, 93, citing J. W. D. Moodie, *Ten Years in South Africa*, 2 vols., London, Richard Bentley, 1835, I, 103.

[37] These will be discussed in chapter 5, below.

property was presented to the Legislative Council by 'inhabitants of hire houses' in the city. A high proportion, probably as much as 40 per cent, of the signatories were illiterate, and a number of others barely so. Nearly a third had obviously slave names – of the Cape, Van Mozambique and so forth – and many others were undoubtedly of slave descent, including those with evidently Islamic names. Hardly any of them appear in the Cape Town street directory of 1840, both suggesting the bias in that source towards those who owned houses and making it impossible to say anything about their occupations. They claimed that the house proprietors would pass on the costs in extra rent: 'Many of us are hard working for our daily bread . . . [but] as we are in want of houses, as of food, we cannot escape the payment of a higher rate of rent, and shall be compelled to suffer with our wives and families.'[38] This is the voice of those struggling for respectability, a struggle in which not all in Cape Town succeeded, or indeed took part.[39]

What mattered for people like this was not so much how their house looked but rather what was inside it: in the first place, the number of people. After emancipation, and the consequent flight of the ex-slaves from their owners' houses, overcrowding became rife. In 1840, a survey of Cape Town by the wardmasters found eight to ten people living in a single room in Rogge Bay. In an alley known as the Diaconies Gang, in the block bordered by Long, Loop, Longmarket and Shortmarket Streets in the centre of Cape Town, 'on a space of about 3,000 square feet, we *were told* ninety-one human beings live, but from what we saw we shd. say that double that number was nearer the truth'.[40] Such comments were made regularly throughout the rest of the century in Cape Town, although the precise locations might vary.[41] They could also be made in other towns within the Colony,[42] and in the

[38] CA LCA 13, item 36. I would like to thank Patricia van der Spuy for her sterling work in trying to decipher these names; see also *SACA*, 23 May 1836, 27 May 1836; *Cape Town Mail*, 17 Apr. 1849, as cited in Katherine Elks, 'Crime, Community and the Police in Cape Town, 1825–1850', MA thesis, UCT, 1986, 73, 109.

[39] Shirley Judges, 'Poverty, Living Conditions and Social Relations: Aspects of Life in Cape Town in the 1830s', MA thesis, UCT, 1977; see also chapter 6, below.

[40] Cited in Judges, 'Poverty, Living Conditions and Social Relations', 74–5.

[41] E.g. Vivian Bickford-Smith, 'Dangerous Cape Town: Middle-Class Attitudes to Poverty in Cape Town in the Late Nineteenth Century', *Studies in the History of Cape Town*, 4, 1981, 32–4.

[42] K. W. Smith, *From Frontier to Midlands: A History of the Graaff-Reinet District, 1786–1910*, Grahamstown, Institute of Social and Economic Research, Occasional Paper 20, 1976, 220–1; Keith S. Hunt, 'The Development of Municipal Government in the Eastern Province of the Cape of Good Hope, with Special Reference to Grahamstown (1827–1862)', *AYB*, 14, 1963 for 1961, 202; Gary Baines, 'The Origins of Urban Segregation: Local Government and the Residence of Africans in Port Elizabeth, c. 1835–1865', *SAHJ*, 22, 1990, 67–8, 70.

countryside.[43] This was what the respectable had to avoid. It is difficult to know how many managed to do so, and in what style, because for obvious reasons the historical record tends to over-emphasise either the top of society, who are the role models and create the information, or the bottom, who are targets of prurient disapproval and offensives from those who, for whatever reason, feel the need to intervene. The main exceptions to this generalisation were those who lived on the mission stations, who are discussed in the next chapter. Nevertheless, the wardmasters' reports of 1849, which were primarily concerned with identifying those areas of the city which were insanitary and threatening the health of the respectable citizens of Cape Town, noted that even in Ward 1, the poorest quarters of the town near the harbour, 'many houses, & especially those of the better classes of Malays were kept in very clean and wholesome condition'. Again in Ward 10, near Plein Street, 'the streets were found in a tolerable state of cleanliness', or again in Ward 13, 'the class of inhabitants are more cleanly in their habits, the greatest part being Mechanics and tradesmen, that occupy small Dwellings the greater part of which have been recently built'.[44]

The second diagnostic requirement for a house to be considered respectable was in a sense negative. Both it, and the street in front of it, had to be free from dirt. The same reports of the overcrowding of Cape Town are full of complaints about the insanitary nature of these slums. By the late nineteenth century, Cape Town municipal politics had even come to polarise between the 'Clean' and the 'Dirty' parties, on the issue not of electoral probity but of municipal sanitation (in part expressed in terms of English and Afrikaner ethnicity, with the 'coloureds' on the side of the Afrikaners).[45] But the insides of the houses were another matter. Lady Duff Gordon, one of the most sympathetic observers of the Cape population, noted of the farm labourers around Caledon that:

Their cottages are far superior in cleanliness to anything out of England, except in picked places, like some parts of Belgium; and they wash as much as they can, with the bad water-supply, and the English outcry if they strip out of doors to bathe. Compared to French peasants, they are very clean indeed, and even the children are far more decent and cleanly in their habits than those of France.

Despite this, the people of whom she was writing were at best on the edge of respectability, and when they had the wherewithal they would get roaring

[43] Pamela Scully, *The Bouquet of Freedom: Social and Economic Relations in the Stellenbosch District, South Africa, c 1870–1900*, Cape Town, Centre for African Studies, UCT, Communication no. 17, 1990, 84–5.
[44] CA CO 490, 159, Wardmasters' reports with regard to smallpox.
[45] Vivian Bickford-Smith, *Ethnic Pride and Racial Prejudice in Victorian Cape Town: Group Identity and Social Practice, 1875–1902*, Cambridge, Cambridge University Press, 1995, 58–9.

drunk. They were, moreover, poorer and less able to keep up appearances than those Muslims she had met in Cape Town and with whom she had very good relations – a herbal tea they had provided had proved a good palliative for her consumption. Of these she wrote: 'The great mania of the poor blacks about Capetown is a grand toilet table of muslin over pink, all set out with little "objects", such as they are, then a handsome bed with at least eight pillows.'[46]

This emphasis on textiles may have been a rather later development, or one that was specific to the Muslims with whom Lady Duff Gordon had most contact. The inventories of the middling sort of people – craftsmen, fishermen, small shopkeepers, often Free Blacks, or descended from them – that have been studied for the first half of the nineteenth century in Cape Town, tend to suggest that such wealth as they possessed was displayed more with furniture and cabinets containing pottery than with cloth.[47] Also, in part because their space was limited, the degree to which the various rooms of their house were differentiated by function was not great. As Patricia Scott noted of the artisans and working men of Grahamstown, their interiors were characterized by 'a generally haphazard inclusion of extraneous items in the rooms . . . Usually . . . one room was furnished as a parlour-dining room, with basic sofa, table and chairs, possibly a carpet, rarely curtains, ladies' work box, mirror and clock, together with incidental items.'[48] Equally, Afrikaner farming households at what was clearly neither the highest nor the lowest reaches of the economic scale are depicted, for instance by J. C. Poortermans, as cluttered and devoid of privacy.[49]

This was not merely a question of economic status. Through the first half of the nineteenth century there was a steady trend among the elite away from the multi-purpose *voorkamers* of the eighteenth-century Dutch towards a much greater specialisation in the use of rooms and a greater emphasis on the space around the individuals. This can be seen in the representations of the rooms inhabited by the Governor and his ladies, the Chief Justice, or indeed by Major George Pigot, an (illegitimate) scion of the British aristocracy.[50] The style was taken up by those of lower status as their circumstances improved. This was in part a question of ethnic affiliation.

[46] Lucy, Lady Duff Gordon, *Letters from the Cape*, annotated by Dorothea Fairbridge, London, Oxford University Press, 1927, 72, 96.
[47] Antonia Malan, 'Households of the Cape, 1750–1850: Inventories and the Archaeological Record', Ph.D. thesis, UCT, 1993, 114–15.
[48] Patricia E. Scott, 'An Approach to the Urban History of Early Victorian Grahamstown 1832–53, with Particular Reference to the Interiors and Material Culture of Domestic Dwellings,' MA thesis, Rhodes University, Grahamstown, 1987, 246.
[49] See reproduction in Hattersley, *Social History*, after p. 126.
[50] These can be found conveniently in Scott, 'Approach to the Urban History', plates 1–4.

English houses had English interiors. But it was also a question of the definition of refinement. In this way, outward style manifested the acceptance of the standards of behaviour deemed appropriate to the higher layers of society.

The outward signs: clothing

Even more than housing, clothing, and other forms of body decoration, forms probably the most universal medium whereby people all over the world make statements to claim status, in the widest meaning of that term. As any fashion magazine makes plain, clothing is seen as an extension of the personality, and can thus be chosen to project the sort of personality its wearer would desire. What might seem to be the primary functions of clothing, to provide protection against the sun, rain, heat, cold or the hardness of the ground, are usually less important, as reasons for the choice of a particular garment or whatever, than the less material, and more social, connotations that it may have at any given time or place.[51]

Two further points need to be made on this. The first is that the claim need not be based on some universal truth, if such a concept is allowable, but rather may establish that truth. To give a South African example, no matter what his biological sex may have been, and it is still in doubt, by his clothing (and other behaviour) Dr James Barry, head of the army medical service at the Cape between 1822 and 1827, established that he was a man, and was generally accepted as such. Of course, the fact that his sex can be doubted shows that the claim he made was not perfect. Secondly, the claims that are made through clothing need not be universally accepted. Take the statements made by Pixley Seme, one of the founders of the African National Congress (ANC). He had himself photographed in full court dress, with frock coat, top hat and umbrella,[52] a costume in which, indeed, many of the delegates to the founding meeting of the ANC in Bloemfontein appeared.[53] Evidently he was claiming equality, at least, with all the lawyers of South Africa. This was not accepted by his white fellows. He was not a member of their clubs, did not dine with them, and there was no question that he would ever be appointed a judge. On the other hand,

---

[51] Jack Schwartz, 'Men's Clothing and the Negro', MA thesis, University of Chicago, 1958, 27, cited in Marshall Sahlins, *Culture and Practical Reason*, Chicago and London, University of Chicago Press, 1976, 183.

[52] The photo can be found in André Odendaal, *Vukani Bantu: The Beginnings of Black Protest Politics in South Africa to 1912*, Cape Town and Johannesburg, David Philip, 1984, illustrations before p. 1.

[53] Peter Walshe, *The Rise of African Nationalism in South Africa: The African National Congress, 1912–1952*, London, Hurst, 1970, 33; at that stage, the ANC was of course still the South African Native National Congress.

the claims for superiority enhanced his prestige among his various black constituencies.

To return to the Cape in the early nineteenth century, the first distinction that had to be made was between the clothed and the undressed. The bodies of respectable men, women and children were totally covered, except for the face, parts of the rest of the head and neck, depending on the style of hat and collar worn, and, usually, the hands. This was civilised; the display of bare skin in the torso, arms, legs or feet, let alone near-nudity, was savage. Both the raggedness of Cape Town's poor and the very different conventions of dress employed by the Sotho, the Xhosa or the Zulu could be so categorised. The savagery (or as Thomas Pringle put it, with awareness for the evolutionary theory of his day, the barbarity[54]) could be seen as noble, as when the French Protestant mission, which approved of him, portrayed Moshoeshoe in a garment bearing more resemblance to a Roman toga than to any Sesotho clothing – and incidentally with a nose to match.[55] It could also be exaggeratedly wild, as Sandra Klopper's analysis of G. F. Angas's portrait of a Zulu chief makes clear, notwithstanding his use of poses from Ancient Greek sculpture, notably the *Apollo Belvedere*.[56] But African leaders claiming acceptance by, and some degree of equality with, the Cape Colony's leaders had to put on the dress of the Europeans.[57] With the possible exception of the notorious bare-headedness of the eccentric missionary, Johannes van der Kemp, the reverse was not the case.[58]

Among the clothed, a number of major distinctions were developed. Some were gradual, for instance in the way that clothing mirrored the wealth of its wearer. Most, though, followed the axes of binary division by which the social order of the Colony was regulated, between slave and free, Christian and Muslim, young and adult, man and woman, town and country, military and civilian, Dutch-speaker and English-speaker, the mourning and the celebrating, clergy and laity, and no doubt others. That between the slave and the free disappeared in the 1830s, or rather was sub-

---

[54] Thomas Pringle, *Narrative of a Residence in South Africa*, reprinted Cape Town, C. Struik, 1966, 267.

[55] This portrait, 'drawn by a Parisian artist under Eugène Casalis's supervision' (Leonard Thompson, *Survival in Two Worlds: Moshoeshoe of Lesotho, 1786–1870*, Oxford, Clarendon Press, 1975), was first published in Eugène Casalis, *Les Bassoutos*, Paris, C. Meyrneis, 1859.

[56] Sandra Klopper, 'George French Angas' (Re)presentation of the Zulu in *The Kafirs Illustrated*', *South African Journal of Cultural and Art History*, 3, 1989, 63–73.

[57] Robert Ross, 'The Top Hat in South African History: The Changing Significance of an Article of Material Culture', *Social Dynamics*, 16, 1990, 90–100.

[58] There was a twist to this story at the end of the nineteenth century. With the rise of migrant labour especially for the mines, employers displayed a preference for the 'red-blanketed' Africans, uncontaminated by European influences – and the demands for higher wages that went with them – over the dangerous, dressed 'mission boys'.

sumed into others, those of wealth and religion above all. The others became in general more pronounced during the first half of the nineteenth century. Thus before then, once the boys had been breeched, at the age of three to four, elite children, at least in their best clothes, were dressed more or less as their parents were.[59] Only during the nineteenth century was the dress of childhood always used to delineate a stage in the life-cycle. Girls were allowed to wear their skirts shorter than would have been seemly for young, or older, women, though they did have to keep their legs covered by stockings. Boys too could wear short trousers. In particular, the sailor suit came to be accepted as their typical wear. This was an innovation, congruent with changes in the way children were imagined, and largely imported into South Africa from England. Short trousers were symbolic of the temporary freedom accorded to boys – and short skirts of the lesser freedoms of girls. In South Africa, though, there was to be an ironic shift. Around 1890 the fashion developed for clothing black male house servants in simplified versions of white boys' dress. They were known as 'piccanin suits', and were marketed commercially after an enterprising draper had visited a household where the servants were dressed in this fashion. This signified not their freedom, but rather their infantilisation.[60]

During the nineteenth century a similar accentuation of difference occurred between the clothes worn by men and by women. This may seem to be a remarkable comment. Both Western culture and those of South Africa have made such distinctions for at least as long as there are records of the matter, and probably ever since dress and ornamentation codes began to be elaborated. Only in the late twentieth century have these become less pronounced, but nevertheless they still survive.[61] And before the nineteenth century, the basic forms of male and female clothing were much as they would be later. What changed was the colour, and to some extent the fineness. As photographs of, for instance, the first Members of Parliament after 1854 make clear, men were increasingly incarcerated in black broadcloth and white linen,[62] and even the coloured necktie, later the only release from drabness, was not adopted until the last years of the

---

[59] See the portrait of Hendrik Storm on p. 12 above. I hope that the formulation I have used here would escape the strictures made by G. R. Elton against Philippe Ariès in *Return to Essentials: Some Reflection on the Present State of Historical Study*, Cambridge, Cambridge University Press, 1991, 58.   [60] Strutt, *Fashion in South Africa*, 348.

[61] I recommend, as a way of alleviating boring academic lectures and seminars – whether given by yourself or someone else – checking the number of women in the audience who are wearing some item of clothing, or these days more usually ornament, which would not be worn by men, and the number of men whose clothes would not be worn by a woman. Such audiences are drawn from the group that in my experience displays the least pronounced sexual division of clothing.

[62] See, for example, the photos of MPs, e.g. in Le Cordeur, *The Politics of Eastern Cape Separatism*, facing p. 187.

century. Only the military could escape this tyranny, rejoicing in the splendour of their uniforms.[63] Women mirrored in their dress the delicacy of character that Rebecca Schreiner accused her daughter of lacking. Lace, for instance, became exclusively female. It is difficult to imagine a Voortrekker man wearing one of the embroidered *kappies* that were his sisters' or his wife's pride – or indeed that he would have put on any other garment made with the same attention to detail.[64]

Neither the Voortrekker nor his wife, though, would have worn the black broadcloth suits which Cape Members of Parliament felt appropriate to their dignity. This was not a matter of ethnicity. Rather it reflected one of the sharpest divisions in the mental mapping of South Africa, that between the town and the country. Away from the towns men and women were allowed to be scruffier, and less formally attired. Men might wear other colours, notably browns, and other materials, including leather on their bodies. They might also wear wide-brimmed hats, rather than the toppers of the townsmen.[65] But this showed a lack of formality. When they went to church, for instance, they would do their best to emulate in drabness their urban counterparts.

Education

Gentility, for men and women, had to be acquired, and thus taught. Education at the Cape was in part concerned with matters of literacy and numeracy, which, if not exactly neutral, are of fairly wide cultural application. As much as this, though, education was about the moulding of 'character', or in other words about socialisation into a set of very specific roles which the children would be expected to play in later life. It was indeed seen as the main way in which the Colony could be racially and culturally homogenised. In 1842, the *SACA* editorialised that 'the distinction between *black* and *white* was in every sense *superficial*. The only practical

---

[63] Another exception was Roualyn Gordon Cumming, a Scots elephant hunter, who on occasion appeared in town or at a ball in full Highland dress, complete with kilt and sporran, and on another was refused entry to an inn until he wore at least a cloak to cover his complete nakedness. See A. Gordon-Brown (ed.), *The Narrative of Private Buck Adams, 7th (Princess Royal's) Dragoon Guards on the Eastern Frontier of the Cape of Good Hope, 1843–1848*, Cape Town, Van Riebeeck Society, 1941, 96–7, 282.

[64] Strutt, *Fashion in South Africa*, 223–9; see also L. M. Chaveas, 'A Study of the Quilted and Corded Kappies of the Voortrekker Women and their Resemblance to French White Work Quilting of the 17th and 18th Centuries', *Navorsinge van die Nasionale Museum, Bloemfontein*, 1993.

[65] See, for example, Thomas Baines's painting, 'Mr Hume's wagon with ivory and skins from the interior of Africa on the Grahamstown market, 1850', in the 1820 Settlers' Memorial Museum, Grahamstown, reproduced in Strutt, *Fashion in South Africa*, facing p. 325.

distinction in this case is in training, in habits, in custom, in a word EDUCATION.'[66]

This process began early in life. In 1830, Rebecca Schreiner's half-sister, Elizabeth Lyndall, brought out to the Cape by Dr. John Philip, opened an infant school in St George's Street, Cape Town. It was for children between the ages of eighteen months and eight, and attracted pupils from all classes in Cape Town. The boy she remembered best when she wrote her reminiscences forty years later was Frederic Rutherfoord, son of one of Cape Town's leading merchants, but she also remembered many young slaves responding 'in a wonderful manner to the language of kindness and to the gentle influences of the Pestalozzian system'. Many of these, though, were taken away, because, so their owners claimed: 'Slaves they still were and slaves they should remain, but they were becoming too "*slim*" under the English teacher!' The parents of other children in the school, including the immediate family of John Philip, found that the infant school had failed to inculcate sufficient discipline. All the same, the school was a temporary tourist attraction, and increased its reach by attracting a number of young women, 'mainly missionaries' daughters', who were trained in the system and would later open similar schools in the various towns of the Cape Colony.

For all 'the gentle influences of the Pestalozzian system', Elizabeth Lyndall's school was a disciplining institution, of both the children and their parents. Time was strictly imposed. No children were admitted after the doors shut at ten and two precisely. Cleanliness in 'persons and clothes' was stressed. As she wrote in the institution's first annual report, 'the principal subjects brought before the children, in order to employ, amuse, and instruct them – are Spelling, Numbers, Grammar, Natural and Scripture History; – and for the Girls, Needle-work; – but as the chief object is to teach them to *think, act* and *speak* correctly, many others are introduced as opportunity occurs'. Socialisation had been well taken in hand.[67]

The infant school in Cape Town was not segregated by sex (nor by race) even if, within it, only the girls learnt sewing. Thereafter, in general, boys and girls were taught separately, at least among the elite, though the Dutch school in Cape Town, *Tot nut van 't Algemeen*, was a (poor) exception. Even

---

[66] *SACA*, 7 May 1842, cited in Elks, 'Crime, Community and the Police in Cape Town', 78 (original emphases).

[67] This section is based on Karel Schoeman, 'Elizabeth Rolland (1803–1901), pioneer van kindertuinonderwys in Suid-Afrika', *QBSAL*, 40(1), 1985, 32–9; Karel Schoeman (ed.), *The Recollections of Elizabeth Rolland (1803–1901)*, Cape Town and Pretoria, Human & Rousseau, 1987, 55–7; Edna Bradlow, 'Children and Childhood at the Cape in the 19th Century', *Kleio*, 20, 1988, 19, and 'Women and Education in Nineteenth-Century South Africa: The Attitudes and Experiences of Middle-Class English-Speaking Females at the Cape', *SAHJ*, 28, 1993, 123.

in the undenominational public schools, where possible the two sexes were taught in separate rooms, with a mistress for the girls. The expectation was that girls were not being prepared for one of the professions, but for a life as a wife and mother. In this context, subjects such as domestic economy and sewing were thought to be more essential, and the 'accomplishments' that Maria Bouwer presumably acquired at Mrs Eedes's in Grahamstown more valuable.[68] Moreover, the characters that were to be inculcated were somewhat different. When she was staying in Cape Town, on holiday from boarding school, Henriette Schreiner, who came between Katie and Olive in the family, was criticised by her hostess, Mrs Dale, for being 'far too self-opinionated & womanish for her age, not 15'.[69] Her life in the wilds of Herschel district, and no doubt keeping her end up in what was, by any standards, a remarkable family, had given her an independence that might well have been appreciated in a boy of her age, but which was not compatible with ideas of femininity.

There was a certain discrepancy between the high moral character expected of young ladies and the view that 'no greater calamity can befall us than that . . . our daughters not be given in marriage'.[70] Emma Rutherfoord, Frederic's sister and a member of a family notable both for its mercantile wealth and its piety, expressed the matter clearly in a letter to her married sister:

It is true many girls here do waste their time and minds in falling in love etc. etc., but the fault is in their education and not having better things set before them, not in the place. A mind bent on trifles and follies here would be the same in England. I question whether there are not as many girls bent on folly and vanity of dress or anything else as here. As to Ellen [her younger sister] she is not quite so foolish as to be full of such things. Her feelings are strong but childish and transient and now she is beginning to find happiness in promoting the welfare and happiness of those around her, works hard in making caps etc. for the working society, indeed is an able coadjutor in all labors and has not time for vanity and is being weaned from the desire for admiration, etc. etc. Indeed we are as quiet as she could possibly be kept anywhere and will grow up more natural and simple-minded than elsewhere, at least I think so.[71]

---

[68] Bradlow, 'Children and Childhood', 16–17.

[69] Joyce Murray (ed.), *Mrs Dale's Diary*, Cape Town, Balkema, 1966, 85. Mrs Dale's husband was the Colony's Superintendent-General of Education. For a photo of Henriette, taken about this time, see Schoeman, *Olive Schreiner*, plate 15. She was later to become a formidable temperance campaigner, and 10,000 people are said to have attended her Cape Town funeral in 1912. See Karel Schoeman, *A Debt of Gratitude: Lucy Lloyd and the 'Bushman Work' of G. W. Stow*, Cape Town, South African Library, 1997, 55–8.

[70] J. S. H., 'Mechanics' Institutes – Their Social Role', *CMM* 8 Dec. 1860, cited in Edna Bradlow, 'Women at the Cape in the Mid-Nineteenth Century', *SAHJ*, 19, 1987, 56.

[71] Joyce Murray (ed.), *In Mid-Victorian Cape Town: Letters from Miss Rutherfoord*, Cape Town, Balkema, 1968, 24–5.

At the time she wrote this, Emma Rutherfoord was seventeen. While her letters are mainly concerned with family news, descriptions of the obligatory climbing of Table Mountain and her pious works on behalf of the Bible Society, they do on occasion note the style of the bonnets that she and Ellen were wearing.[72] Her work, perhaps not very serious, as a schoolmistress, on the other hand, scarcely receives a mention. All the same, the ideas she had of the proper character for women, as exemplified in these comments, were not empty. Some three years later, she received a proposal of marriage from the Rev. Andrew Murray, a young minister of the Dutch Reformed Church (DRC) living in Bloemfontein. In the first instance she was uncertain, as she had only known him for three weeks, and felt that, for all his learning, he lacked 'heart cultivation'. She soon came round, however, and her sense of duty and her Christian piety made her an ideal wife for the man who was to dominate the DRC in the later nineteenth century.[73] The educational work that had been begun, probably by Elizabeth Lyndall, had achieved success.

Education for sons of the elite, at least once they had passed beyond the infant schools, was likely to be more academic. Entry into the professions or the civil service, neither of which were open to young women, required the passing of fairly stringent examinations. The curriculum for Cape secondary education was developed by Sir John Herschel, a man of formidable intellect and learning (he was made a fellow of the Royal Society at the age of twenty-one, after winning all the prizes available for his year as an undergraduate at Cambridge) who was consulted while he was living in Cape Town to catalogue the stars of the southern hemisphere – his father had done the same for the northern.[74] He set out the principles on which education should be based as follows:

I cannot but think that what is good education in a highly civilised & peopled country is also good education in a colony and considering how much below the standard of what should be considered *good* is the *best* usually afforded in England, I cannot regard that – (or rather that improved by omitting much that is useless and inserting many things of primary importance which are never thought of at home, or at least in schools) – a bit too good for the Cape. In education as in coinage to lower the standard is suicidal. The finest principles – the correctest knowledge – the soundest maxims and the most elevating associations are not too good for the humbles, and the highest can have no better, though they may and ought to ornament them more. In effect one great object of education considered in a public light is so far to civilise the mass of a community & to spread so universal a standard of intellectual attainment as well as moral feeling that when a man rises in life by his industry, he shall not find himself above his level of knowledge & ideas and vice

[72] Murray, *In Mid-Victorian Cape Town*, 37.
[73] J. du Plessis, *The Life of Andrew Murray of South Africa*, London, Marshall Bros., 1920.
[74] The district where Olive Schreiner was to grow up was named after him.

versa that when a man sinks by misfortune he shall be spared a wish to divest himself of his intellectual habits and associations. The bitterness of adversity would be infinitely alleviated to a man of cultivated mind if it did not of necessity bring him into contact with ignorance and vulgarity while on the other hand prosperity would lose much of its intoxicating quality were the mind prepared by previous culture for the wider sphere into which it is an introduction. A practical equality of moral and intellectual culture[,] could it be established, so far from having tendencies inimical to a due subordination of stations and wealth would operate as a powerful correction of some of their worst evils, by smoothing the intercourse between distant ranks, and facilitating that perfect interfusion of classes which is essential to the harmony of society where free institutions prevail.[75]

Sir John Herschel's ideas were put into practice. From 1839, government-aided public schools were set up throughout the Colony, although only in the larger centres were there the '1st class' secondary schools that were envisaged here. But this high-minded liberalism was probably too much for any society, colonial or otherwise. Like many liberalisms, it was in its application seriously exclusionist. In order to benefit from the best, scholars had to come from families with, at the every least, enough wealth to forgo the immediate incomes of their sons and to pay school fees. Also they had to live in or close to one of the few schools able to offer tuition at such an exalted level. Except for Cape Town, Stellenbosch, Port Elizabeth and Grahamstown, these could not be found. The only alternatives were the boarding schools which emerged from the 1840s and 1850s, either resolutely Anglican such as Diocesan College ('Bishop's') near Cape Town, and St Andrew's College, Grahamstown, which were modelled on Dr Arnold's Rugby and consciously thought of themselves as schooling the future elite,[76] or one of the non-conformist academies. The latter might be of high quality. The Schreiner boys enjoyed superb education from the Rev. Robert Templeton in the tiny *dorp* of Bedford.[77] But even the government schools were not egalitarian in intent. According to Sir Langham Dale, the Superintendent-General of Education in the Colony, the high quality schooling provided for instance by the South African College School in Cape Town was designed to 'keep the children of the higher and middle classes up to the standard of their peers in Europe', thus ensuring their 'unquestionable superiority and supremacy in this land'.[78]

In this way, Herschel's ideals, probably against his own intentions, worked to entrench a particular group in social power within the Colony.

---

[75] Ferguson and Immelman, *Sir John Herschel*, 47.
[76] Peter Randall, *Little England on the Veld: The English Private School System in South Africa*, Johannesburg, Ravan, 1982, 61–6.
[77] Schoeman, *Olive Schreiner*, 201–2.
[78] Sir Langham Dale, 'The Cape and its People', in R. Noble (ed.), *The Cape and Its People*, Cape Town, J. C. Juta, 1869, 9, cited in Bradlow, 'Children and Childhood', 14.

The universality that had been granted to certain culturally determined particularities, notably the learning of Latin, ensured this. But this could not be left unchallenged. The ideas of respectability and gentility, in terms of possessions, education and behaviour, were not so group specific. They provided ideals to which all could aspire. Moreover, they contained within themselves the assumption that everyone should attempt to follow such examples. In this, such ideas were the secular side of a set of religious tenets which were of great importance through the nineteenth century in South Africa and which led to a whole series of political and social conflicts.

5 Christianity, status and respectability

That polymath millenarian Dr Johannes van der Kemp, the first missionary to the Eastern Cape, taught his Khoisan converts to sing the psalms. One of the favourites of these men and women struggling to escape from their *de facto* bondage to European settlers was Psalm 118, which runs in part:

The Lord is on my side; I will not fear: What can man do unto me?/ The Lord taketh my part with them that hate me./ It is better to trust in the Lord than to put confidence in man./ It is better to trust in the Lord than to put confidence in princes./ All nations compassed me about: but in the name of the Lord will I destroy them./ They compassed me about; yea they compassed me about but in the name of the Lord I will destroy them . . . The stone which the builders refused is become the head stone of the corner./ This is the Lord's doing; it is marvellous in our eyes. (verses 6–11; 22–3)

They also appreciated Psalm 134:

Behold, bless ye the Lord, all ye servants of the Lord, which by night stand in the house of the Lord/ Lift up your hands in the sanctuary, and bless the Lord./ The Lord that made heaven and earth, bless thee out of Zion.

This they sang in the church of Graaff-Reinet in June 1801, when, at a moment of high political tension during the Servants' Revolt, they gained access to that building for the first time. This was not appreciated by the Boers, who had gathered in the town for safety and as a basis from which to smash the revolt. They too knew their Bibles, and sang back, from Psalm 74:

Thine enemies roar in the midst of thy congregations; they set up their ensigns for signs . . . They have cast fire into thy sanctuary, they have defiled by casting down the dwelling place of thy name to the ground . . . O God, how long shall the adversary reproach? Shall the enemy blaspheme thy name for ever? (verses 4; 7; 10)[1]

[1] Ido H. Enklaar, *Life and Work of Dr J. Th. van der Kemp, 1747–1811: Missionary Pioneer and Protagonist of Racial Equality in South Africa*, Cape Town and Rotterdam, Balkema, 1988, 112; Susan Newton-King, 'The Rebellion of the Khoi in Graaff-Reinet, 1799 to 1803', in Susan Newton-King and V. C. Malherbe, *The Khoikhoi Rebellion in the Eastern Cape (1799–1803)*, Cape Town, Centre for African Studies, 1981, 24. Biblical citations are taken from the Authorised Version.

This dramatic contest of voices was a struggle for control over the title of 'Christian'. The Graaff-Reinet farmers claimed a monopoly over this most potent of symbols, and protested against the Khoi and the Xhosa 'being instructed by [the missionaries] in reading, writing and religion, and thereby put upon an equal footing with the Christians [and] especially that they were admitted to the church of Graaff-Reinet'.[2] Other farmers could assert to a converted Khoi that 'your baptism is not as good as ours'.[3] Van der Kemp and the Khoikhoi contested this, and indeed would later assert that they represented the only true Christians in the country.[4] Christianity clearly was a source of social power, well worth the costs entailed in entering it, or, alternatively, in keeping others out.

This may seem a sterile way in which to approach the religious history of South Africa. That history must surely be first of all about belief, about theology, about communion, about spirituality, about the inner power which Christianity has given its adherents to change society, not necessarily for the better. A history of Christianity which does not include such matters – and this chapter will only do so peripherally – is impoverished and incomplete. Nevertheless, Christianity, or rather the church, provided both a terrain on which the divisions within society were accentuated and the possibility, eventually vain, for overcoming them.

Who? The social politics of baptism

Baptism is the rite by which an individual is admitted to the Christian church. It entails the application of water, in greater or lesser quantities, symbolically to wash away the pre-Christian life, and is often the moment at which a 'Christian' name is bestowed, either as a replacement for a previous one or to take a new-born child out of anonymity. Baptism is in general administered to the children of Christians shortly after birth, and thus without their active consent, or alternatively is a public sign of an adult's conversion to, and acceptance by, the Christian church.

In the aftermath of the Reformation, there were those, known as Anabaptists, who believed that baptism should only be given to those who were of an age at which they could consciously accept Christianity. Perhaps because of the Anabaptists' political excesses in the early sixteenth century, this was not a position which was held by other Protestant theologians. Reformed theologians in the Calvinist tradition invariably allowed the

---

[2] *Transactions of the Missionary Society*, 1, 1804, 481–2, cited by Hermann Giliomee, *A Question of Survival: A Social History of the Afrikaners*, forthcoming.
[3] Genadendal diary, 28 Sept. 1813, *PA*, VI, 39.
[4] Elizabeth Elbourne, ' "To Colonize the Mind": Evangelical Missionaries in Britain and the Eastern Cape, 1790–1837', D.Phil. thesis, University of Oxford, 1991, 143, 153–4.

baptism of the children of Christians. For the Dutch at least, the covenant that God had made with his church was passed down from generation to generation. Even the children of parents under censure from the church, even children 'wrought in adultery', should be baptised.[5] The attempt of one minister in South Africa to refuse baptism to the children of those members of his congregation with whom he was in conflict was condemned by the superior ecclesiastical authorities in the Netherlands, and the children in question, who included the future Voortrekker leader Piet Retief, were baptised.[6] It was a rite that in practice could be claimed for all those both of whose parents were Christians, however loosely.

Within the context of the Netherlands, where nearly everyone was Christian, even if many were Roman Catholics, this argument did not cause great problems. In South Africa, with numerous slaves and Khoikhoi who were not of Christian descent, further difficulties arose. It was as if there was a theological foreshadowing of the 'nature versus nurture' debate. Was it enough for children to be born and brought up in a Christian environment, or was the acknowledged descent from Christian parents a requirement for infant baptism? There were those who took the former position, notably Dominee Johan van Arckel who ministered at the Cape for six months until his death in 1669. He was prepared to baptise a Khoikhoi child who had been adopted by Europeans, and he established the policy, which would continue throughout VOC rule, that all babies born in the VOC slave lodge were to be baptised.[7] Thus at the end of the eighteenth century, a listing of the Company's slaves shows that all those born at the Cape, and no others, had been admitted to the first rite of the Reformed Church.[8] Although the Company did at times make fairly desultory efforts to instruct its slaves in the faith, it is difficult to believe that this ritual had any practical significance.

The Company's practice was not followed by the mass of colonists. The baptism of infant slaves belonging to free burghers and Company officials was very rare indeed. St Paul had told his gaoler at Philippi that, if he believed, 'thou shalt be saved, and thy house'. Whatever Paul may have meant, the States Bible, as used in South Africa, glossed 'house' as 'family, your wife and children, as children of the covenant'.[9] In the Netherlands,

[5] Jonathan Neil Gerstner, *The Thousand Generation Covenant: Dutch Reformed Covenant Theology and Group Identity in Colonial South Africa, 1652–1814*, Leiden, New York, Copenhagen and Cologne, Brill, 1991, 194, citing the decisions of the Synod of North Holland for 1583.   [6] Gerstner, *Thousand Generation Covenant*, 234–9.
[7] Gerstner, *Thousand Generation Covenant*, 203–5, citing C. Spoelstra, *Bouwstoffen voor de Geschiedenis der Nederduitsch-Gereformeerde Kerken in Zuid Africa*, 2 vols., Amsterdam, Hollandsch-Afrikaansche Uitgevers-maatschappij, 1907, II, 259. The baby in question died within a few weeks.   [8] See the list in ARA VOC 4347.
[9] Gerstner, *Thousand Generation Covenant*, 111, citing Acts 16; the Dutch word used was *huis-gezin*.

where, in contrast to England, servants were not thought of as part of the family, this was perhaps an unthinking gloss. In South Africa, where the commentaries to the States Bible were often thought to have the force of holy writ, it could only strengthen the limitation of the family to the acknowledged kinship group, thus excluding the slaves.[10]

As Robert Shell has pointed out, the debates at the Synod of Dort on this matter only strengthened the slave-holders' interests in not having their slaves baptised. It was laid down at Dort that Christian slaves could not be sold to others.[11] This was no problem for the Company, which never sold any of its Cape-born slaves, and hardly any of those it imported. For private owners, this was a different matter, since even if they did not intend to sell their slaves, they wished to maintain the possibility of doing so, or for instance of raising a loan using slaves as security. Slaves could only be baptised or admitted to full church membership 'with a letter of permission from their owner'.[12] Only when the missions began to work towards the conversion of the slaves, in the early nineteenth century, were the rules changed, and in 1812 the Government specifically made it possible for baptised slaves to be sold.[13] This removed a brake against baptism. In 1823, the Government even provided an incentive, as henceforth only unbaptised slaves were taxed.[14] However, this measure did not result in mass, more or less enforced baptism of slaves at the orders of their owners eager for a tax break.[15]

There were various reasons for this. The Cape's clergymen would not have relaxed their fairly strict criteria for the baptism of 'heathen' and their children, nor would the masters have been prepared to abandon one of the marks of distinction between them and their slaves for a relatively minor financial gain. The masters themselves were not enthusiastic. One slave-owner in Graaff-Reinet, otherwise 'one of the best-intentioned members of the church', told Van der Kemp that he was afraid of having a slave baptised, not for pecuniary reasons but because of 'his apprehension

[10] Ross, 'Paternalism, Patriarchy and Afrikaans', 34–47.
[11] Shell, *Children of Bondage*, 332–43.
[12] *Kerkenraad* Cape Town to J. I. Rhenius, Acting Governor, 4 June 1792, published in Spoelstra, *Bouwstoffen*, II, 340. It was specifically mentioned that, were it to be required that baptised slaves be manumitted, this would lead to a 'hindrance to the progress of Christianity'. On the other hand, the fact that the *Kerkenraad* of Drakenstein needed elucidation on the matter demonstrates that the question did not arise with any regularity.
[13] Cradock to Bathurst, 25 Jan. 1813, in *RCC*, IX, 130.
[14] Proclamation of 18 Mar. 1823, *RCC*, XV, 336.
[15] Gerstner, *Thousand Generation Covenant*, 211, suggests otherwise, claiming 'by 1827 most frontier congregations had larger slave membership than free', but the figures on which his claim is based, deriving ultimately from A. M. Hugo and J. v. d. Bijl, *Die Kerk van Stellenbosch, 1686–1965*, Cape Town, Tafelberg, 1963, 126–7, refer to the total population within the area served by the church of Stellenbosch, not the congregation in the strict ecclesiastical sense of the word. The Dutch word 'gemeente' is used in both senses.

lest her pride should grow unsupportable by her admission among Christians'.[16] Even the secretary of the Paarl Auxiliary Missionary Society is said to have commented that baptised slaves were worth nothing, although it is not clear whether this was his own judgement of the detrimental effects of baptism or rather that of his fellows reflected in the market price.[17] Nor, in all probability, would the slaves have accepted it. At least one slave, a decade later, refused to be baptised until she was emancipated.[18] For close on two centuries, there had been a close association between emancipation and baptism. The Abbé de la Caille commented, of the situation around 1750, that 'when an owner wishes to free his slave, he is baptised and becomes a Christian', and there are other examples that the two changes in status, the religious and the legal, were closely linked.[19] It was not automatic, as Gerstner seems to think. Some of those who were manumitted became, or remained, Muslims, and others did not become members of any religious denomination.[20] Others again failed to satisfy the church council that their knowledge of the tenets of the Reformed faith was sufficient for them to be admitted to the church, 'and this congregation, alas, already has more than enough of such ignorant members'. At a later date it was laid down that potential converts had to demonstrate that they had received instruction from designated catechists.[21] Nevertheless, the symbolic connotations of that practice could not be done away with.

The baptism of those who were neither slaves nor of full Christian descent was another matter. All Christian churches have always been prepared in principle to welcome converts into their midst. Christ is said to have commanded his disciples to 'Go forth into all the world and preach the gospel to all nations.'[22] This is one of the foundational texts of the faith, and was regularly used, in South Africa as elsewhere, as a text for sermons

---

[16] *Transactions of the Missionary Society*, 1, 1804, 491, cited by Giliomee, *A Question of Survival*.

[17] Journal of James Kitchingman, 5 Jan. 1831, in Basil le Cordeur and Christopher Saunders (eds.), *The Kitchingman Papers: Missionary Letters and Journals, 1817 to 1848 from the Brenthurst Collection Johannesburg*, Johannesburg, Brenthurst Press, 1976, 105.

[18] Brian Warner (ed.), *Lady Herschel: Letters from the Cape, 1834–1838*, Cape Town, 1991, p. 82.

[19] Nicolas Louis de la Caille, *Travels at the Cape: 1751–53*, trans. and edited by R. Raven-Hart, Cape Town and Rotterdam, Balkema, 1976, p. 35, cited in Gerstner, *Thousand Generation Covenant*, 210.

[20] Elphick and Shell, 'Intergroup relations', 190; they comment that in only 8.4 per cent of cases was an application for manumission accompanied by a comment that the slave had been baptised. What matters, in the context of the argument I am making at the moment, is rather the proportion who *would be* baptised once manumission was granted. I know of no statistical evidence on this matter, so that I have to rely on the impressionistic comments of foreign visitors.   [21] Spoelstra, *Bouwstoffen*, II, 332, 366.   [22] Mark 16:15.

by ministers concerned with the mission.[23] However, to understate matters, the Cape church in the eighteenth century was not one of the most eager to put this precept into practice. Undermanned as it was, the Cape hierarchy was only very rarely prepared to engage actively in proselytisation among the Colony's 'heathen'. As was mentioned above, it also brought about the abandonment of the only attempt at missionisation before the last decade of the century, driving the Moravian Georg Schmidt out of the Colony because his work constituted an attack not just on the ecclesiastical but also on the social order.[24]

Those who were of Christian parentage on both sides were baptised as a matter of course; for those only whose father was a Christian, and whose parents were therefore not married, matters were uncertain. Some were baptised and accepted unquestioningly into the full Christian community, others were recorded as 'baptised Bastards'.[25] Men in this category, though poor, were apparently able to attract wives of European descent as often as their fellows who were not so designated.[26] The women probably had little difficulty in marrying up the social scale, given the chronically imbalanced sex ratio in the Colony. Others again were not baptised at all, probably as the result of the chance of circumstances rather than for some deeper sociological reason. All the same, it mattered enough for one man to spend money on it, as we have seen.[27] Others again were able to claim specific benefits on the grounds of their membership, at the most basic level, of the church.[28] At least through the eighteenth century, being a Christian meant social acceptance.

Where? Seating in church.

The church service, weekly in Cape Town and the small towns, less often attended in the thinly settled countryside, was an opportunity for the confirmation of status. It could begin competitively. A Cape Town woman of standing would have her personal chambermaid, who was better dressed than the rest of her slaves, carry her psalm book behind her as she went to church.[29] The slaves, though, did not stay to hear the service. There were regular complaints of the irreverent and rowdy behaviour of slaves outside the church disturbing the worship, while the seats in the gallery reserved for

---

[23] G. and G. Fagan, *Church Street in the Land of Waveren*, Tulbagh, Tulbagh Restoration Committee, 1975, 33; T. N. Hanekom, *Helperus Ritzema van Lier: Die Lewensbeeld van 'n kaapse Predikant uit die 18de Eeu*, Cape Town and Pretoria, N. G. Kerk-Uitgewers, 1959, 247.   [24] See above, p. 31.

[25] As pointed out earlier, in Dutch 'bastard' means 'mongrel' in addition to, and probably before, it means 'illegitimate'.   [26] Giliomee, 'The Eastern Frontier', 458.

[27] Sparrman, *Voyage*, I, 264; see above, p. 30.   [28] Giliomee, 'The Eastern Frontier', 457.

[29] De Jong, *Reizen*, I, 143. See the illustration printed in Shell, *Children of Bondage*, 249.

slaves in the *Groote Kerk* in Cape Town were always empty.[30] They had to be back by the end of the service, to carry their owners' Psalm books and also their owners in the sedan chairs which could cause such a scrimmage outside the church that a new door had to be made in 1796 to allow the congregation an orderly exit.[31] The evil did not disappear, however. In the 1840s the police had to be sent to ensure that church-goers were not plagued by the begging of 'swarms of filthy, ragged, disgusting children' as they came out of church.[32]

Once in church, though, competition gave way to affirmation. The seating plan was as regulated and as much a reflection of official status as at any formal banquet. With his usually accurate memory of how things had been in Cape Town during his stay there in the 1730s, Mentzel described how, beneath the armorial bearings of former governors, rank and precedence were confirmed weekly.

The Governor's pew is to the right of the pulpit and is occupied by him and his son, if he has one. The floor between this pew and the pulpit is covered with a handsome carpet upon which armchairs are placed for the Governor's lady and her daughters. The pew opposite that of the Governor is for the Upper-merchants, namely: the Vice-Governor, the *Fiscaal* and the Captain; the other merchants or members of the Council of Policy are also accommodated in the same pew. The two remaining pews along the columns are reserved for the military and civil officers of the Company. Along the side walls are two rows of benches: those in front for persons of distinction, those at the back for the citizens of the town. There are besides many rows of open benches under the organ that are available for all-comers without distinction. The ladies sit in the centre of the Church directly facing the minister at the pulpit. They sit upon their own chairs that are drawn up in regular rows one behind the other by the verger and his assistants before the service, but which are on other occasions pushed away in a corner. The ladies' seats are arranged in a definite sequence of precedence.

Communion was taken, by those who were full members of the church, with the same attention to rank, and to division between the sexes.[33] Since

---

[30] E.g. *Case against Jefta v.d. Caap*, 15 Aug. 1754, ARA VOC 4196; *Kaapse Plakkaatboek*, III, 64, IV, 13; J. S. Marais, *The Cape Coloured People, 1652–1937*, reprinted Johannesburg, Witwatersrand University Press, 1968, 168.

[31] Resolution of the Cape Town *Kerkenraad*, 1 Aug. 1796, published in C. Spoelstra, *Bouwstoffen*, II, 354. It should not be thought that this crush of sedan chairs was a consequence of the liberalisation of status markers after the British conquest; by the *pracht en praal* regulations, provided they were not adorned with gold or silver, such chairs were allowed to all under the VOC. See Van der Chijs, *Nederlandsch-Indisch Plakkaatboek*, VI, 773.

[32] Elks, 'Crime, Community and the Police in Cape Town', 39, citing *SACA*, 11 Dec.1841.

[33] Mentzel, *Description*, I, 123–4; cf. P. B. Borcherds, *An Autobiographical Memoir*, 1861, reprinted Cape Town, African Connoisseurs Press, 1963, 205, for similar discussions of Stellenbosch during his youth around the turn of century. His father was the dominee.

it was by no means automatic that every adult had that right,[34] there were times when the top of the Company hierarchy were not admitted to the 'Lord's Supper Table'.[35] It would be reasonable to suppose, although there is no confirmation of this, that at such times the display of rank during communion was less pronounced.

A seat in church in conformity with one's rank continued to be a major matter of concern well into the nineteenth century. There were occasions when the church had to discipline those who took too much freedom,[36] and others when individuals complained that they, or their sons, were not accorded the seat which was their due.[37] The distribution of seats was indeed one of the tasks of the Political Commissioner appointed by the Government to oversee the actions of the *Kerkenraad*. At least after 1795, individuals who felt that they had not received their due appealed to the British governors. The British, however, did not wish to become involved in such matters, perhaps because they thought them to be too trivial for their attention, or, more likely, because they felt their intervention could only lead to needless acrimony directed against them. Whatever decision the *Kerkenraad* might take, Governor Dundas wrote in 1801, 'shall be considered as final', a remarkable but tactful abdication of responsibility.[38] All the same, the Government's retreat from involvement in such questions did not diminish their importance. The third Synod of the DRC in South Africa, in 1829,[39] is most famous in the historiography for the refusal of the Political Commissioners, the Government's representatives, to allow any discussion of the question whether there should be any distinction on the grounds of colour as to when the members of the church took communion.[40] However, it also spent much of its time discussing the question of the seat in church to which the wife of the District Surgeon in Worcester, who was not a member of the church, was entitled. As the report of the Political Commissioners commented:

---

[34] Gerstner, *Thousand Generation Covenant*, 214–18; D. van Arkel, G. C. Quispel and R. J. Ross, 'Going Beyond the Pale: On the Roots of White Supremacy in South Africa', in Ross, *Beyond the Pale*, 80; G. J. Schutte, 'Tussen Amsterdam en Batavia: De Kaapse samenleving en de Calvinistische kerk onder de Compagnie', unpublished paper presented to the Conference of Dutch and South African Historians, Johannesburg, 1997.

[35] Francois Valentyn, *Description of the Cape of Good Hope with the Matters Concerning it*, edited by R. H. Raven-Hart, 2 vols., Cape Town, Van Riebeeck Society, 1971 and 1973, II, 259.   [36] E.g. Leibbrandt, *Requesten*, I, 73.

[37] Jeffreys, *Kaapse Archiefstukken, 1781*, 139.

[38] B. Booyens, 'Kerk en Staat, 1795–1853', *AYB*, 28, 1965, II, 40–3.

[39] Full Synods of the Cape church, demonstrating its independence of the churches of the Netherlands and its growing ability to govern its own affairs, had been instituted in 1824.

[40] E.g. Chris Loff, 'The History of a Heresy', in De Gruchy and Villa-Vicencio (eds.), *Apartheid is a Heresy*, Grand Rapids, Mich, Eerdmans, 1983.

In most of the Country Districts there exists a jealousy among the female part of the congregation as to Rank of Seats in the Church and the indulgence which for the sake of peace it has been found necessary to use in this respect has given rise that by the augmentation of places of distinction the seats of respectable women, but whose husbands accidentally did not fill any situation of distinction in Church or State, have constantly been removed further and further back from the hearing of the Minister, which circumstance often gives rise to unpleasant feelings, and consequent quarrels among the Congregation.

Henceforth only the wives of government officials in office and of Church Wardens would be allowed special seats, and on the expiry of their husbands' term of office, they would have to go back to the seats they had previously occupied.[41] It was a conflict which the inhabitants of the Colony a hundred years earlier would have understood.

In the more distant districts, matters were not so formally organised, probably because the mass of the congregation often lived too far from the church to attend every Sunday. Rather, once every quarter, there was a great gathering in the church town to celebrate *nagmaal*, or Holy Communion. This provided opportunities for trade, and for social activities, including courting. In the course of these, naturally enough, the relative status and wealth of those attending *nagmaal* could be easily demonstrated.[42]

Which? Denominational strife

In 1801, Egbertus Bergh, an embittered scion of one of the Cape's leading official families, wrote a long memorandum on the state of the Colony which he presented to the Government of France. He argued that it would be possible for the French to capture the Colony since the British had not defended it strongly, whereafter it might be ceded to the Batavian Republic, France's client state in the Netherlands. Further, by vilifying the Cape's previous Dutch rulers, he hoped to be rewarded with a position in the new regime. Indeed, after the Batavian Republic took over the Cape two years later, not by conquest but through the short-lived Peace of Amiens, he was appointed Auditor-General of the Cape.

In these circumstances it is not surprising that Bergh's memorandum consistently criticised the policies which had been pursued at the Cape by the VOC, which was in many ways the embodiment of the old Dutch order which the Batavian Republic had replaced. It included a scathing attack on the attempts by the VOC to maintain the religious monopoly of the DRC. Bergh wrote:

---

41 Dreyer, *Boustowwe*, 322–3.
42 B. Booyens, *Nagmaalsweek deur die jare: 'n kerkhistoriese studie*, Cape Town, N. G. Kerk-Uitgevers, 1982.

The intolerance with regard to religion at a spot where all the faiths of the world could easily be found was . . . so strong that fairness, sound policy and the interest of both the Colony and its rulers was sacrificed to it. After having requested it for half a century, the Lutherans had been granted the freedom to practise their religion, but this honey was mixed with gall by also laying down that the members of this church might no longer be promoted to the highest positions. The fate of the Roman Catholics was still less pleasant; cut off from all services, they were allowed neither church nor building in which to demonstrate their praise of the Almighty, and, as regards the Easterners who confess to the Mohammedan faith, they were watched with such care that I have several times seen them dispersed with sticks by the servants of the [department of] Justice,[43] on the orders from higher up, while, at a great distance from the town, or in the mountains, they were honouring their God in their usual way, or burying their dead, without causing annoyance or offending in any way.[44]

Bergh had a reason for this harangue. Although not a member of any church, he had admitted that his views were closer to the Augsburg confession than to any other, and probably for this reason his preferment within the VOC service had been blocked.[45] Nevertheless, his complaints were justified. There had been Lutherans at the Cape ever since 1652. By the end of Dutch rule almost two-thirds of those officials who were members of any church were Lutherans.[46] All the same, only in 1780 were they allowed to establish a congregation and to convert into a church the warehouse which Marten Melck, the richest burgher at the Cape, had built anticipating this decision. And indeed, as Bergh mentioned, religious freedom for Lutherans had to be set against the erection of barriers to their political advance. It was not impossible for Lutherans to be promoted to the Councils of Policy and Justice but this could only be done with the explicit permission of the *Heren XVII* in the Netherlands.[47]

The monopoly, as opposed to the predominance, of the DRC at the Cape for so long was not a reflection of metropolitan Dutch practice,[48] nor of that of the VOC in Batavia. In such a small society, the power of individuals' prejudices could be considerable and the long domination of the Cape by Rijk Tulbagh, first from 1739 as *Secunde* to his brother-in-law Hendrik Swellengrebel and then, from 1751 to 1771, as Governor, delayed the

---

[43] Presumably the kaffers, who were under the orders of the *Fiscaal*.

[44] Egbertus Bergh, 'Memorie over de Caap de Goede Hoop, aan het Gouvernement der Fransche Republiek gepresenteerd', 22 Aug. 1801, published in Theal, *Belangrijke Historische Dokumenten, III*, 118.

[45] J. Hoge, 'Die Geskiedenis van die Lutherse kerk aan die Kaap', *AYB*, 1(2), 1938, 135; in general, information in this section is taken from this work.

[46] Hoge, 'Geskiedenis van die Lutherse Kerk', 145–6.   [47] Spoelstra, *Bouwstoffen*, II, 350–1.

[48] S. Groenveld, *Was de Nederlandse Republiek verzuild? Over segmentering van de samenleving binnen de Verenigde Nederlanden*, Leiden, Leiden University Press, 1995; Jonathan I. Israel, *The Dutch Republic: Its Rise, Greatness and Fall, 1477–1806*, Oxford, Oxford University Press, 1995, 1019–38.

recognition of the Lutherans. It is clear, however, that more than the quirks of individual conscience, if that is what it was, drove his stubbornness. Church membership was also a marker of ethnicity. Lutherans were, with few exceptions, Germans or Scandinavians. Of the 106 men who signed petitions in 1742 and 1743 for the establishment of a Lutheran church at the Cape, only four were born in the Dutch Republic, and four more at the Cape, but then as the children of Germans.[49] They formed much of the middle management of the Company and also on occasions the senior officers in the armed forces. With one exception, however, the governors and the other high officials of the civilian administration were Dutchmen.[50] The long refusal of the Cape's rulers to sanction the establishment of a Lutheran church was as much a demonstration of the relative power of Dutchmen and Germans in the Colony as it was an expression of religious intolerance.

After the ending of VOC rule, such concerns no longer mattered. Through De Mist's *Kerkorde*, the Batavian Republic maintained state control over the DRC, and over the appointment of elders in the Lutheran Church. However, De Mist equally did not see that the state had any role in denominational strife. As he said in a meeting of the Batavian National Assembly in 1799, while the state's 'dearest duty' was to maintain and further religion, 'Whether this should be taught according to the ways and particular tenets of the Roman Seat, of Calvin, Luther, Menno Simons or Arminius – as a Christian I can make my own choice in the matter – but as a Statesman I may not, according to the currently accepted principles, give preference to any of these various ideas.'[51]

The British, taking over the Cape permanently in 1806, were committed to maintaining the institutions of their Dutch predecessors, thus including the Cape Church. Since they also introduced British churches, and had to do so, this meant that any overt political favouritism was impossible. In 1816, Lord Charles Somerset attempted to prevent Methodists, as dissenters, from ministering to the troops. It was no problem if they worked among the Africans beyond the borders, but the established Church of England, he felt, should have a monopoly with regard to the British in South Africa.[52]

---

[49] Hoge, 'Geskiedenis van die Lutherse Kerk', 32–3, 42–3.

[50] The exception was Hendrik Swellengrebel, whose grandfather had been a German merchant in Moscow and whose father, in Company service, had signed the 1742 petition. He himself, though, was born at the Cape – which led the German army commander Rudolf Alleman to accuse him of parochialism – and was fully assimilated to the Dutch. He eventually retired to become a country gentleman and rentier living outside Utrecht.

[51] Cited in J. P. van der Merwe, *Die Kaap onder die Bataafse Republiek, 1803–1806*, Amsterdam, Swets & Zeitlinger, 1926, 10–11. Menno Simons and Arminius were the founding figures of the Mennonite and Remonstrant (or Arminian) Churches, respectively.

[52] Somerset to Bathurst, 30 Jan. 1816, *RCC*, XI, 62.

It was not a policy that he was able to maintain. Religious intolerance which would not be permitted in Britain could not be allowed in the colonies. Obviously there was a certain amount of unofficial preferential treatment for the Anglicans. It is not by chance that the Anglican cathedral occupies the prime site in Cape Town, astride the city's main street and close to Parliament. In general, though, the Government slowly divested itself of responsibilities towards the Colony's Protestant churches, finally ending government representations in the synods in 1843. By then, as the Attorney-General William Porter pointed out, the DRC 'does not claim peculiar privileges', so that specific surveillance was 'out of place'.[53]

The only exception to this toleration of Christian denominations at the Cape related to the position of Catholics in the Government. In itself this was no problem. In 1818, Lieutenant-Colonel Christopher Bird, of an old Catholic family and with a Jesuit priest for a brother, was appointed Colonial Secretary, the head of the Cape administration. On doing so, he took the so-called Canada oath of loyalty, which had been introduced as an alternative to the standard formula which required adherence to the Church of England. This only began to cause controversy with the arrival in the Colony of William Parker, a militantly Protestant 1820 settler from County Cork in Ireland. Before he knew that Bird was a Catholic, he expressed his pleasure at coming to a country free of the influence of Catholic priests. When he discovered that the region of South Africa which had been assigned to him and his party, in the Oliphants River valley of the Western Cape, was particularly harsh, and that he was unable to live the life there that he had envisaged, he came to believe that this was the result of a Catholic plot against him. A stream of vitriolic attacks on Bird followed, which went all the way to the British House of Commons. They were not initially taken seriously. The acting governor, Sir Rufane Donkin, commented that 'a strong opinion prevails here, that this individual is suffering from a degree of mental derangement', paranoia in modern parlance.[54] However, when Lord Charles Somerset returned as Governor in 1821, he was able to use Parker's attacks as a weapon in his vendetta against Donkin, whom he thought not to have shown sufficient respect for Lord Charles's son, Colonel Henry Somerset, who had remained in the Colony in his father's absence. As a result, Bird, who took Donkin's side in the controversy, was hounded from the Colony.[55]

Anti-Catholic prejudice survived, but decreasingly as the century wore

[53] Porter to Maitland, 31 Dec.1844, cited in Booyens, 'Kerk en Staat', 166, and more generally, *ibid.*, 156–66.   [54] Donkin to Bathurst, 30 Oct. 1820, *RCC*, XIII, 308.
[55] This controversy can be followed through a series of letters published in *Records of the Cape Colony*, notably Parker to Goulburn, 8 Dec. 1821, *RCC*, XIV, 200–6, Parker to Bathurst, 17 Dec. 1821, *RCC*, XIV, 216–18, and many subsequent effusions.

on. Sir Harry Smith refused to allow the submission of a memorial from the Catholic bishop claiming the same rights (and stipends) for Catholic priests as were granted to dissenting ministers.[56] The village of Burghersdorp, founded in 1843 at the instigation of the DRC and on land owned by the church, refused to allow the building of a Roman Catholic (or any other non-Calvinist) church within its bounds.[57] One of the ways in which his opponents attempted to defame Andries Stockenström during his time as Lieutenant-Governor of the Eastern Province was by claiming that he had converted to Catholicism.[58] The Mother Superior of the first congregation of nuns in the Eastern Cape commented in 1850 that '*we have to fight for every inch of ground* in this hotbed of prejudice and protestantism', and a dissenting minister in Grahamstown preached against the popish danger every week.[59] Matters came to a head when Elizabeth Heavyside, the daughter of a leading Grahamstown Anglican clergyman, herself decided to take the veil. The more evangelical of the Anglican clergy in the Colony at the time commented that this was a consequence of the father's Puseyite leanings.[60] Again her family was decidedly unhappy when, after Gottlob's death, Rebecca Schreiner sought solace from her hard life in the Grahamstown convent.[61] All the same, by this time, such animosities were personal (and in this case soon smoothed over), not general or political, at least in the Cape Colony. The head of the convent, known to all as *Notre Mère*, was a much respected figure in Grahamstown by this time, and the convent could count on subscriptions from all sectors of the town's population.[62]

The decrease of political discrimination against or in favour of any denomination reached its logical conclusion in 1875, when, after many years of campaigning, the Cape Parliament adopted the 'Voluntary Principle' for church financing. By this measure, which took the Cape's leading parliamentarian Saul Solomon twenty-one years to get passed,

---

56 Mary Young (ed.), *The Reminiscences of Amelia de Henningsen (Notre Mère)*, Cape Town, Maskew Miller Longman for Rhodes University, Grahamstown, 1989, 189.

57 E. J. C. Wagenaar, 'A Forgotten Frontier Zone – Settlements and Reactions in the Stormberg Area between 1820–60', *AYB*, 45, 1982, 153.

58 C. W. Hutton (ed.), *The Autobiography of the late Sir Andries Stockenström, Bart.*, 2 vols., Cape Town, J. C. Juta, 1887, II, 59. The Grahamstown gentry also reminded the Afrikaner farmers of his role in the Slagters Nek affair, thereby resuscitating this matter which would become a major plank of Afrikaner nationalist mythology. This was two decades before the examples of this found by Leonard Thompson in his *The Political Mythology of Apartheid*, New Haven and London, Yale University Press, 1985.

59 Mother Gertrude to Sister Thérèse Emmanuel, 15 Sept. 1850, cited in Young, *Reminiscences*, 189 (italics in original).

60 A. F. Hattersley, *A Victorian Lady at the Cape, 1849–51*, Cape Town, Maskew Miller, n.d. [1951], 63; for a Catholic perspective, see Young, *Reminiscences*, 312.

61 Schoeman, *Olive Schreiner*, 478–9; Young, *Reminiscences*, 280–1.

62 Young, *Reminiscences*, 53.

state support for all ministers of religion, of whatever denomination, was finally removed, and churches had to maintain their clergy entirely on the basis of the contributions of their members.[63]

Divisions between the various churches remained, of course. In part these were a matter of language, perhaps of ethnicity. Membership of the DRC was effectively reserved for those who could understand its services, and who felt part of the Dutch community. In part, too, certainly among the English-speakers, church membership reflected social status. The Anglicans might on occasion receive their first adherents in a town from Khoi who claimed finally to have a church where they would not be shown the door, but the colour prejudice in the Anglican Church was as great as in the DRC.[64] Much more generally, though, the Anglicans were at the top of the social pyramid, certainly in the larger towns, and as men and their families found their social and economic position improving they would be likely to switch their allegiance to the Church of England, as it was imprecisely known. By the mid-nineteenth century, most of the leading merchants in Cape Town were Anglicans, prepared to pay rents for the pews in the city's cathedral.[65] It was a demonstration of the rank they had by then attained.

Wherein? Church architecture

Leiden, the city in which I am writing this book, has three great churches. Two of them are Late Gothic symbols of civic pride, both completed more or less in their current form before 1540. Like all medieval Catholic churches they were built along a west–east axis, as the architecture takes the eye to where the altar once stood. With the Reformation, this literal orientation disappeared, although the chancel might be used for the serving of communion to full church members. Instead, the arrangement of seating and so forth in the buildings was focused around massive pulpits placed between pillars of the nave, creating a tension between fabric and interior

---

[63] W. E. Gladstone Solomon, *Saul Solomon: THE Member for Cape Town*, Cape Town, Oxford University Press, 1948, 34–47, 173–9; Philip Le Feuvre, 'Cultural and Theological Factors affecting Relationships between the Nederduitse-Gereformeerde Kerk and the Anglican Church (of the Province of South Africa) in the Cape Colony, 1806–1910', Ph.D. thesis, UCT, 1980, 89–93. Part of the argument used by Solomon and his ally William Porter was that subventions to Christian churches would have to be balanced by ones to mosques and synagogues. See McCracken, *New Light*, 126–7.

[64] Le Feuvre, 'Cultural and Theological Factors', 69. The Khoi adherence to the Anglican Church occurred in Burghersdorp, while racism was rife in the churches in the Cape peninsular: see N. J. Merriman, *The Cape Journals of Archdeacon Merriman*, edited by D. H. Varley and H. M. Matthew, Cape Town, Van Riebeeck Society, 1957, 7, 11.

[65] Digby Warren, 'Merchants, Commissioners and Wardmasters: Municipal and Colonial Politics in Cape Town, 1840–1854', *AYB*, 55, 1992, 129; Hattersley, *Social History*, 122.

design which I at least, schooled in an Anglican church architecture which has preserved the medieval form, find exceedingly discomforting.

The third church, the *Marekerk*, was completed in 1639 as one of the first specifically Protestant churches in the Netherlands, and one of the most radical rejections of Catholic architecture.[66] Here, fabric and interior design are in harmony. In plan, it is an octagon. The pulpit, with its great sounding board, fills one of its sides. Next to it is the font, and the seating is arranged around and in front of it without doing violence to the space in which it is found. The sober space is roofed by a great dome, on whose support, on the outside, in an apparent concession to those used to gauging direction from the local church, are affixed the letters of the eight cardinal points.[67]

While the plan of the *Marekerk* was exported to Batavia, none of the Cape churches matched its simple grandeur. The principles of their interior architecture were however the same. They were also built clean, in the Protestant style, without what the Calvinists would have seen as popish frippery. The Lutherans, and later the Methodists,[68] could convert warehouses into places of worship without in any way offending against the Colony's ideas as to what a church should be. So did the Catholics, but they disguised their origin by gothicising the windows and adding functionally valueless buttresses.[69] The Anglicans, on the other hand, no doubt sinned aesthetically when they borrowed the *Groote Kerk* of the DRC and imported a portable altar for their services, which had to be hastily removed before the subsequent Dutch service.[70]

Given this background, it is most surprising to find that Dutch Reformed churches built after the middle of the nineteenth century at the Cape generally seem to have more in common with medieval tradition than with that of the Reformation. Even the church in Heidelberg, a town near Swellendam which by its very name resonates to its Calvinist background, was built in a Mock Gothic style.[71] By the second half of the nineteenth century, the Cape Colony had taken over what were by this time English ideas as to how sacred space should be conceived.

This was a process which began early in the century. The LMS church

---

[66] The Westerkerk in Amsterdam, built somewhat earlier by Hendrik de Keyser, in contrast combines a Protestant floor-plan with a Gothic shell.

[67] J. J. Terwen, 'De ontwerpgeschiedenis van de Marekerk te Leiden', in *Opus Musivum*, Assen, 1964; in more general terms, see Van Swigchem *et al.*, *Een Huis voor het Woord*.

[68] Barnabas Shaw, *Memorials of South Africa*, 2nd edn, London, Adams & Co, 1840, reprinted Westport, Conn., Negro Universities Press, 1970, 212.

[69] See the plate in Viney and Brooke Simons, *The Cape of Good Hope*, 106.

[70] Dreyer, *Boustowwe*, 155–6.

[71] Desirée Picton-Seymour, *Victorian Buildings in South Africa, including Edwardian and Transvaal Republican Styles*, Cape Town and Rotterdam, Balkema, 1977, 63.

at Pacaltsdorp, near George, was built in the 1820s with a battlemented tower and pointed windows, so that the first Anglican bishop of Cape Town, Robert Gray, was moved to call it 'the most church-like edifice I have seen in the Colony'.[72] This was a matter of considerable concern to the bishop, and even more to his wife, Sophy, to whom he was writing. As high church Anglicans in the England of the 1840s, they had been caught up in the movement for the Gothic Revival, and had read the standard texts by Pugin, Rickman and Bloxam.[73] Arriving in South Africa with the goal of constructing an Anglican diocese, they conceived their task as comprising church fabric as much as the immaterial institutions of ecclesiastical organisation. In this they were aided by extensive grants of land and money from the Colonial Treasury, organised by the Colonial Secretary, John Montagu.[74] Sophy Gray was herself a gifted and enthusiastic draftswoman and architect – she would also have made an outstanding clerk-of-the-works, if the proprieties and her other duties had allowed. She designed at least seventeen churches in South Africa, in medieval, mainly Early English, style, and took pains to ensure that they were, as she saw it, 'correct'.[75] She had, of course, portfolios of designs, including some by George Butterfield, from which those intending to build churches could choose, but increasingly what went up was her own interpretation, generally rather mangled by uncomprehending local builders. It was an imposition onto the landscape of a particular vision of what places of worship should be. Sophy Gray saw it as in some way sacralising the Cape, and there were others, of many denominations, who shared this vision. They may not all have realised how much it was also Anglicising the landscape.[76]

[72] Thelma Gutsche, *The Bishop's Lady*, Cape Town, Howard Timmins, 1970, 76; on the building of Pacaltsdorp church, see Anderson to Directors, 7 Jan. 1823, 22 Oct. 1824 and 28 July 1825, in LMS-SA 9/1/A, 9/2/D and 9/3/C, respectively.

[73] Gutsche, *The Bishop's Lady*, 36; presumably the works were Augustus Pugin, *An Apology for the Revival of Christian Architecture in England*, London, J. Weale, 1843 and *Contrasts: Or a Parallel between the Noble Edifices of the Fourteenth and Fifteenth Centuries and Similar Buildings of the Present Day*, London, for the author, 1836; M. H. Bloxam, *The Principles of Gothic Ecclesiastical Architecture, elucidated by Question and Answer*, London, Whittaker, Treacher & Co., 1829; Thomas Rickman, *An Essay on Gothic Architecture: An Attempt to Discriminate the Styles of English Architecture from the Conquest to the Reformation*, London, Longman, 1819 (the first of many editions, originally published only under the sub-title).   [74] Kirk, 'Self-Government and Self-Defence', 306, 337.

[75] Gray churches are to be found in Claremont (near Cape Town), Stellenbosch, Clanwilliam, Caledon, Bredasdorp, Robertson, George, Stanford, two in Knysna, Oudtshoorn, Graaff-Reinet, Port Elizabeth, Cradock, King William's Town and also in Pietermaritzburg and Bloemfontein. See Picton-Seymour, *Victorian Buildings*, and Hans Fransen and Mary Alexander Cook, *The Old Buildings of the Cape*, Cape Town, Balkema, 1980.

[76] In general on church architecture, see Dennis Radford, 'South African Christian Architecture', in Richard Elphick and Rodney Davenport (eds.), *Christianity in South Africa: A Political, Social and Cultural History*, Claremont, David Philip, 1997, 327–36.

What? Missions, the reformation in manners and the struggle for acceptance

The church – any church – prescribed certain behaviour, as well as propagating particular beliefs and being a community of those who held them. The formal sanctions which churches at the Cape could impose on those who transgressed against their rules were generally not great, at least not in a material sense. Those who were in receipt of poor relief, which was administered by the church, were obviously most vulnerable to interference from the church officials, particularly if they were seen as sexually promiscuous or as alcoholics.[77] Otherwise the church could do little more than reprimand offenders and exclude them from communion, sometimes imposing conditions before they were readmitted to the benefits of full church membership.[78]

Such matters might of course cause considerable embarrassment in a small community. In 1784, the 24-year-old Johan Gerhard Cloete, whose father Hendrik was the richest man in the Colony and had served terms both as *Heemraad* and in the *Kerkenraad*, was called before the Stellenbosch *Kerkenraad* and accused of fathering a child on Elizabeth Smalberger. Her father had apparently complained of the matter to the landdrost, after which it had come to the attention of the church. Cloete, however, refused to answer the question, exclaiming that he was not a Catholic and therefore he was not obliged to confess. He was therefore excommunicated.[79] His father did not bring a civil action against the *Raad*, so he claimed out of respect for that body, but rather directed a memorial to the Colony's Governor and Council. As he supplied them with barrels of Constantia wine from his vineyard, he obviously had the necessary connections. He asked that the Minister and *Kerkenraad* of Stellenbosch be ordered

to abandon their absolutely unauthorized and directly inquisitorial researches, summonses and interrogatories, etc. etc.! and to stop them, the more so as his son has never appeared before his competent and daily judge for such an affair[80] on which the minister and Kerkenraad had wished to question him, and much less proved against him, as it appears 'Luce meridiana clarius' (clearer than noonday) that Minister and Kerke[n]raad had proceeded on no other grounds than loose

---

[77] Marais, 'Armesorg', 25–7.

[78] In 1716, the *Kerkenraad* of Drakenstein demanded as such a condition that Etienne Bruël present written evidence that he had sold a certain slave with whom his wife Anne du Puis was leading 'a most evil life' before she could be readmitted to Holy Communion. Spoelstra, *Bouwstoffen*, II, 431.

[79] CA G2 1/3, Stellenbosch DRC: Resolutieboek des Kerken Raads, Notule, 11 Jan. 1784, 23 Feb. 1784. The individual in question was probably Elizabeth Magdalena Smalberger, then seventeen, who later married Matthias Johannes van Eyssen.

[80] Presumably Cloete is referring to himself, as head of the household.

rumours and conversations, which does not become anyone, much less a 'Kerke[n]raad,' and to leave his son unmolested, to delete from the minutes every-thing connected with the case, and to permit memorialist's inspection of the same, (to see that it has been done), or to order such other course to be pursued, as the Council may deem fit, for the maintenance of good order and peace, and the preservation of the honour and reputation of memorialist and his numerous family.

The Council noted that they had to take cognisance of the accusations, out of duty 'and from reverence for the Holy Communion', but had no inten-tion of insulting Cloete 'much less his minor son'.[81] All the same, as they well knew, the summons must have had that effect. The Government there-upon managed to calm matters down.[82] Perhaps it is significant that Johan Gerhard never married, although he lived until 1806.[83]

After the establishment of mission stations in the Cape, from 1792 onwards, the missionaries had temporal powers which their colleagues working in the parishes of the various denominations lacked. They could not merely excommunicate; they could also expel miscreants from the Christian communities that the stations were designed to be. Since the sta-tions functioned as refuges from the harsh world beyond their bounds, these were powers that had to be respected. The mission stations provided benefits, in terms of spiritual succour, kinship, education and so forth, and these should not be discounted in any attempt to understand the develop-ment of missions at the Cape. Equally, for most of those who had come to live on the three dozen or so stations which had been established in the Cape Colony by the mid-nineteenth century, the alternatives were grim. Even around 1850, expulsion would mean a harsh, brutish and exploited life as a tied farm worker for all but a very few, and those few would prob-ably have acquired the skills they needed to survive as an artisan in the country dorps on a mission station.[84] And even in some of the towns the

---

[81] It is notable that a 24-year-old should be described as 'minderjarig'. Perhaps he would only have obtained his (social) majority on marriage.

[82] Based on Leibbrandt, *Requesten*, I, 276–8.

[83] C. C. de Villiers, *Geslagsregisters van die Ou Kaapse Families*, edited by C. Pama, 3 vols., Cape Town and Amsterdam, Balkema, 1966, I, 142.

[84] For studies of labour conditions on Cape farms after emancipation, a subject which, prob-ably as a result of the retreat from Marxism, still awaits a full-scale study, see John Marincowitz, 'Rural Production and the Labour in the Western Cape, 1838 to 1888, with Special Reference to the Wheat Growing Districts', Ph.D. thesis, University of London, 1985; Wayne L. Dooling, 'Agrarian Transformations in the Western Districts of the Cape Colony, 1838–c. 1900', Ph.D. thesis, University of Cambridge, 1996; for suggestive studies, see various chapters in Nigel Worden and Clifton C. Crais (eds.), *Breaking the Chains: Slavery and its Legacy in the Nineteenth-Century Cape Colony*, Johannesburg, Witwatersrand University Press, 1994, notably the chapters by Robert Ross, '"Rather Mental than Physical": Emancipations and the Cape Economy'; Pamela Scully, 'Private and Public Worlds of Emancipation in the Rural Western Cape, c. 1830–42'; and Clifton C. Crais, 'Slavery and Emancipation in the Eastern Cape'.

influence of missionaries could not be discounted. By 1850, the Rev. Adam Robson of the LMS was in full charge of the 'Hottentot' location in Port Elizabeth, receiving applications from those who wished to settle there and arranging for the expulsion of squatters and other undesirables.[85]

There was a certain ambivalence which was occasionally evident in missionary attitudes to the temporal advance of their converts. Second only to the Bible as one of the foundational texts of nineteenth-century Protestantism was, after all, John Bunyan's *The Pilgrim's Progress*. This is among other things a virulent attack on the dangers of the world and on the perils of wealth. A famous lithograph, much loved by the German pietists, illustrated the distinction between the 'Broad and the Narrow Ways', with the former leading through Vanity Fair to the fires of eternal damnation.[86] At the Cape, Van der Kemp once famously proclaimed, 'all civilisation is from the devil'.[87] He went about bare-headed and lightly dressed, and ate the same food as the Khoisan at Bethelsdorp, because it was his 'fixed idea that in order to raise the natives to his own level he must in everything which was not reprehensible go down to theirs – a principle of which', a later missionary wrote 'experience has demonstrated the falsity'.[88] Others were less extreme than the eccentric doctor, if for no other reason than that they did not share his patrician background, but generally stemmed from the respectable artisanate and were personally upwardly mobile, in social terms. All the same, in 1830, the first Huguenot missionaries described the dress of the most substantial male inhabitants at a great dinner in Bethelsdorp, noting that they 'arranged their cravats according to Parisian fashion with a square knot and the large corners crossed or held in place by a pin with a sparkling head'. However, it is symptomatic that this section was censored out of the published version by the editors of the *Journal des Missions Evangéliques* in Paris.[89]

All missionaries were, and are, engaged in an attempt to change their potential converts' behaviour as well as their beliefs. The question is, what to? The first missionaries to the Cape Colony were members of the

---

[85] Baines, 'Origins of Urban Segregation', 74–6.

[86] Birgit Meyer, 'Translating the Devil: An African Appropriation of Pietist Protestantism: The Case of the Peki Ewe in Southeastern Ghana, 1847–1992', Ph.D. thesis, University of Amsterdam, 1995, 25–31.

[87] F. A. Steytler (ed.), 'Minutes of the First Conference held by the African Missionaries at Graaff-Reinet (1814)', *Hertzog-Annale van die Suid-Afrikaanse Akademie vir Wetenskap en Kuns*, 3, 1956, 110.

[88] Eugène Casalis, *My Life in Basutoland*, reprinted Cape Town, Struik, 1971, 104. Casalis had his information on Van der Kemp from James Kitchingman.

[89] Rolland's journal, 17 Feb. 1830. I am currently preparing a translation and edition of the first letters of Prosper Lemue and Samuel Rolland, the missionaries in question, for the Van Riebeeck Society. The editors also cut Rolland's mouthwatering description of the dinner menu.

Moravian Brotherhood. Their aim was to create in South Africa the sort of Christian communities which were equally their central European ideal. Often described as villages, such settlements had at times more in common with small towns. Genadendal, the first and most important Moravian mission station, was for a time the second largest settlement in the Colony, and in its knife works it had the Cape's first substantial workshop. All the same, the accent of the Moravians was always on agriculture and its associated crafts.[90] The behaviour that was inculcated was seen as simple, rather than proud, and was rural rather than urban. In 1837, Brother Lemmerz, the missionary at Groenkloof (modern Mamre), complained that the mission's proximity to Cape Town – a full day's journey away – was partially responsible for the spiritual dangers to which his flock was exposed.[91] The Moravian ideal was one of a settled agricultural community, cut off from the world and as far as possible self-sufficient. To this end, the construction of irrigation channels was a holy act. At the foundation of Shiloh, in the upper Kei valley, the simple diversion of water 'recreated a nomadic people as an agricultural one, without which step Christianity cannot take root'.[92]

This was consonant with the self-image projected by the converts to the Christian faith in the Moravian missions, as found in the numerous accounts of their lives and conversions to be found in Moravian missionary publications.[93] This sort of material has of course gone through a whole range of processes of selection before it reached the form now available. Men and women cast their spiritual experiences in terms that the missionaries wanted to hear, translation may well have shifted them still further in

---

[90] Of the 1,093 adults (excluding the missionaries) who were *de jure* resident in Genadendal in 1849, 82 were infirm (including one man described as a pensioner), 896 were unskilled labourers, a catagory taken to include those women engaged in 'housework' or as washerwomen, 114 were tradesmen and women, one man was a teacher and two women (including the teacher's wife) were described as assistant teachers. The tradesmen were tailors, carpenters, masons, shoemakers, thatchers, cutlers, wheelwrights, brickmakers and layers, tanners, waggonmakers and drivers, smiths, coachmen, a cooper and a miller. Women noted as having trades were all either sempstresses or cooks, except for two midwives and one mat-maker. See Cape of Good Hope, Legislative Council, *Master and Servant: Addenda to the Documents on the Working of the Order in Council of 21st July 1846*, Cape Town, Saul Solomon, 1849, 191ff.

[91] In general, see Krüger, *The Pear Tree Blossoms*; see also Robert Ross, 'The Social and Political Theology of Western Cape Missions', in Henry Bredekamp and Robert Ross (eds.), *Missions and Christianity in South African History*, Johannesburg, Witwatersrand University Press, 1995, 97–112; on·Groenkloof, *Berichten uit de Heidenwereld*, 2, 102.

[92] *Berichten wegens de zending der Broedergemeente*, 20, 1831, 25.

[93] In particular successive volumes of the *Periodical Accounts*. It was a Moravian tradition that members of the community should regularly rewrite their spiritual autobiography, which would then serve as their obituary. For one particularly rich example, see 'Memoir of Sr. Wilhelmina Stompjes, a Kaffir native-assistant, who departed this life at Shiloh, July 9th 1863', *PA*, XXVI, 153–63, 209–22.

that direction, and the missionaries only published those passages which suited them. For some purposes, though, such considerations do not matter. The representations given may not be accurate in some abstract sense – has anyone anywhere ever written an 'accurate' autobiography? – but they do provide evidence of what was culturally acceptable within the mission-dominated communities. It is thus striking that so many are entirely concerned with the state of the convert's soul, and with his or her delivery out of the bondage of sin, and even more that ideas of temporal advance, or progress in civilisation, are totally absent.

In 1836, the Rev. H. P. Hallbeck, first bishop of the Moravian Church in South Africa and one of the outstanding missionaries of his generation, gave a vision of the ideal Christian community that he and his fellows were trying to create. He did this by imagining Genadendal as it would be a century later, if its inhabitants followed the path of righteousness. He wrote:

I see a pleasant town with long streets and beautifully built houses, in the shadow of noble old trees and surrounded by fine gardens and fertile fields. The peaceable and happy inhabitants walk, tidily dressed, through the streets and lanes, or rest in small groups under their vines and fig-trees,[94] while the youth hurries off together to the schools. There are no police, prison judge or magistrate: because love reigns amongst them. Without din or disturbance everyone goes about his business, no sluggard is found among them, no drunkard pollutes their streets; and, although all are active, no-one sees the work of his hands as all-important. I approach their groups, I hear the content of their conversations; and everywhere only two questions are discussed: 'What must I do to be saved?' and 'What can we do to honour our God?'[95]

The Moravian ideal of a mission community in South Africa was important not merely because it was the first; it also provided a model for most subsequent missions. A visit to Genadendal was one of the obligatory parts of new missionaries' introductions to South Africa, from Van der Kemp onwards. The conservative, nostalgic vision of a Christian community, divorced from the world, was much more widely spread among missionaries than is sometimes thought.[96] It was, however, not the only one. An

---

[94] Hallbeck, like two other missionaries quoted later in this chapter, is here making an implicit reference to the vision of peace of the Prophet Micah (4:4), when, after the swords had been beaten into ploughshares and the spears into pruning-hooks, 'But they shall sit every man under his vine and under his fig tree; and none shall make them afraid: for the mouth of the Lord of hosts hath spoken it.'

[95] *Berichten uit de Heidenwereld*, 2, 1836, pp. 73–80.

[96] E.g. Terence Ranger, 'The Local and the Global in Southern African Religious History', in Robert W. Hefner (ed.), *Conversion to Christianity: Historical and Anthropological Perspectives on a Great Transformation*, Berkeley, Los Angeles and Oxford, University of California Press, 1993, 67–72, 88–92. Their failure to understand this is one of the (many) faults in Jean and John Comaroff, *Of Revelation and Revolution: Christianity, Colonialism and Consciousness in South Africa*, Chicago and London, University of Chicago Press, 1991, I.

alternative idea of Christian witness, much more aggressively concerned with the affairs of this world, also developed in South Africa, above all under the impetus of a minority of representatives of the LMS, led by Dr John Philip, whose prominence and extensive writings make it reasonable to treat him as exemplary for a tendency whose ideas he may have articulated but in which he was certainly not alone.[97]

During the three decades in which he was the Superintendent of the LMS in South Africa, John Philip was involved in numerous political controversies. Sir Lowry Cole, Governor of the Cape, famously described him in 1830 as 'more a *politician* than a missionary',[98] and such comments have been made ever since by historians, either approvingly or, more usually, in condemnation.[99] It was not a comment with which Philip himself would have agreed, except in so far as his position required that he take a more active part in public affairs than did his colleagues whose prime work was pastoral. At least as would have justified his actions to himself, his entries into the public arena were driven by two main impulses. The first was the Christian tenet that anything tending to increase human poverty and misery was inherently sinful. Since he accepted the argument, deriving essentially from Adam Smith and the Scottish enlightenment, that perfect liberty of trade and persons would maximise wealth, it followed that agitation to remove all forms of bondage and to extend civil rights was an act of Christian charity.[100] The second derived from his understanding of the necessary conditions for salvation.

For Philip there was an intimate connection between Christianity and civilisation, which ran in both directions. As he wrote in 1825:

While I am satisfied, from abundance of incontrovertible facts, that permanent societies of Christians can never be maintained among an uncivilized people without imparting to them the arts and habits of civilized life, I am satisfied, upon ground

[97] It should not be thought that the Moravians were averse to commenting and quietly agitating on temporal matters involving their flock. Hallbeck in particular recorded his strong opposition to a proposed vagrancy law, both in private correspondence with the Government in 1834 – he was careful not to be seen 'intruding myself on the public, or engaging in a newspaper discussion' (*PA*, XIII, 189) – and in his evidence before the British Parliamentary Select Committee on Aborigines a couple of years later. British Parliamentary Paper 538 of 1836, *Report from the Select Committee on Aborigines (British Settlements)*, 335–45.

[98] Cited in W. M. Macmillan, *Cape Colour Question*, London, Faber & Gwyer, 1927, 96, emphasis in original. Philip himself specifically rejected the charge; see Andrew Ross, *John Philip (1775–1851): Missions, Race and Politics in South Africa*, Aberdeen, Aberdeen University Press, 1986, 103.

[99] The most recent, and contrasting, examples are Ross, *John Philip*, and P. H. Kapp, 'Dr John Philip: Die Grondlegger van Liberalisme in Suid-Afrika', *AYB*, 48, 1985.

[100] Istvan Hont and Michael Ignatieff, 'Needs and Justice in *The Wealth of Nations*: An Introductory Essay', in Hont and Ignatieff, *Wealth and Virtue: The Shaping of Political Economy in the Scottish Enlightenment*, Cambridge, Cambridge University Press, 1983.

no less evident, that if missionaries lose their religion and sink into mere mechanics, the work of civilization and moral improvement will swiftly retrograde.[101]

Or again, writing a few years later:

Civilization bears to religion a relation similar to what the foliage bears to the tree. Trees are not planted in our gardens for the sake of their leaves; but without leaves, in their season, the garden would be without beauty, and the fruit neither well flavoured nor abundant.[102]

Now, Philip's view of civilisation was limited and ethnocentric, or to put it more charitably, he exemplified the ideas of his age, nationality, class and creed, but did not rise above them. Peter van Rooden has recently argued that the missionary movement of Protestant Europe from the late eighteenth century was closely related to the emergence of distinctions between the public and private spheres. For the Protestants of this milieu, he writes, 'Christianity [is located] within individual conscience. Therefore, the distinction between private and public sphere, the hallmark of civilization, is the most important social aspect of Christianity, too, because it is the precondition of sincere conversion.'[103] At least as an analysis of the values propagated by the missionaries in South Africa, this seems accurate. The privacy given by covering oneself up with modest clothing and by living in the closed space of a cottage was the outward sign of that concern with one's individual soul without which true Christianity could not be experienced. Thus, in the rhetoric of the missionaries and increasingly in the internal experience of their converts, the Protestant virtues of cleanliness, tidiness, sobriety, modesty and chastity were allied to the quintessentially Protestant skill of literacy, and eventually to scientific curiosity and enquiry. None of these, though, was possible in the smoky hovels in which the Khoikhoi of many mission stations had been living when Philip first arrived in the Cape in 1819, and the building of neat cottages was one of the main improvements he urged upon their residents.[104] Christianity and civilisation could best flourish in South Africa under British rule, and he opposed the retrocession of the Ciskei to the Xhosa in 1836.[105] However, this could be the case if the system of government was as lawbound and concerned for the promotion and preservation of civil liberties in South Africa as it was in Britain.

There was a political side to this, in the wider, modern sense of the word,

[101] Letter to the Rev. George Burder, secretary of the LMS, 5 July 1825, cited in John Philip, *Researches in South Africa illustrating the Civil, Moral and Religious Condition of the Native Tribes*, 2 vols., London, James Ducan, 1828, I, 219.
[102] Philip, *Researches*, I, 204.
[103] Peter van Rooden, 'Nineteenth-Century Representations of Missionary Conversion and the Transformation of Western Christianity', in Peter van der Veer (ed.), *Conversion to Modernities: The Globalization of Christianity*, New York and London, Routledge, 1996, 70.   [104] Philip, *Researches*, I, 209–12.   [105] Ross, *John Philip*, 140.

not in that connected with party politics which was employed at the time. On the one hand, his political campaigns were designed to remove the feeling of despair which had gathered over the mission stations, notably Bethelsdorp, and which was hindering the advance of Christianity and civilisation. On the other, he urged on the Khoikhoi of Bethelsdorp

> the advantage which an improvement in their houses, and in their industry and mode of living, would afford to their friends, in pleading their cause. I stated to them, that it was vain to attempt to plead their cause, while their enemies could point to Bethelsdorp in its present state; that the world, and the church of Christ, looked for civilization and industry as proofs of their capacity and of the utility of our labours; that the men of the world had no other criterion by which they could judge the beneficial effects of missions.

He justified this line of argument by quoting from the Gospel: 'By their fruits ye shall know them.'[106]

In retrospect, Philip was more succinct on what was behind the struggle. Writing in the 1840s, he commented: 'The question between us and the government was one of civilisation. The criterion of a people's civilisation with Lord Charles Somerset [the Governor of the Cape from 1812 to 1827] was whether the people used knives and forks.'[107]

In the short term, this strategy paid off, or at least to the Khoikhoi it seemed to do so. By the end of the decade, the Cape Government had enacted Ordinance 50, which removed all civil disabilities for the free people of colour, thus including, and especially, the Khoikhoi. This was further entrenched by the metropolitan authorities in London, who laid down that it could not be amended without their permission and who tested subsequent legislation against its provisions. The Khoikhoi saw it as the guarantor of their liberties. In 1834, Platje Jonker of Bethelsdorp exclaimed at a meeting to protest against the introduction of a Vagrancy Act, which would have laid the Khoi open to arbitrary arrest, 'Every nation has its screen: the white men have a screen, the colour of their skin is their screen, the 50th ordinance is our screen.'[108] Another man kept a copy of the Ordinance carefully folded away in his Bible.[109]

Whether or not Philip should be given the credit for this measure,[110] he

---

[106] Philip, *Researches*, I, 212–13; the biblical citation is from Matthew 7:20.
[107] John Philip, 'A Narrative Written for Buxton', LMS archives, Africa Odds, Philip Papers, Box 3, folder 5.   [108] George Barker to LMS, 6 Oct. 1834, LMS-SA 14/2/B.
[109] Tony Kirk, 'Progress and Decline in the Kat River Settlement, 1829–1854', *JAH*, 14(3), 1973, 424.
[110] For dissenting views, see Susan Newton-King, 'The Labour Market of the Cape Colony, 1807–28', in Marks and Atmore, *Economy and Society*, 171–207; Kapp, 'Dr John Philip', 86–78. The Ordinance itself was promulgated in his absence and not as a result of his influence; its entrenchment in London, on the other hand, was at his suggestion, although it may have been accepted by the Colonial Office because of its application to other British colonies, notably in the Caribbean.

claimed it, and his claim was accepted by its prime beneficiaries. When Philip returned to Bethelsdorp in February 1830, he was greeted 'as a prince entering the capital of his kingdom'. For two days the men of the village had waited with their horses 12 kilometres up the road, and escorted his waggon to Bethelsdorp. One league from the station, the boys and girls were waiting, in their best clothes, and escorted him in, singing

hymns of recognition, first to the god who has ransomed them, and from whom they receive all their blessings, then to the honour of Dr Philip, whom God had used to procure their liberty, and thirdly to the honour of the King of England who gave it to them and whose bounty they celebrated by singing the national anthem *God save the King*.[111]

Philip then went on a tour of the station, where he was glad to notice that 'not a single vestige of [the Khoikhoi's] former condition was to be seen'. Specifically he was glad to note that 'not one sheepskin caross' was worn in the school.[112] A day or two later, the men and women of Bethelsdorp gave Philip a great dinner. They were dressed in their best. The men, as has been noted, wore cravats tied in the best Parisian fashion, and also cotton trousers and waistcoats of striped calico, or cloth suits; the women 'wore dresses of printed calico, with white stockings and small black shoes . . . all had neat handkerchiefs of silk or red and yellow cotton on their heads'. Rolland, who reported on this, was also surprised to note that they had fully met Somerset's criterion for civilisation. Served up were

beef, mutton, kid, goose, duck, chickens etc., all prepared as in Europe, whether boiled, roast, stewed or fried. The vegetables were perhaps less diversified; there were only cabbages, potatoes, carrots and rice. Dessert, in contrast, was abundant. There were plates of all sorts of puddings, tarts, sweets and pastries, all made by the Hottentots at the institution; grapes, melons, and apples and wine in proportion, to such an extent that we could almost say of this what Moses said of the manna in the desert: it was there in abundance and in taste to suit everyone.[113]

There followed speeches in which Philip and his companions exhorted the company to continue in the faith and in civilisation, and the Khoikhoi gave thanks that in contrast to the time when 'the misery and sufferings of the Hottentots were at the highest', they now had liberty. Indeed, as Piet Manuel said: 'One of the blessings he now enjoyed through the Gospel

---

[111] See the description of Samuel Rolland, one of the first French missionaries, who accompanied Philip on this occasion, *JME*, 5, 1830, 237–8; on a former occasion, when the cornerstone of the new school at Theopolis was laid, the assembled gathering sang 'Rule Britannia'; see V. C. Malherbe, 'The Cape Khoisan in the Eastern Districts of the Colony before and after Ordinance 50 of 1828', Ph.D. thesis, UCT, 1997, 157.

[112] Cited in Malherbe, 'Cape Khoisan', 226, from *Evangelical Magazine*, Philip to Read, 5 Apr. 1830, and Rhodes House, Oxford, Mss. Afr. s. 219A, f. 178. A caross is a fur cloak.

[113] In Rolland's journal, 17 Feb. 1830, forthcoming with the Van Riebeeck Society. This was the passage cut before publication in the *JME*.

was that he could sit at ease in his own house and at his own table.'[114] Christianity had given him the chance of privacy.

This dinner celebrated the conjunction between Christianity, respectability, loyalty to Great Britain and political advance in a way that was never repeated. All the same, for at least the next two decades this vision of the benefits of Christianity prevailed among the mission converts, in contrast to the more militant version their parents had learnt from Van der Kemp. Also, undoubtedly, the levels of conduct which the missionaries advocated – and indeed generally practised themselves[115] – required a self-discipline which provided a degree of certainty in what was still a dangerous and threatening world. On the basis of this, those claiming political rights had the confidence to express pride in their Khoikhoi descent and to make their demands as 'Hottentots', an ethnonym which for a time could be used without the negative associations it had before, had still, in the eyes of their enemies, and was to acquire again.[116]

Throughout the Colony, and indeed beyond its borders, this combination of Christianity and respectability was attractive to a considerable number of the free people of colour and, after 1838, of the ex-slaves. It enabled them to make statements and claims within the same arena as those of their white fellow-colonists who were arguing about ethnic affiliation, individual status and the sacredness of the landscape through and within their churches, or by emphasising the respectability of their lifestyles. The struggle to maintain what was now seen as a Christian lifestyle would be rewarded in this world with material and political advance, to say nothing of the rewards it was thought to make possible in the next. It was not an easy option. Henriette Külpmann, the wife of a Rhenish missionary in Worcester, graphically described to friends in Germany the efforts that had to be made:

Most of the heathen who came straight to the town to be able to attend the church and the school have begun to build houses, or rather cottages, and also to lay out a bit of garden, which later, when they can, they will enlarge. Several are now building, at which they help each other. Thus first they construct the walls of clay and cover them over with bushes, shrubs and so on. Once they have got so far, and as

---

[114] These speeches were printed in *SACA*, 20 Mar. 1830.

[115] The scandals which had caused many problems for the LMS in particular during the 1810s did not recur to anything like the same extent after 1830, probably because the missionaries who came to South Africa from Great Britain and elsewhere had assimilated the behavioural message of their churches more thoroughly, and had put behind them the more enthusiastic features of the early missionary movement. For the scandals, see Doug Stuart, ' "Of Savages and Heroes": Discourses of Race, Nation and Gender in the Evangelical Missions to Southern Africa in the Early Nineteenth Century', Ph.D. thesis, University of London, 1994, particularly pp. 247–73.

[116] Stanley Trapido, 'The Emergence of Liberalism and the making of "Hottentot nationalism", 1815–1834', *SSA*, 17, 1992, 34–60.

their supplies of money are seldom great to begin with, the men and boys go out again to the farmers in the region, where they work particularly at ploughing and harvest time, until they have earned a few more dollars, and then they continue building. As you can imagine, this all goes very slowly. Once they have finally got the cottage finished from the outside, including a roof, also in time they try to improve and beautify it. As it is being built, a square hole is made in the wall, to serve as a window. At first, particularly in the winter, it is blocked up with stones, so that it is then quite dark; then, later, they can make a wooden shutter, which can be closed in bad weather and opened in good. Later, if they get on, they put in a glass window (all of which they can do themselves, as they learnt it as slaves). This is the way it goes with everything at the beginning, and for many it stays that way. As the house consists of a single room, they are able, later, to build a wall inside, also of clay, so that two rooms are formed. The floor is also of clay, and, instead of being scrubbed, it is smeared with thinned cow-dung every week, so that it becomes hard and fast. The door of the house is made of a number of planks nailed together or of canes and branches woven or tied together. Those who do well are then able to improve their houses and enlarge their gardens. Some already have a fine vine growing against their cottage, and rather more have planted fig and cherry trees, and so forth, and take such care of their garden that it is a pleasure to see it.[117]

As Mrs Külpmann made clear, respectability entailed expense, and the cottages which those who lived in the small towns and on the mission stations wished to construct were costly investments. Nevertheless, at least some of them were able to realise their hopes. In his great tour of South Africa in 1838–9, the Quaker James Backhouse visited most of the Colony's mission stations and in many he reported on the physical state of the housing. Genadendal, naturally, was the best provided, in part because the church had given everyone who built a house a grant of £1 17s 6d, and laid down that possession of such a house was a condition for office in the church or village. It had '260 neatly thatched cottages, of unburnt brick, or mud and gravel, which stand well in this climate'.[118] In Zuurbraak, a poor settlement, he entered

most of the cottages of the Hottentots, as well as some of the scattered hovels. The latter were poor places indeed for the residence of human beings. Some of the cottages were neatly whitewashed inside, and had a coloured surbase of French grey. The material used for colouring, as well as that used for whitewashing is clay, found

---

[117] *Schwester* Henriette Külpmann to friends in her home town, Altena, near Wuppertal, 19 June 1844, *Das Missionsblatt, herausgegeben von der Missions-Gesellschaft zu Barmen*, 19, no. 23; for descriptions of the sort of buildings they made, see James Walton, *Cape Cottages*, Cape Town, Intaka, 1995.

[118] Backhouse, *Narrative*, 97. Backhouse, too, referred to the vines and fig-trees around the houses, under which 'the poor and oppressed having found a refuge under the banner of the cross, were literally sitting . . ., none making them afraid'. See also Pamela Scully, *Liberating the Family? Gender and British Slave Emancipation in the Rural Western Cape, South Africa, 1823–1853*, Oxford, James Currey, 1997; Tessa van Ryneveld, 'Merchants and Missions: Developments in the Caledon District, 1838–1850', BA Hons. thesis, UCT, 1983, 48.

on the Zuurbraak property. The walls of the cottages were of mud, the roofs thatched: few of the cottages had chimneys: the fires were generally made in the middle of the floor; the inside of the thatch was consequently black with smoke.[119]

In Pacaltsdorp, near George, 'some . . . now have comfortable cottages, but a large number live in rude, thatched huts, of interwoven branches and mud'. The inhabitants expressed a desire to have the station granted to them in freehold, 'that they might build better houses', a wish which was only granted a generation later in 1873.[120] In Bethelsdorp, where Philip had once exhorted the Khoikhoi to build houses which would impress visiting British dignitaries, and later had to admonish them to maintain their houses as they had once been,[121] the inhabitants lived in 'houses and cottages, arranged as little streets'.[122] In the Kat River Settlement's villages,

[some of] the neat cottages of those who have become more prosperous . . . would not discredit the more respectable of the labouring class in England. The walls are of brick, externally, of that which has been burnt, and internal, of such as is only sun-dried: they are plastered on both sides with mud and whitewashed internally. The roofs are thatched with reeds.[123]

Finally, among the Griquas in Philippolis, outside the Colony to the north of the Orange River, there were few substantial houses, in part because of the cost of timber, which had to be brought 200 miles from the Kat River, but also in part because those used to living in the mat huts of the Khoi 'complained of the closeness of houses'. As yet they had not fully appreciated the message of the missionaries, dividing the private from the public, but eventually this would change. By the mid-1850s, the richest of the Philippolis Griquas were building new houses, both in the town and on the farms, 'of stone and burnt brick and some of them very excellent houses – one in particular is an excellent comfortable dwelling containing parlour, dining room, 3 bedrooms, kitchen, pantry and store room – all the timber used in the house is good English deal and the house has cost the proprietor about £300'.[124]

Backhouse's view of clothing worn by the mission converts was more complimentary. On none of the mission stations did he comment that the inhabitants were ill-dressed and on most he noted that they were all wearing English – perhaps he only meant English-style – clothing. It might be a bit scruffy, but they also always had a costume of best clothing to wear to church on Sundays. The iconographic evidence confirms this pattern. From

---

[119] Backhouse, *Narrative*, 109–10.
[120] Backhouse, *Narrative*, 128–9; on the transfer of the mission stations to freehold property, see Elizabeth Elbourne and Robert Ross, 'Combatting Spiritual and Social Bondage: Early Missions in the Cape Colony', in Elphick and Davenport, *Christianity in South Africa*, 31–50.   [121] See above, and *SACA*, 20 Mar. 1830.   [122] Backhouse, *Narrative*, 154.
[123] Backhouse, *Narrative*, 189.   [124] Solomon to Tidman, March 1857, LMS-SA 30/3/A.

Angas's famous print of Genadendal, made in 1847, to the first mission photographs, taken by the Rev. W. B. Philip in Philippolis in the late 1850s,[125] all the evidence suggests that the respectable clothing could be worn by everyone when they so wished. They might not always want to. In 1838, 'H. B.' made a sketch of a 'Kat River Bastard and his afterider [sic]'.[126] The former was well dressed in the country style of the Cape, with a jacket, trousers, veldschoen and a wide-brimmed hat. The latter, the *agterryer* or servant, seems only to be wearing a flamboyant wide-brimmed hat, complete with a long feather, and a waistcoat. But even so, there is no way of knowing what he might have worn when not out on a hunting expedition. Among the Khoikhoi and the ex-slaves, at least, nakedness had become rare.

Progress towards respectability in less tangible spheres was as steady as in these outward matters. The ideas on gender, on the division of labour, on responsibilities and on power between the sexes, which lay at the heart of respectability, were shared by the missionaries and their wives.[127] The behaviour which these ideas entailed was therefore required of those who came to live on the missions. In some villages, for example, housing was not available to single women. In Genadendal in 1849, for example, all but one of the seventy-one widows in the village were living in households headed, at least in theory, by men, as were all eight 'spinsters'.[128] However, this does not mean that the regulations were necessarily unwelcome, nor that the ideas were not shared by those who lived by them, both men and women, perhaps particularly the latter. On the farms of the Cape before emancipation, the sexual exploitation of young women slaves by their owners and their owners' families was regular. In the 1860s, Lady Duff Gordon heard stories of Rosina, an emancipated slave woman of considerable spirit, who accosted her former master (by whom she had had two children) in the streets of Caledon with the words: 'Aha! when I young and pretty slave-girl you make kiss me then; now I ugly, drunk dirty old devil and free woman, I kiss you!'[129] Except that 'kiss', or its Dutch equivalent, was probably not the word used, this story rings true. There were mission station residents,

---

[125] G. F. Angas's print has been reproduced many times, for instance in Isaac Balie, *Die Geskiedenis van Genadendal, 1738–1988*, Cape Town and Johannesburg, Perskor, 1988, 97; W. B. Philip album, Manuscript collection, Jagger Library, UCT.

[126] In the Africana Museum, Johannesburg, reproduced in J. C. Visagie, 'Die Katriviernedersetting, 1829–1839', Ph.D. thesis, UNISA, 1978, 87a.

[127] Natasha Erlank, 'Letters Home: The Experiences and Perceptions of Middle Class British Women at the Cape 1820–1850', MA thesis, UCT, 1995, ch. 4; for an occasion when matters went wrong, see Karel Schoeman, *'A Thorn Bush that Grows in the Path': The Missionary Career of Ann Hamilton, 1815–1823*, Cape Town, South African Library, 1995.

[128] Scully, *Liberating the Family?*; *Master and Servant: Addenda*, pagination missing.

[129] Duff Gordon, *Letters from the Cape*, 112.

both ex-slave and (part-)Khoi who were biological products of such exploitation.[130] For people with such experiences, the constraints and formal subordination of mission monogamy may not have chafed much. Equally those who had grown up while their mothers cared for other people's children may have been only too glad to care for their own, and, given the alternative, and the past, of physical agricultural labour, the maintenance of one's own household and the performance of 'womanly' work was probably attractive. Their own childhood experiences may have made it difficult for them to live up to their ideals, but that is another matter.[131]

Necessarily, these comments are speculative. Nevertheless, it is suggestive that nuclear family structures were generally to be found throughout the Colony's mission stations, according to the 1849 census,[132] and that a rash of infanticide cases testifies to the pressure young women were under to be seen to be conforming to sexual norms, a pressure applied both by the missionaries, who had to be exhorted by the Government not to expel unmarried mothers from their homes, and by their parents and peers.[133] There are hints that among the would-be respectable Christians of the towns, where the social control of the clergy was less, cohabitation preceding marriage – but eventually leading to it – was more readily accepted.[134] But this should not detract from the argument that, in general and in principle if not always in practice, those wishing to be considered respectable agreed with the gender norms of respectable white society.

They also did what they could to become literate. Protestantism, in its various varieties, is a religion of the book, one which stresses that everyone should be able to read the Bible for themselves. The missionaries took at least this part of their work seriously. In Stellenbosch in 1841, the Rev. P. D. Lückhoff noted that, together with a teacher and their respective wives, they taught 80 to 90 children in class one, 130 to 160 in class two, and between 400 and 500 adults, including 60 to 80 in the day school, 120 to 140 in the night school and 250 to 290 in Sunday school.[135] At least among the ex-slaves there was clearly a widespread desire to acquire the rudiments of literacy.

How far those who came to listen to them, and to learn from them, had

---

[130] See, for example, the comment by Esau Prins in the 1834 meeting at the Kat River to protest against the Vagrancy Ordinance, *SACA*, 3 Sept. 1834; Merriman, *Cape Journals*, 105; Duff Gordon, *Letters from the Cape*, 102, 110–11.

[131] This paragraph differs somewhat in emphasis from, but is nevertheless heavily dependent on, Pamela Scully's work, particularly her *Liberating the Family?*

[132] *Master and Servant: Addenda.*   [133] Scully, *Liberating the Family?*, ch. 7.

[134] Smit to LMS, 30 Aug. 1844, LMS-SA 20/2/C; the issue is discussed further in Elbourne and Ross, 'Combatting Spiritual and Social Bondage', 49–50.

[135] *Berichte der Rheinischen Missionsgesellschaft*, 12, 1841, 40–1; for a description of the syllabus, see *Berichte*, 13, 1842, 116–17.

more secular concerns, is of course difficult to say, and at the very least the advantages of literacy had to be balanced against the alternative uses which could be made of the time invested in acquiring it. Philip had to exhort the men of Bethelsdorp not to take their sons with them on their expeditions outside the station, mainly waggon-riding, because the boys should be in school.[136] Who should be assisting with the oxen was not an issue which concerned him, but undoubtedly exercised the waggon-riders.

The success which the missionaries had with their literacy campaigns can be gathered, to some extent, from the mission census of 1849, although the material is not invariably easy to interpret. The magistrates were instructed to take a Dutch Bible with them on their inspection visits, and to test whether those who claimed to be able to read could indeed do so.[137] In the long-established stations of the Eastern Cape, literacy rates among adults were considerable. The proportions who could read in Enon, Bethelsdorp (men only), Pacaltsdorp and Hankey were 52 per cent (substantially more for women than for men), 49 per cent, 44 per cent and 40 per cent respectively. In the Western Cape, the proportions were substantially lower. The Rhenish stations of Stynthal and Saron had rates of 13 per cent and 7 per cent literacy for adult men. As to the old Moravian stations, in Genadendal, 20 per cent of men and 30 per cent of women could read, in Elim 9 per cent of men and 16 per cent of women and in Groenkloof 14 per cent of men. This would seem to have been a temporary phenomenon, for the literacy rate in Genadendal for boys above twelve was 61 per cent, and for girls 78 per cent, and in Elim the respective figures were 59 per cent and 83 per cent.[138] The training college for teachers, which had been established in Genadendal in 1838, was beginning to yield results.[139]

By the late 1840s, clearly, a significant minority of the mission stations' inhabitants had given heed to the missionaries' call for an outward reformation of manners as well as an inner realignment of their beliefs. In their housing, clothing, sexual mores and attitudes and schooling, they were behaving as their mentors wished. How far they were able to reap the political rewards of their behaviour was of course an entirely different matter.

---

[136] *SACA*, 6 Mar. 1830.
[137] In the following figures, I have included those who were said to read 'indifferently' among the readers.
[138] *Master and Servant: Addenda*. The raw figures from which these proportions were taken are: Enon, men 40 literates out of 94, women 67 out of 111; Bethelsdorp, 40 men out of 82 (only 80 children out of 250 could read, but this included all children, including those under twelve); Pacaltsdorp, 92 out of 209; Hankey, 111 out of 278; Genadendal, men, 110 out of 546, women, 163 out of 547, boys above twelve, 177 out of 291, girls above twelve, 149 out of 191; Elim, men, 16 out of 179, women, 44 out of 193, boys above twelve, 62 out of 114, girls above twelve, 76 out of 92; Groenkloof, 33 out of 237; Stynthal, 8 out of 62; and Saron, 9 out of 122.   [139] Balie, *Geskiedenis van Genadendal*, 50–1.

6   Outsiders

The antithesis to respectability was drunkenness. When Dr Philip's opponents wished to ridicule him and those he worked with, they portrayed the
mission Khoikhoi as simplistic drunks. South Africa's oldest surviving
play, C. E. Boniface's *De Temperantisten* (1832), for instance, portrays, a
number of Khoi ex-convicts drinking and brawling in the streets before
heading off to the canteen, or liquor shop, to prepare themselves for the
inauguration of the local temperance society. The meeting where this would
happen was run by Dominee Humbug Philipumpkin (John Philip) and Sir
John Brute (Fairbairn). It was, apparently, a most successful farce, though
naturally enough it was not appreciated by its targets.[1] Equally a few years
later, Andrew Geddes Bain made use of the same motifs in *Kaatje
Kekkelbek*, a sketch that was heavily influenced by Boniface, but was now
transferred to the setting of Grahamstown and was largely in English. The
drunkenness of the 'Hottentot' characters, for all their connections with the
missions, was just as evident.[2]

What they wrote, they also drew. Almost all the significant artists of the
nineteenth-century Cape could present some vicious images of slave and
Khoikhoi drunkenness and debauchery. In the 1820s and 1830s, H. C. De
Meillon drew slaves smoking dagga (marijuana) and Sir Charles D'Oyly
portrayed drunken slaves on the streets of Cape Town above the title: 'The
South African besetting sin'.[3] Charles Davidson Bell was a gifted artist who

---

[1] Andrew Bank, 'Liberals and their Enemies: Racial Ideology at the Cape of Good Hope,
1820–1850', Ph.D. thesis, University of Cambridge, 1996, 178; C. E. Boniface, *De Nieuwe
Ridderorde of de Temperantisten*, Cape Town, P. A. Brand, 1832; F. C. L. Bosman, *Drama
en Toneel in Suid-Afrika*, I: *1652–1855*, Cape Town and Pretoria, HAUM and J. H. de Bussy,
1928, 299–320. The identification of the persons caricatured is on pp. 302–3.

[2] Bank, 'Liberals and their Enemies', 212–15; *Kaatje Kekkelbek* is reprinted in M. H. Lister
(ed.), *Journals of Andrew Geddes Bain*, Cape Town, Van Riebeeck Society, 1949, 193–202. It
would be fascinating to know who played the drunken Khoi, just as it would be to learn who
played the Moor in the contemporary Cape Town productions of Othello. David Johnson,
Shakespeare and South Africa, Oxford, Clarendon Press, 1996, 36.

[3] Andrew Bank, *The Decline of Urban Slavery at the Cape, 1806 to 1843*, Cape Town, Centre
of African Studies, UCT, Communication no. 22, 1991, esp. 118, 124; C. Pama, *Regency
Cape Town*, Cape Town, Tafelberg, 1975, 129; A. H. Smith, *Cape Views and Costumes:
Water-Colours by H. C. de Meillon*, Johannesburg, Brenthurst Press, 1978, 89; Shell, *De
Meillon's People of Colour*.

had accompanied Andrew Smith on his great expedition to the north in the 1830s and later rose quickly through the ranks of the civil service, as might be expected of the nephew of the Colonial Secretary. His drawing was not for profit, and thus he could have had no inhibitions in producing works such as 'Hottentot Woman with Bottle', 'Hottentot with Bottle' and so forth.[4] Frederick I'Ons, on the other hand, is more difficult to pin down, precisely because he needed to satisfy a variegated market. On the one hand, he could produce paintings celebrating the triumphs of British liberalism, such as his idealised portrait of a slave on emancipation day. On the other, he produced (to commission) savage (and no doubt well-selling) prints lambasting Philip, Fairbairn and Stockenström – with some of the clearest contemporary comments about Sir Andries's slave ancestry – or depicting 'Romance and Reality, or Hottentots as they are said to be and as they really are', where the Romance shows John Philip and Sir Thomas Fowell Buxton viewing the Khoi learning the Greek alphabet and Latin declensions and the Reality a scene of drunken fighting and sexual looseness in and around a canteen.[5]

This sort of representation, in drama, in drawing, later in other genres of literature, was stereotyping of the most blatant variety.[6] It was, moreover, a presentation in artforms of a stigmatisation of the Khoi and ex-slaves as drunken, lazy, dangerous good-for-nothings, an idea which was widely spread within the white community as a whole.[7] It worked to maintain boundaries, to prevent an elision of categories. To the extent that it purported to describe complete classes of people, to make claims about the Khoikhoi, the ex-slaves, the proto-coloureds or whoever, *as such*, it was of course inaccurate and pernicious. Temperance societies on the Eastern Cape mission stations, in particular, did exist and were in no way the sort of ridiculous inanities that Boniface portrays.[8] Indeed, it was the prejudice

---

[4] F. R. Kennedy, *Johannesburg Africana Museum Catalogue of Pictures*, Johannesburg, Africana Museum, 7 vols., 1966, nos. B754–5, B762–5, B779–80. See above all Bank, 'Liberals and their Enemies', 290.

[5] Bank, 'Liberals and their Enemies', 298; the print is reproduced in Viney and Brooke Simons, *The Cape of Good Hope*, 107.

[6] V. A. February, *Mind Your Colour: The 'Coloured' Stereotype in South African Literature*, London and Boston, Kegan Paul International, 1981; at times, the fear of the underclass could be displaced into metaphors, as for instance in the long-running complaints about stray dogs in Cape Town, just as today the British, unable to keep foreigners out, resort to keeping their dogs out on the dubious excuse that they might be rabid. See Kirsten McKenzie, 'The *South African Commercial Advertiser* and the Making of Middle Class Identity in Early Nineteenth-Century Cape Town', MA thesis, UCT, 1993, ch. 2.

[7] See, for example, Elks, 'Crime, Community and the Police in Cape Town', ch. 2; Van Arkel *et al.*, 'Going Beyond the Pale', 81–6; Clifton C. Crais, *White Supremacy and Black Resistance in Pre-Industrial South Africa: The Making of the Colonial Order in the Eastern Cape, 1770–1865*, Cambridge, Cambridge University Press, 1992, 125–46.

[8] See, for example, James Read to William Ellis, Philipton, 3 July 1834; Read to Philip, Bethelsdorp, 16 Nov. 1835; Read to Kitchingman, Bethelsdorp, 24 Sept. 1838, all printed in Le Cordeur and Saunders, *Kitchingman Papers*, 142, 159, 202.

shown by Boniface, by Bain, by Bell or by I'Ons, and their fellows, which made the living of what they saw as a virtuous life more difficult, and less rewarding, than it would otherwise have been. Equally it ignored the heavy drinking of the upholders of law and order, such as the Superintendent of Cape Town's police, who was once accused of 'drunkenness and rowdy behaviour', an occurrence which was hushed up, or the high court judges described as 'notable bottle men'.[9] A missionary, with different perceptions of the proprieties of class, would describe Cape Town as 'Sodom', where 'drunkenness and fornication both in high and low life are scarcely considered as sins, and the Sabbath seems scarcely known'.[10]

On the other hand, what Bell and I'Ons drew was not entirely a figment of their imagination. There is no doubt that they reflected scenes which they had seen around them, even if they may have exaggerated them for comic effect. Drunkenness and degradation were, and are, common South African phenomena. They are no more to be ignored than are the upright, sober, God-fearing men and women of whom the missionaries were so proud.

The respectable saw the drunken as helpless victims of their race or as targets for redemption. Historians, who are only occasionally half-naked and drunk in public, and who, if they are prostitutes, hide their prostitution under some other name, have tended to do the same. We have written of degradation, and have tried to find explanations for that degradation, believing that it needed an excuse. It does not. For the men and women concerned, it was a defiant rejection of the values which those who saw themselves as their betters attempted to foist upon them. As Ivan Karp has put it, in another context, drinking became the 'social theory' of the Cape's underclass, 'expressing ideas about the nature of their social world and their experience of it'.[11]

The making of an underclass community in Cape Town[12]

Cape Town was a port city. It owed its life to the ships which put into Table Bay for a week or more, mainly in the first three months of every year. Before 1770, between sixty and 100 ships a year visited the Cape, and

[9] Elks, 'Crime, Community and the Police in Cape Town', 46, 138; Hattersley, *Victorian Lady*, 27.

[10] Letter by Anne Hodgson, 7 Feb. 1822, Historical Papers Department, University of the Witwatersrand, Johannesburg, A 567, cited in Erlank, 'Letters Home', 178.

[11] Ivan Karp, 'Beer Drinking Experience in an African Society: An Essay in Formal Sociology', in I. Karp and Charles S. Bird (eds.), *Exploration in African Systems of Thought*, Bloomington, Indiana University Press, 1980, 85, cited in Emmanuel Akyeampong, 'What's in a Drink? Class Struggle, Popular Culture and the Politics of *Akpeteshie* (Local Gin), in Ghana, 1930–67', *JAH*, 37(2), 1996, 234.

[12] Aficionados will appreciate that by this very title I have accepted some of the criticisms made in Bank, *Decline of Urban Slavery*, 99–101, of my *Cape of Torments*.

thereafter the numbers rose to an eighteenth-century peak of 183 in 1791. Some of the ships were small, but others were manned by large crews. There were, for instance, on average around 200 voyagers on board the Dutch ships on the voyage from the Netherlands to Asia, and just over 100 on the return voyage.[13] After the demise of the VOC, the numbers certainly did not decline, and probably grew. There were times, then, when there were at least 5,000 extra people in Cape Town and its harbour, almost all male members of what has always been one of the roughest and rowdiest occupations.

The presence of so many people from outside the Colony was always a major source of income for Capetonians. The more prosperous among the mariners might take up temporary lodgings with Cape Town's householders. They were also the source of most of the Colony's new slaves and of many foreign commodities, both of which Capetonians would later resell to people from the countryside when the latter brought their agricultural produce to market. Even if they did not contribute thus directly to the city's commerce, the sailors had money in their pockets which they could spend on the traditional delights of seamen ashore, women and drink.

Prostitution is, surprisingly, not a subject on which information is readily available. In the eighteenth century, the Company government generally did not take any action against it, and indeed was said to have profited from the activity. Mentzel described how

Female slaves are always ready to offer their bodies for a trifle; and towards evening, one can see a string of soldiers and sailors entering the lodge where they misspend their time until the clock strikes 9. After that hour no strangers are allowed to remain in the [Company slave] lodge. The Company does nothing to prevent this promiscuous intercourse, since, for one thing, it tends to multiply the slave population, and does away with the necessity of importing fresh slaves.[14]

This was blatant, but casual prostitution was probably more common. Again according to Mentzel, the motto of the slave women was 'Kammene Kas, Kammene Kunte',[15] and one slave, Fortuyn van Ceylon, was charged with assaulting and attempting to rape Sara van de Caab after his offer of six *schellingen* for her to lie with him was refused with the crushing comment: 'Jou swart canailje, wie wil met jou te saamen gaan?'[16] Only two

---

[13] Figures taken from Coenraad Beyers, *Die Kaapse Patriotte gedurende die laatste kwart van die agtiende eeu en die voortlewing van hul denkbeelde*, 2nd edn, Pretoria, J. L. van Schaik, 1967, 333–5, and J. R. Bruijn, F. S. Gaastra and I. Schöffer, *Dutch-Asiatic Shipping in the 17th and 18th Centuries*, 3 vols., The Hague, Martinus Nijhoff, 1987, I, 144.

[14] Mentzel, *Description*, II, 125. Given the likelihood that such practices would spread venereal disease, the VOC's demography was probably mistaken.

[15] Translation: 'No cash, No cunt'; Mentzel, *Description*, III, 99.

[16] Translation: 'You black trash! Who would want to go with you', Victor de Kock, *Those in Bondage: An Account of the Life of the Slave at the Cape in the Days of the Dutch East India Company*, Pretoria, Union Booksellers, 1963, 45.

cases of more organised prostitution have turned up, both of which refer to Free Black women – who may well have accumulated the money by which they purchased their freedom in this fashion – hiring out a few small rooms to soldiers and sailors and the girls they were with for a short time. In one of these, Flora van Rio de la Goa, one of the few Mozambicans to be emancipated, was sentenced to five years in the slave lodge after, on a Sunday afternoon in 1766, during the time of the church service, one of the constables had found eight or ten soldiers in the house she had rented. They had purchased a barrel of wine together, they said, and were carousing noisily. Also in the house were two slave women, one of whom had run away from her master.[17]

In the nineteenth century, prostitution remained a casual profession. It had become an offence, but was relatively rarely prosecuted. In ten years between 1840 and 1850, for instance, 107 convictions were obtained for prostitution, an average of under one a month, and apparently nearly half of these were against a single woman, Catherine Wood from Scotland.[18] As the police force itself contained a number of sufferers from venereal disease, it is quite likely that, like police forces the world over, they took bribes in kind from the women in question.[19] Only 1 per cent of offenders, for all classes of misdemeanours, were described as prostitutes.[20] While a majority of these women were described as 'Afrikander' (or Cape coloured, in later terminology), by the 1860s the registered prostitutes reflected the city's increasing cosmopolitan make-up, including English, Irish, Scots, French, Spanish and Dutch ladies.[21]

Inebriation could be a much more public occurrence than prostitution,[22] and was of course only a problem when not in the privacy of a gentleman's house. The Government was necessarily somewhat ambivalent about the matter, since a very substantial proportion of its income came from the sale of licences to sell wine, brandy and, to a lesser extent, beer, and from the tax on wine brought into Cape Town. The various drinking shops in the city were nevertheless regularly the scene of drunken brawls which disturbed the

---

[17] Case 27 of 13 Nov. 1766, ARA VOC 4247; see also case 27 of 19 Dec. 1737, *contra Clara Tant*, ARA VOC 4135.

[18] Elks, 'Crime, Community and the Police in Cape Town', 55, 155. Some of her convictions may of course have been for other offences.

[19] Elks, 'Crime, Community and the Police in Cape Town', 34.

[20] Elks, 'Crime, Community and the Police in Cape Town', 56.

[21] Elizabeth van Heyningen, 'The Social Evil in the Cape Colony, 1868–1902: Prostitution and the Contagious Diseases Act', *JSAS*, 10(2), 1984, 182; also Van Heyningen, ' "Gentoo" – A Case of Mistaken Identity', *Kronos: Journal of Cape History*, 22, 1995, 73–86.

[22] In the nineteenth century, admittedly, there were occasions when women (though not their male partners) were sentenced for having 'carnal connection' in the streets, even in the middle of the Parade or Hottentot Square (now Riebeeck Square). See Elks, 'Crime, Community and the Police in Cape Town', 156.

peace of the respectable. Two cases may be exemplary for many. In 1745, Adolf van der Caab, a 26-year-old slave living on a small market garden high in Table Valley, had been to the funeral of a fellow slave. Afterwards he went to the drinking house (*schaggerij*) to return the black skirt he had worn to the funeral and to pick up his coat. He then settled down to drink brandy with other slaves and Khoi, so much that on his way home, he had to lie down and sleep it off. On coming to, he came across a European from whom he removed a snuffbox, and was then arrested. He claimed that the man had already been assaulted, and was lying unconscious. The court seems to have agreed, and sentenced him to five years in chains, presumably only for the theft.[23] Two years later, Joumath van Maccassar returned, rather drunk, to the *schaggerij* where he lived. A fellow slave, who served drinks there, refused to let him in, and after a row Joumath started throwing rocks through the windows, breaking thirteen panes of glass, for which he was flogged and sent to Robben Island for ten years, despite his mistress's offer to pay for the glass.[24]

Both of these affrays occurred at legal drinking establishments, supplied through the liquor licensees. Equally, the soldiers who met at Flora van Rio de la Goa's house were behaving legally, at least in that they had purchased their wine in a half-aum (*c.* 77 litre) barrel, the smallest receptacle which a private person could sell. The legal licensees had continually to be on their guard against the illicit sale of wine by the bottle, with some success during the eighteenth century,[25] but increasingly little thereafter, as Cape Town became larger, more variegated and less controlled. By the early 1840s, there were seventy-one licensed drinking houses in Cape Town, while the city's magistrate, probably exaggerating, claimed there were also 300, illegal, 'smuggling houses'.[26] Even the legal drinking establishments were not appreciated by the sober. Residents living near The Anchor, in Waterkant Street, for instance, complained in 1840 that a wall shielded the tavern from scrutiny by the police, but did not stop the neighbours being plagued by the 'unbecoming language' used by its drunken habitués.[27]

Other drugs besides alcohol also circulated in Cape Town. Probably because it does not tend to make its users violent, historians have not found unequivocal evidence for the smoking of dagga, except for suggestive iconographic material. Opium, on the other hand, is known to have found

---

[23] Case 26 of 8 July 1745, ARA VOC 4165.   [24] Case 9 of 23 Mar. 1747, ARA VOC 4172.

[25] E.g. cases 20 and 25, in both cases *Relaas van J. J. Doeksteen*, 12 Sept. & 2 Nov., 1757, VOC 4209.

[26] Elks, 'Crime, Community and the Police in Cape Town', 133, 139. This is a translation of *smokkelhuisen*; in Dutch, *smokkel* refers to the evasion of any form of duty, not merely that on imports and exports.

[27] Letter to Municipality, 15 Dec. 1840, CA 3/CT/1/5/1, cited in Elks, 'Crime, Community and the Police in Cape Town', 40.

its way to Cape Town, to the house of an Indonesian political leader banned
to the Cape, Soera Dioromo, and, before he ran amok in 1786, killing
several people, Soera Brotto is said to have built up his courage with the
drug.[28]

Slaves were able to partake in the alcoholic life of the city because the
occupations of many of them allowed them considerable mobility and
absence from supervision. Some of course worked as house-servants, and
had little chance to escape from constraints imposed by their owners.
Others might be rented out, for instance to building contractors.[29] Rather
more were required by their owners to move about the town, and its surrounding areas, fetching wood and water, washing clothes, working in the
docks or earning *coeligeld*. This was, in effect, an arrangement by which the
slaves rented their own labour from their owners. The slaves were required
to hand over a fixed sum at the end of each week, which they earned either
as casual labourers, as skilled craftsmen or as petty traders. In particular
the retail trade in foodstuffs was in their hands. Those who failed to accumulate sufficient cash, or who had gambled or drunk it away, were likely to
be beaten, and there are a number of cases where slaves ran away rather
than face this punishment. On the other hand, those who were assiduous,
frugal and lucky were able to accumulate sufficient capital to purchase their
own emancipation and then to go into business on their own account. Since
they continued in the same line of business, in the early nineteenth century
all Cape Town's cheap restaurants ('chophouses') were run by emancipated
slaves. Eventually, in the early nineteenth century, this fluidity in Cape
Town's occupational structure, coupled with the increasing presence of
non-slaves among the labour force, would lead to what Andrew Bank has
termed the 'erosion' of urban slavery.[30]

The mobility which slaves enjoyed as a result of this sort of occupational
structure was not appreciated by the master class, even though the city
could not have functioned as it did without it. Proclamations laid down
that: 'After dark, and also during the night no slaves shall appear in the
street, or in the neighbourhood of the town, unless with those under whose
charge they are, without having a lighted lantern in their hand, on pain of
being apprehended the same as runaways.' After eleven at night, even those

---

[28] Resoluties van de Raad van Politie, 18 Aug. 1761, ARA VOC 4225; Bradlow, 'Mental
Illness'; Bank's reference, *Decline of Urban Slavery*, 123, seems to me to refer to opiates
used medicinally as a soporific, not for the alteration of consciousness. Furthermore, his
comment that the import of opium was banned following the Soera Brotto case seems mistaken. In 1792, six years later, the VOC issued two decrees maintaining the VOC's monopoly on the import of the drug, thus tacitly admitting that it could be sold. *Kaapse
Plakkaatboek*, IV, 141, 151.   [29] *RCC*, XXIX, 457–63.
[30] Robert Ross, 'The Occupations of Slaves in Eighteenth Century Cape Town', *Studies in the
History of Cape Town*, 2, 1980, 6–12; Bank, *Decline of Urban Slavery*, esp. 20–45, 208–13.

with a lantern had to have a pass from their master explaining why they were abroad. And, even during the day, the constables were to drive apart with their canes groups of three or more slaves belonging to different owners.[31] In part such provisions were an attempt to control slave theft, which was seen, probably rightly, as rampant. There was a world of house-breaking, receiving and shipping out of stolen goods which the officials of the Court of Justice rarely penetrated, and in which Chinese exiles from Batavia and elsewhere seem to have played a major part.[32] In part, though, these measures were designed to give the masters the illusion that they controlled what went on in the city, even though they no doubt recognised that this illusion had little basis in fact. Nevertheless, it was backed up by a range of brutal punishments, ranging downwards from capital punishment in deliberately sadistic forms to working on the treadmill, which required daily defaulters to grind corn to make the city's bread.[33]

Despite this, the slaves were able to find and to exploit space, both social and physical, within the city. Two small vignettes from the first half of the eighteenth century can illustrate this. In the first, in 1727, a group of slaves and Free Blacks who had been out fishing in Table Bay spent from four in the afternoon till around midnight tending to their lines, drinking and building fires to warm themselves and dry their clothes, until their gathering was broken up by one of the kaffers with his stick.[34] Nine years later, in 1736, two groups of slaves, sitting at night in houses in the Gardens, were arrested by the watch patrolling the Gardens above Cape Town. One set were eating rice and curry and drinking arak. They were flogged and sentenced to work in chains for three years at the public works. The others, who claimed that they had been sent out to find some pigs which had escaped, were sitting drinking coffee in apparent peace, but were nevertheless sentenced to be flogged and put in chains for a year. It was only because at the time the Cape Town slave-owners were in a panic, caused by the activities of Leander Bugis and his gang of runaways who had attempted to burn the town down in March of that year, that the reaction was so sharp, and the case came to court, and thus to historians' cognisance.[35] In general, such gatherings remained outside the purview of the authorities, or were dealt with so summarily that no record has remained.

Towards the end of the eighteenth century, such surveillance was begin-

---

[31] D. Denyssen, 'Statement of the Laws of the Colony of the Cape of Good Hope regarding Slavery', 16 Mar. 1813, *RCC*, IX, 156–8.   [32] Ross, *Cape of Torments*, 23.

[33] Ross, 'Rule of Law'; M. D. Teenstra, *De Vruchten Mijner Werkzaamheden gedurende mijne Reize over de Kaap de Goede Hoop, naar Java, en Terug, over St Helena, Naar de Nederlanden*, edited by F. C. L. Bosman, Cape Town, Van Riebeeck Society, 1943, 195.

[34] Case 7 of 8 May 1727, *re Marlang van Madagascar*, ARA VOC 4112.

[35] Case 5 of 22 Mar. 1736 *contra Bellesoor van Bengalen c.s.* and case 9 of 26 Apr. 1836, *contra Pieter v. d. Caab c. s.*, ARA VOC 4131. On Leander, see Ross, *Cape of Torments*, 54–72.

ning to break down. Thus, for instance, slave gambling was becoming ever more evident. A decree first issued in 1794 laid down that: 'No slave is allowed to join gamblers either in the houses or in the streets or in any secret places, on pain of being flogged, and if found gambling near the public water pump he will be immediately tied to a pole erected there for the purpose, and flogged by the constables.'[36] This decree was issued after François Duminy, a ship's captain in the service of the VOC and a resident of Cape Town, had complained that slaves gambled with dice and held cock-fights behind his garden, and when they were dispersed by the officers of justice often took flight through his property.[37] A few years later, though, an anonymous British officer could describe how he wandered around Cape Town

till I at last found myself in the middle of a crowd of Malay slaves, who, having formed a circle, were enjoying the pleasures of a *cock-fight*, and, after the idle part of our countrymen, had bets depending on the match. The keen expression of their countenances, and the warm interest of the spectators, excited my curiosity. I mingled with the crowd, . . . The conflict was obstinate, and the strength and spirit of the poor animals were totally exhausted. They are commonly armed with artificial spurs, and seldom separated till one of them receives the mortal blow. The crowd separated into several lesser circles, and a new scene of gambling commenced. The dice-box was forthwith produced, and the young, middle-aged, and old, pressed close upon each other and staked their various sums.[38]

While the gamblers had to beware of the officers of justice breaking up the gathering, they were evidently not worried by the presence of a European they did not know.

Slave dancing, and music in general, follows a similar pattern. Hidden from view, or only surfacing during the eighteenth century in the slave orchestras of the very rich,[39] by the 1820s it was out in the open, and one of the exotic attractions of the city for an overseas visitor. W. W. Bird, for instance, wrote that

there are other [dances], in which the negroes are engaged; and although a few of these dances take place every night, yet the grand display is in the outskirts of the town, to which the black population rush, on a Sunday, . . . and go through their various awkward movements in quick or slow time, according to the taste of the

[36] *RCC*, XII, 156.
[37] Petition of Duminy to Raad van Politie, 18 Sept. 1792, CA C207, 276–80.
[38] *Gleanings in Africa*, 244–5.
[39] De Kock, *Those in Bondage*, 94–5; in the nineteenth century, too, the musicians for formal dances, for instance at the Castle, were blacks in British uniforms playing European instruments, at least according to a drawing made of them for the wife of a former governor. See P. R. Kirby, *The Musical Instruments of the Native Races of South Africa*, London, Oxford University Press, 1934, 254. The dancing at Government House was so vigorous that the 'long sustained vibration' it entailed caused the walls to crack and a large portion of the ceiling to collapse. Viney and Brooke Simons, *The Cape of Good Hope*, 70.

dancers. The Sunday dance is accompanied by native music of every description.
The slave boys from Madagascar and Mozambique bring the stringed instruments
of their respective tribes and nation, from which they force sounds, which they
regard as melodious. The love of dancing is a ruling passion throughout the Cape
population in every rank; but music, though a pursuit favoured by a small part of
the society, is here a passion with the negro alone.[40]

There are other such comments from travellers,[41] and several famous draw-
ings of such events.[42] Equally, one slave commented that he regularly went
to Mr Griffin's wine-house on a Friday 'to listen to a band playing music'.[43]
This is clearly the beginnings of the tradition of Cape Town music which
has lasted to the present. Unfortunately, the texts of the songs that were
sung do not seem to have survived, or at least there is no unequivocal evidence that any modern song was composed in the slave period. It would
however be surprising if the satirical tradition of the *ghoemaliedjes*, which
were still sung of the Electoral Commission by those waiting to vote in
Bo'kaap in April 1994, did not have its roots before 1834.[44]

The most notorious of Cape Town's early nineteenth-century dances
were the events known as 'Rainbow Balls':[45]

The females are chiefly slave girls of the first class, and girls who have acquired their
freedom; and amongst the men are seen officers, merchants, and young Dutchmen.
It cannot be pretended that these meetings add to the morals of the town. However
that may be, everything during the ball is conducted with due decorum. The ladies
imitate the manner, conversation, and dancing of their mistresses, and nearly equal
them in dress; and when the dance is over, it is not necessary to follow the parties
into retirement.[46]

While these events were not necessarily exploitative – it would at any rate
be difficult to be sure who was exploiting whom – they were certainly not
examples of equality. On the other hand, that culture of drinking, dancing

[40] Bird, *State of the Cape of Good Hope*, 166.
[41] Cowper Rose, *Four Years in Southern Africa*, London, Richard Bentley, 1829, 3–4.
[42] D'Oyly's drawing of 'South African Hop' in Pama, *Regency Cape Town*, 28; Bell's 'Slave
      Dance on a Free Sunday', in Viney and Brooke Simons, *The Cape of Good Hope*, 50; and
      'The Dark Fantastic', in Kirby, *Musical Instruments*, plate 71.
[43] Cited in Bank, *Decline of Urban Slavery*, 140. Since the only two Griffins in the Cape Town
      Almanacs were a wheelwright living in Dorp Street and a blacksmith in Stil steeg, this wine
      shop was presumably one of many 'smuggling houses'. The Cape Town Almanacs have
      been entered on database files by the Jagger Library of UCT, and I am most grateful to
      them, and to Antonia Malan who acted as intermediary, for sending the files to me.
[44] Given the paucity of research into Cape oral literature, evidence for survivals may yet turn
      up. For a beginning, see C. Winberg, 'The "Ghoemaliedjes" of the Cape Muslims:
      Remnants of a Slave Culture', unpublished paper, UCT, 1992, cited in Vivian Bickford-
      Smith, 'Meanings of Freedom: Social Position and Identity among ex-Slaves and their
      Descendants in Cape Town, 1875–1910', in Worden and Crais, *Breaking the Chains*, 301–2.
      Nigel Worden told me of the singing of *ghoemaliedjes* during the elections: personal
      communication.
[45] Cf. Desmond Tutu, *The Rainbow People of God: South Africa's Victory over Apartheid*,
      London, Doubleday, 1994.   [46] Bird, *State of the Cape of Good Hope*, 165–6.

and music, what Andrew Bank has called a 'canteen culture', increasingly came to comprehend individuals from all of Cape Town's legal categories. The respectable came to believe that those involved were Irish, soldiers and sailors as well as slaves and Khoi.[47] This is a list which is only inaccurate in that it is incomplete, as can be seen, for instance, from the list of 'regular offenders' drawn up by the Cape Town police in 1843, which included five Irish, four English, three Scots, nine 'Bastard-Hottentots', one 'bushman' and five Mozambicans.[48] Anyway soldiers might be demobilised in Cape Town, and not return to Europe. They were indeed suspected of running many of Cape Town's 'smuggling houses'.[49] In any event, the participants within this 'canteen culture' displayed cross-racial solidarity. In 1843, the police attempted to clean up Zieke Street, which ran alongside the main barracks on the site which has since become the Caledon Square Police Station. They were, however, prevented from carrying out their orders by a group of soldiers who issued from the barracks to the defence of their civilian friends.[50]

Grahamstown

The double standard is usually a term used in reference to a level of sexual licence allowed to, even encouraged in, young men which is simultaneously condemned in their female partners. Something similar happened with regard to drinking. The law officers were not the only drunkards and revellers among those with a reputation in society. On 4 February 1824, a large party of the male white citizens of Grahamstown, including some of the most prominent settlers such as Thomas Philipps, celebrated the arrival of the Commissioners of Inquiry, whom they expected would castigate the Cape Government, and specifically the landdrost of Albany. They made merry and fired off their guns in the air with such abandon that the army turned out to repel an attack by the amaXhosa. At least that was the explanation which they later gave. It was after all only five years since the town had nearly fallen to Xhosa attack. The revellers' reaction was that of an angry mob. Philipps and Alexander Biggar were heard to damn the landdrost 'while their tempers were inflamed'. The incident caused a temporary scandal but was soon forgotten, or rather, Grahamstown being what it is, considered inconsequential.[51]

---

[47] E.g. Elks, 'Crime, Community and the Police in Cape Town', 59.
[48] Report of Inspector King, 19 Sept. 1843, CA CO 520, cited in Elks, 'Crime Community and the Police in Cape Town', 82.
[49] Evidence of Inspector King, Apr. 1846, CA LCA 17, cited in Elks, 'Crime, Community and the Police in Cape Town', 87.
[50] *Case of Erfurt*, 10 Nov. 1843, CA 1/CT 6/18, cited in Elks, 'Crime, Community and the Police in Cape Town', 156.
[51] Malherbe, 'Cape Khoisan', 101–2; Keppel-Jones, *Philipps*, 208–9.

The lower orders did not have this freedom. The Commissioners of Inquiry were silent about their over-enthusiastic welcome into Grahamstown, but wrote that 'scenes and disorders of the most disgusting kind . . . arising from the intemperate use of spirits, were very frequent in the streets of Graham's Town, not confined to the Hottentots alone, but comprising individuals of the lower order of European settlers, who upon these occasions did not disdain association with them'.[52] Evidently what mattered was not how drunk a man was, but who he drank with.

Liquor sales in the canteens were obviously to the material advantage of those who sold drink, and to the wine and brandy farmers. All attempts at their prohibition were bound to fail, except on mission stations and in the Kat River, where by the agreement of the settlers canteens were banned. Elsewhere, the scenes of disorder, 'indecency' and 'licentiousness in language' around such drinking shops were widely condemned in public, though surreptitiously maintained both for the profit of those concerned and for the confirmation of racial hierarchies which they provided. The only way to curb the 'vicious propensities' of the Khoi when inflamed by drink was to condemn them to hard labour.[53] This was however clear class discrimination. Philipps and Biggar did not suffer for their public drunkenness. Saul Rondganger, a Khoi arrested in Grahamstown for drunkenness and breach of the peace, had a point when he protested that 'he was a freeman and as good as any Englishman'.[54]

The culture of the farm labourers

In 1836, the English soldier and big-game hunter William Cornwallis Harris was spending a night in his waggon at a farm near Somerset East, in the eastern part of the Cape Colony. He did not sleep well, if at all, since he was kept awake

by the drunken merriment and boisterous singing of a lame Irish cobbler, who was 'keeping it up' in a roofless mud outhouse with two Hottentot 'boys' neither of whom was under fifty years of age. The cobbler apologised next morning for not inviting us to the wassail, on the score that we were *gentlemen*, adding that not being at the time altogether 'compos mentis', he hoped that we would excuse his apparent want of politeness.[55]

In itself, this was a trivial incident. Nevertheless, it does provide an insight into an aspect of Cape life which is otherwise exceedingly hard to docu-

[52] 'Report of the Commissioners of Inquiry . . . upon the Police at the Cape of Good Hope', *RCC*, XXXV, 185.

[53] *Graham's Town Journal*, 13 June 1833, cited in Malherbe, 'Cape Khoisan', 299.

[54] *Graham's Town Journal*, 3 Feb. 1832, cited in Malherbe, 'Cape Khoisan', 299.

[55] W. Cornwallis Harris, *The Wild Sports of Southern Africa*, London, Henry G. Bohn, 1852, 12–13, italics in original.

ment.[56] Drunks do not write, at least outside rarefied literary circles, and thus historians have difficulty in escaping from the representations of them given by the sober, whether the stereotyping of the racists or the censoriousness of the missionaries and temperance advocates. But representation is not all; indeed to over-emphasise it is to reiterate elitist historiography in a form only altered by tone, not by content.

The incident between Harris and the drunken Irish cobbler makes two things clear. First, the Irishman enunciated the expectation that gentlemen would not be involved with the alcoholic revelry of those who were not behaving respectably. Secondly, the cross-racial nature of the rural variant of 'canteen culture' is made plain. This is something which went far back into the Cape's past. In 1742 the landdrost and *heemraden* of Stellenbosch reported

that many of the Drakenstein people dare not send their corn to the Mill there, as both 'Knechts' and slaves drink themselves drunk in the neighbouring tap [drinking establishment] kept by the burgher Johan Wit; so that they not only remain away days longer than they ought to, but also lose a quantity of the meal without the possibility as yet of finding evidence to show what has become of it; the present miller, Jan Gabriel Visser, has also often complained that the slave in whose charge the mill is often placed, has often been found intoxicated.[57]

The power relations on the farms often led to conflicts between the slaves and the 'knechts' or overseers.[58] Evidently, though, at least some of them could find much in common.

It is not so surprising that the main elements of rural working-class culture in the Cape were alcohol and music. Wine was one of the Colony's main agricultural products. As in vineyards the world over, the labourers were accustomed to drink during the harvest, for instance, a period of considerable physical labour. As the nineteenth century wore on, and quite possibly earlier, this was transmuted into the standard provision of wine to the farm labourers in quantities that were literally staggering. Eventually, farm labourers were receiving a *dop*, half a bottle of bad wine, five times a day.[59] Equally, music, dancing and all-night gatherings had been part of Khoikhoi culture, and indeed came to symbolise that which the newly converted Christians thought to be heathen within that culture. When Hendrik

---

[56] According to a supplementary *stelling* accompanying Peter Kloos's 1971 Ph.D. thesis for the University of Amsterdam, 'The Maroni River Caribs of Surinam', anthropologists engaged in participant observation may also have problems in this regard, if of a rather different nature.

[57] Leibbrandt, *Requesten*, I, 373.   [58] E.g. Ross, *Cape of Torments*, 32–3.

[59] Elizabeth Anne Host, 'Die Hondje Byt: Labour Relations in the Malmesbury District, *c.* 1880 to 1920', Honours thesis, UCT, 1987; Pamela Scully, 'Liquor and Labor in the Western Cape, 1870–1900', in Jonathan Crush and Charles Ambler (eds.), *Liquor and Labor in Southern Africa*, Athens and Pietermaritzburg, Ohio University Press and University of Natal Press, 1992, 56–78.

Boesak, one of the first converts, smashed his violin, it was the clearest rejection of his former life.[60] Many followed him, but again many did not. Indeed, the missionaries were regularly plagued by the drunkenness of those whom they believed had renounced wine and brandy as the juice of the devil, as when mission residents who had served as soldiers in the Eastern Cape returned to Genadendal, or when a canteen was opened near to the station.[61] Equally, there were occasions when dagga was smoked on the mission stations, again to the great distress of the missionaries, who considered it to be a reason for expulsion.[62]

It must be admitted that the advocates of temperance and respectability had a point. The alcoholic life on the Cape farms could be very violent and uncertain. Alcohol addiction and venereal disease can only have shortened many lives, and broken many others. The ragged clothes which many labourers wore demonstrated only too clearly their poverty and their dependence.[63] In the long term, the *dop* turned the agricultural working class of the Cape into highly exploitable, if not particularly efficient, tools of the masters, and contributed heavily to the maintenance of forms of bondage after the ending of slavery. A romantic vision of the lives of the rural underclass is not in its place. But for all that, as the next chapter will argue, it was precisely the farm labourers who provided the greatest challenge to the established order of colonial society. In part this was a challenge in the minds of panicking farmers, but in part it was in the deadly earnest of the so-called Kat River rebellion.

Islam: an alternative respectability

Part of the new self-confidence among the slaves and Free Blacks, as control was in practice relaxed, manifested itself in terms of religion. It is not

---

[60] Elizabeth Elbourne, 'Early Khoisan Uses of Mission Christianity', in Henry Bredekamp and Robert Ross (eds.), *Missions and Christianity in South African History*, Johannesburg, Witwatersrand University Press, 1995, 79. For other, very similar examples, see the conversion narrative of Philip, in Genadendal diary, 11 July 1809, *PA*, V, 20; James Read to Directors, 6 June 1844, LMS-SA 17/2/A.

[61] E.g. letter from H. P. Hallbeck to 'Dear Brother' 10 July 1838, *PA*, XIV, 435; Genadendal diary, 24 May 1844, *PA*, XVII, 267.

[62] *Berichte der Rheinischen Missionsgesellschaft*, 2, 1831, 29; Groenkloof diary, 22 Nov. 1811, *PA*, V, 212; Hemel-en-Aarde diary, 8 May 1833, *PA*, XII, 461; Genadendal diary, 24 Nov. 1844, *PA*, XVII, 327.

[63] I have more confidence in iconographic evidence showing respectability than in that showing decrepitude, since the latter is more likely to be a caricature. However, for the state of clothing of the rural poor, see David Colin Crass and C. Garth Sampson, ' "A Few Old Clothes": 19th Century European Attire adopted by the Seacow River Bushmen', *Africana Notes and News*, 30(6), 1993, 219–34; Karel Schoeman, 'Voersis, Bafta en Molvel: 'n Aantekening oor westerse kleredrag in de Oranjerivier-Soewereiniteit, 1850–1854', *Africana Notes and News*, 30(2), 1992, 58–62, which is based on advertisements requesting the recapture of escaped prisoners.

entirely certain whether an Islamic tradition survived underground from the time of Sheikh Yussuf, the Indonesian leader banned to the Cape in 1694, whose tomb on the shores of False Bay was to become a Muslim shrine.[64] At any event, the first clear evidence of Muslim worship comes from the Swedish botanist Carl Thunberg who was at the Cape in 1772.[65] The celebration of the end of Ramadan, which he witnessed, was in no way hidden. Around the turn of the century, the first mosques would be established.[66]

At the same time, slaves and Free Blacks around Cape Town are first recorded as performing the *Ratiep* or *Khalifa*, a sword ritual of Indonesian provenance which was closely associated, at least at the Cape, with Islam.[67] The first clear reference to it which I know of dates from 1813. On 16 August of that year, a Free Black man, Griep from Mozambique, had joined half a dozen others at the house of Hammat van Macasar in Diepe Rivier. There, without any permission from the magistrate, they performed the *Khalifa*

which play (as appeared from the Instruments exhibited in court, as well as from the Marks which were on the Prisoners Head, Arms & upper part of the Body and on those of the abovementioned persons) is played with Sabres, Daggers & other murderous Weapons with which they chop at, cut, & stab one another, & by which therefore their lives are brought into Immediate danger.

[Griep], having in his turn played some time with said Abdul Zagie, had made him lie down on his back, & holding the point of a Sharp Sword on his naked Body with the palm of his hand, he walked round the same repeating some mystic prayers; that he thereupon having removed the Sword, the entrails of said Abdul Zagie projected through his Belly, whereupon the prisoner sewed up the Wound, continually repeating his prayers, but notwithstanding said Abdul Zagie died about an hour after he received the same.[68]

For this, Griep was sentenced to three years' hard labour in chains on Robben Island.

By the middle of the nineteenth century the performance was institutionalised enough to form part of the ethnographic curiosities of Cape

---

[64] S. Dangor, 'In the Footsteps of the Companions: *Sheykh* Yusuf of Macassar (1626–1699)', in Yusuf da Costa and Achmat Davids, *Pages from Cape Muslim History*, Pietermaritzburg, Shuter & Shooter, 1994, 19–46; the case for such an underground survival is argued by Bradlow, 'Imperialism, State Formation and the Establishment of a Muslim Community'. See also diary of the Rev. P. D. Lückhoff, 25 Jan. 1831, *Berichte der Rheinischen Missionsgesellschaft*, 3, 1832, 28–an earlier reference than has hitherto been found.

[65] Thunberg, *Travels*, 47–8.

[66] Achmat Davids, *The Mosques of Bo-Kaap: A Social History of Islam at the Cape*, Athlone, South African Institute of Arabic and Islamic Research, 1980; the development of Cape Town's Islam will be dealt with in more detail later in this chapter.

[67] On the Indonesian provenance, see H. J. de Graaf, 'De herkomst van de Kaapse "Chalifah" ', *Tydscrif vir Wetenkap en Kuns*, 10, 1950.

[68] CA CJ 805, case of 2 Sept. 1813.

Town, fitting in with the growing image of the 'Malays', as the Muslims came to be called by the British, as mysterious and exotic. Thus in the 1840s, Alfred W. Cole described how he had been to such a ceremony where, in a large room decorated with candles and flowers, and perfumed with incense,

Three or four younger Malays kept marching round the room, and they and the old gentlemen . . . kept up a sort of grunting chorus, which, at first, I took to be indicative of severe pain in the abdominal region, but was afterwards informed that they were chanting sentences from the Koran. Suddenly the young gentlemen began to throw themselves about in the most gladiatorial attitudes, singing faster than ever. Thereupon the old gentlemen shouted much louder, as though the internal agonies had vastly increased. Then the young men stripped off their shirts, and I thought they were going to have a regular 'set to' . . . But they were not going to box at all, – they only danced and jumped and shouted, till they left little pools of sudorific exhalations on the floor. Then a boy came in, shouting awfully . . . Two of the young men seized the boy, and plunged a sharp instrument, like a meat skewer, through his tongue – at least, so it appeared – and they led him round to the admiring spectators with the skewer projecting through his tongue . . .

As soon as this interesting youth had departed, one of the young men took a dagger, and then plunged it into the fleshy part of his side, just above the hip, and then walked round and showed himself. There were a few drops of blood apparently flowing from the wound, in which the dagger was left sticking . . . Another man thrust a skewer through his cheek, and came and showed himself also. Then some red-hot chains were brought in, and thrown over an iron beam, when another of the Malays seized them with his bare hands, and kept drawing them fast over the beams. All the while that these exhibitions were taking place, the Malays kept up their hideous shrieking of the Koran sentences; all of them shouting together, and louder and louder the more horrible the experiment was being tried.[69]

These gatherings could be of a large size, and took place in prominent places in the centre of Cape Town, even in John Philip's old chapel in Church Square, now abandoned by the Congregationalist Church and turned into a ballroom and music hall.[70] They were necessarily very noisy affairs, since the trance into which the performers entered was induced by the loud and rhythmical chanting. As a result, the *Khalifa* came to be seen as a public nuisance, as 'especially the white population [of Cape Town] were disturbed during a number of years in the night, whilst asleep, and sick and dying people more particularly had suffered'.[71] A campaign was begun

[69] Cole, *The Cape and the Kafirs*, 44–5.
[70] Anon, 'Islam at the Cape', *Cape Monthly Magazine*, 10, July 1861, 356, quoted in Robert C.-H. Shell, 'The Establishment and Spread of Islam at the Cape from the Beginning of Company Rule to 1828', BA Hons. thesis, UCT, 1974, 58.
[71] Comment by P. E. de Roubaix, Superintendent of Police, Cape Town, in J. Suasso da Lima, *The Chalifa Question: Documents Connected with the Matter*, Cape Town, Van de Sandt de Villiers, 1857, vi.

for its suppression, or at least its restriction to a single day each (Muslim) year, the 11th of Rubier Agier, the birthday of Abu Bakr.[72]

It might be supposed that such a campaign would be opposed by those who had become the leaders of the Islamic community, the imams of the several mosques in Cape Town. The contrary was the case. De Roubaix, the police superintendent mainly concerned with the matter, was supported in his efforts by all the most prominent imams, who eventually presented him with a solid silver inkstand as thanks for his activity – he felt that to accept it would be against the principles of public office and passed it on with his thanks to the South African Museum.[73] Their reasoning was that while the *Khalifa* was performed by Muslims, it was not an Islamic festival. One of the imams wrote: 'I consider the manner in which the Califa is now played as discreditable; it tends to bring our religion into disrepute, and is the cause that many of the Malays become bad characters, and also that the good feeling, which has been subsisting for so many years, between us and the white population, is destroyed.'[74]

This episode is one which has many parallels in Muslim communities, particularly those with relatively large numbers of recent converts. There is often a conflict between the attempts of the imams, and other clerical leaders, to impose a stricter, more rational, text-based orthodoxy on their followers and the continuation among those followers of more 'magical' practices. This can certainly be seen in the late eighteenth- and early nineteenth-century history of Islam at the Cape. The two main figures, Tuan Nuruman and Tuan Guru, represented these two trends. The former, also known as Paai Schaapie, is much revered among Cape Muslims, above all because of his association with the Islamic burial ground, Tana Baru, on the slopes of Signal Hill. He was however also a man who made use of powers associated with Islam in a way which was not strictly rational. After his banishment from Batavia in 1770, he acquired the reputation of giving

---

[72] Rubier Agier is presumably Rabī l-ākhira, the fourth month of the Muslim calendar, more generally known as Rabī al-thānī.

[73] De Roubaix remained a close associate and benefactor of the Muslim elite, although this was not always equally successful. During his term as a parliamentarian, he naively arranged for the coming to Cape Town of an eminent Muslim scholar from Turkey, in the hope that he would sort out the doctrinal disputes which were dividing the Cape Muslim community. In the event, Abu Bakr Effendi, the man in question, who represented the Hanafite school followed in the Ottoman Empire, while all the Cape Muslims were Shafiites, only exacerbated these divisions. See Achmat Davids, 'The Origins of the *Hanafi-Shafi'i* Dispute and the Impact of Abu Bakr Effendi', in Da Costa and Davids, *Pages from Cape Muslim History*, 81–103; Shamil Jeppie, 'Leadership and Loyalties: The Imams of Nineteenth Century Colonial Cape Town, South Africa', *Journal of Religion in Africa*, 26(2), 1996, 151. See also Achmat Davids, 'Muslim–Christian Relations in Nineteenth Century Cape Town, 1825–1925', *Kronos: Journal of Cape History*, 19, 1992, 97.

[74] Suasso da Lima, *Chalifa Question*, 8.

the slaves advice, and also provided them with protection in the form of *azimat*, texts from the Koran which were supposed to protect runaways from recapture. For this, his parole was cancelled and he was sent back to Robben Island.[75]

Tuan Guru (literally 'Mister Teacher'), or 'Abd Allah Qadi 'Abd Al-Salaam, as he was properly known, was a man of a different stamp. Born on Tidore in the Moluccas and banished to the Cape in 1780, he is said to have produced a handwritten copy of the Koran from memory while on Robben Island. Released in 1793, he led the Muslims in prayer in Cape Town from then on, and was imam of the first mosque in the city, which was established in 1804 after the Batavian Government removed the previous prohibitions.[76] He also wrote the *Ma'rifah al-Islam wa al-Iman* (*Manifestations of Islam and Faith*), a work in Arabic and Malay which has never been printed but which has survived in manuscript to this day, and which formed the basis for Islamic education in Cape Town from the early nineteenth century. It positioned the official version of Cape Islam as Shafiite Sunni, firmly at the rational, non-mystic end of the Islamic spectrum.[77]

In their actions with regard to the *Khalifa*, then, the spiritual leaders of Cape Town's Islam were attempting to re-establish their control over the life of the community, and to direct it along paths which they saw fit.[78] In large part, this was achieved through the institution of the *madaris*, private Islamic schools run by the imams, generally at their own homes. These schools inculcated Islamic learning as promulgated by Tuan Guru.[79] The controlled, disciplined lifestyle they propagated was in many ways similar to that advocated by Christian missionaries.

Islam provided an alternative respectability, but not one which differed greatly from that propagated by the Christians. In a variety of ways, Islamic leaders attempted to decrease the social distance between themselves and their followers, on the one hand, and the white Capetonian elite, on the other. In general, at least until the 1870s, when debates on Responsible Government and the Voluntary Principle for ecclesiastical funding forced

---

[75] *Case contra Norman van Batavia*, 23 Nov. 1786, ARA VOC 4323; Achmat Davids, *The History of the Tana Baru: The case for the Preservation of the Muslim Cemetery at the Top of Longmarket Street*, Cape Town, Committee for the Preservation of the Tana Baru, 1985, 35–9.

[76] Davids, *Mosques of Bo-Kaap*, 93, 100–1. As Tuan Guru died two years later at the age of ninety-five, it may be that his position at the Auwal Mosque in Dorp Street was purely honorary.

[77] Achmat Davids, 'Alternative Education: *Tuan Guru* and the Formation of the Cape Muslim Community', in Da Costa and Davids, *Pages from Cape Muslim History*, 47–56.

[78] There is an interesting parallel with the heavily condemnatory reaction of Dominee Andrew Murray to the outpourings of emotion in his Stellenbosch congregation during the religious revival of the late 1850s. See Du Plessis, *Life of Andrew Murray*, 206.

[79] Davids, 'Muslim–Christian Relations', 87–95. *Madaris* is the plural of *madrasah*.

them into the open, they eschewed politics, in the limited sense of the word, to be sure that they did not invoke the wrath of the Colony's ruling elite.[80] In 1846, a Muslim corps was raised to serve against the Xhosa in the War of the Axe, and several imams served in it, as indeed they had also been involved in earlier wars at the Cape. They were shipped off to the Eastern Cape under a green flag emblazoned with the Union Jack and the Arabic legend 'Allah Akhbar' (God is great). This time, though, the failure of the Cape Government to honour its agreement to provide provisions for the soldiers' wives led to a mutiny, and their contribution to the war effort was minimal. Nevertheless, their position as 'citizens', involved for the general good of the Colony, was re-emphasised.[81] On another level, the houses of at least the more well-to-do of the Cape Muslims came to be furnished in ways which did not differ greatly from those of their Christian fellow Capetonians.[82] In general, the social mores of sobriety, religious observance, literacy (albeit in Arabic, or in Cape Dutch written in Arabic characters[83]) and chastity (if not monogamy), which the leaders of the Islamic community demanded of their followers, accorded well with those which the Cape elite hoped to impose on the whole population of the Colony.

Even in their ideas of what sacred buildings should be like the Muslims accepted the dominant ideas of the Colony. The first purpose-built mosque in Cape Town, the Jamia mosque in Chiappini Street, was constructed in the 1850s to the pattern of a Dutch Reformed chapel, and its original minaret resembled a Dutch pulpit. The original Mosque Shafee, also in Chiappini Street, was built a decade later in almost Gothic Revival style. Only when they were rebuilt in the twentieth century, after contacts with the Islamic heartlands had become much stronger, was their sacredness expressed in an idiom more clearly recognisable as Islamic.[84]

This, though, is only half the story. The Cape's Muslims strove for acceptance, not for integration. It could not be otherwise. The total adoption of the lifestyle of the Christian elite, or the respectable Christian working class, would have eliminated much that was central to the practice of Islam, and thus destroyed the whole *raison d'être* of Cape Town's Muslim congregations. It would also have destroyed the distinction between Muslim and Christian, and thus made the choice between the two unnecessary, or random. Since both Muslim and Christian congregations were still expanding, to some extent at each other's expense but largely by

[80] Jeppie, 'Leadership and Loyalties'; Davids, 'Muslim–Christian Relations', 96–9.
[81] Robert C.-H. Shell, 'The March of the Mardijckers: The Toleration of Islam at the Cape, 1633–1861', *Kronos: Journal of Cape History*, 22, 1995, 3–20.
[82] Anlen Boshoff, 'Die interieur van 'n 19de eeuse Kaapse Moslemhuis na aanleiding van dokumentêre bronne', *Bulletin of the South African Cultural History Museum*, 11, 1990, 5–14.   [83] Davids, 'The Afrikaans of the Cape Muslims'.
[84] Davids, *Mosques of Bo-Kaap*, especially the photos on pp. 139 and 149.

recruiting among those both considered to be 'heathen', such choices were still being made, and were not yet matters of habit or of socialisation. Before 1834, conversion to Islam was a way of rejecting the state of slavery in which many Capetonians still lingered.[85] Even thereafter, there were many who continued to accept the adage that 'Slaamse Kerk is die zwart mans kerk' (the Islamic church is the black man's church), a point of view which did not prevent the decisions of a fair number of Europeans, particularly women, it would appear, to become Muslims.[86] The clothing, diet, religious observances, even the *Khalifa*, of the Muslims established the distinction between themselves and the rest of Cape society, without which conversion would have had less content, and would not have proceeded as fast as it did.

From early in the nineteenth century until late in the twentieth, there has been a tradition among white writers to stress the otherness and the exoticism of the Cape's Muslims. Throughout most of this period, the Muslims were known as Malays, thus emphasising their Eastern foreignness. A whole range of artists, from De Meillon on, liked to draw and paint the Muslims, emphasising the distinctiveness of their dress. The section of Cape Town where many of the Muslims lived, and where a number of the mosques were to be found, was known as the 'Malay Quarter', now Bo'kaap. This was not, in the vision of these whites, just another working-class district in the city, perhaps slightly more prosperous than some others. Rather it was mysterious, and its inhabitants had occult powers. It was an area with its own culture, its own folk-tales, its own music, even if much of what was sung there was in fact old Dutch songs. Thus, 'Malay' came to be one of the categories into which the South African population was legally divided by apartheid.[87]

---

[85] See the comment by LMS missionary William Elliott that: 'If the Cape proprietors of slaves were Mohammedans, the majority of slaves would immediately become Xtian.' Elliott to LMS, 12 June 1829, LMS-SA 11/3/C. Elliott was writing about the situation around Paarl, but the point holds, particularly as free Muslims took pride in converting and emancipating their slaves.

[86] Robert C.-H. Shell, 'Rites and Rebellion: Islamic Conversion at the Cape, 1808–1915', *SHCT*, 5, 1984, 1–45, and 'Between Christ and Mohammed: Conversion, Slavery, and Gender in the Urban Western Cape', in Elphick and Davenport, *Christianity in South Africa*, 272–4. It must be admitted that female converts shocked the white elite more than did male ones, and so are perhaps disproportionately mentioned in the records. On the other hand, European men might have been deterred from converting by the subordination to blacks which it would have entailed; a European woman, in contrast, would have expected to be subordinate to men, and might indeed have had more status as the wife of an imam, for instance, than she would have had among the Christians.

[87] Nineteenth-century examples include Duff Gordon, *Letters from the Cape* (none the less a valuable set of letters); John Mayson, *The Malays of Cape Town*, reprinted Cape Town, Africana Connoisseurs Press, 1963; Maximillien Kollisch, *The Mussulman Population at the Cape of Good Hope*, Constantinople, Levant Herald Office, 1867. The twentieth-century image of the 'Malays' has been dominated by the works of I. D. du Plessis, notably

Obviously, this was an exaggerated, orientalising, way of seeing, but it was not entirely inaccurate. At least some of the Cape's Muslims did dress somewhat differently from Christian Capetonians, even if by the end of the century this was only manifested, at least by the men, by their wearing a fez. The Muslims did not reject the dominant mores with the decisiveness of the drunkards. They strove for a respectability, both according to Muslim tenets and to those of the Colony as a whole. All the same, their otherness, marginal though it may have been, was in part a result of conscious decisions.

The Cape Malays, Cape Town, Maskew Miller, 1944 (reprinted as *The Cape Malays: History, Religion, Traditions, Folk Tales: The Malay Quarter*, Cape Town, Balkema, 1972), and I. D. du Plessis and C. A. Lückhoff, *The Malay Quarter and its People*, Cape Town, Race Relations Series of the Sub-Department of Coloured Affairs, Department of the Interior, 1963. See also Hilda Gerber, *Traditional Cookery of the Cape Malays*, Amsterdam and Cape Town, Balkema, 1957, significantly with a foreword by I. D. du Plessis. On Du Plessis, see especially, M. Shamil Jeppie, 'Historical Process and the Constitution of Subjects: I. D. du Plessis and the Reinvention of the "Malay"', BA Hons. thesis, UCT, 1987.

7   Acceptance and rejection

The celebration and disappointments of emancipation

On 1 December 1834, large numbers of men, women, boys and girls who until that day had been slaves 'promenaded the streets' of Cape Town, 'many of them attended by a band of amateur musicians'.[1] They had paraded before, to celebrate the New Year, a day on which they had been 'permitted to enjoy the day with their own friends; on which occasion they dress in all their best clothes', and perhaps followed bands round the streets.[2] On this day, though, matters were different – joyous, not drunken, but tinged with sadness for those who had not lived to see their freedom, and whose tears, at least according to later tradition, caused it to rain, unseasonably, on Emancipation Day.[3]

Some decades later, J. G. Steytler recalled the parades as follows:

I saw a number of processions of Coloured people with two or three sympathisers at their head, parading Cape Town, singing a Dutch song, in which every verse ended 'Victoria! Victoria! Daar waar de Engelschen vlag' [There the English flag is flying]. My mother asked a Coloured girl to go on an errand for her, she said 'No, I won't, we are free today!'[4]

In its details, this cannot be a fully accurate account. Queen Victoria was not on the throne in 1834, and even if Steytler was actually describing the ending of Apprenticeship, four years later, the Queen had not yet acquired the mythic status she would later have. Rather Steytler has undoubtedly conflated in his mind the original event with the annual celebrations of its anniversary.

[1] *SACA*, 6 Dec. 1834.
[2] Burchell, *Travels*, I, 27. There are a number of claims in the recent literature to musical parades by slaves in Cape Town to celebrate the New Year of 1823; these all refer back eventually to G. M. Manuel and B. Frank, *District Six*, Cape Town, Longman, 1967, 111, who unfortunately do not mention which 'chronicler of life at the Cape' gave this information. So far, the reference has not turned up. See also Bank, *Decline of Urban Slavery*, 127.
[3] John Edwin Mason, ' "Fit for Freedom": The Slaves, Slavery and Emancipation in the Cape Colony, South Africa, 1806 to 1842', Ph.D. thesis, Yale University, 1992, 527; Shell, *Children of Bondage*, 415.
[4] John George Steytler, 'Remembrances from 1832–1900', *QBSAL*, 25, 1971, 23.

146

Such parades may not have begun straight away. In 1838, when with the ending of Apprenticeship emancipation became real, the only demonstration in Cape Town was by a 'few individuals, who had masqueraded themselves as blacks, riding through the streets in a chaise, . . . and a small band of young boys, proceeding through the streets with a flag'.[5] Later, the celebration of 1 December by the former slaves developed, and was maintained until at least the 1880s. In 1856, it was described as follows:

The Negro boy sang a ballad and a large waggon drove up to the house of the washer-woman where all the young Malay girls, who used to wash and iron for her, congregated from all directions. They wore silk dresses with white waists and sleeves and they had put shining silver arrows in their dark hair. The waggon was open and braided with leaves and ribbons. In the back it flew a large red standard. The brother of beautiful Lini, with his skin like gilt bronze, mounted the coachman's seat. After the waggon had been loaded with a dozen girls, under much staring and chatter in the large crowd of people, he lashed out the large whip and off it went to the country. Even black Abdul and his master, together with their wives (you will recall that he is a Moslem), mounted a waggon and drove off to the country. When they had left I dressed and went out in the streets.

Everywhere there was movement in the same direction. The entire coloured population of The Cape appeared to stream to the country. Horsemen and pedestrians crossed each other, colossal waggons, drawn by four, six or eight horses and packed with scores of persons of all ages and complexions, rumbled along the streets. None missed a flying standard and the music of violins or clarinets was heard from many of them. Especially the lively beautiful Malays, with their Chinese hats and scarfs, were busy making music. Some of the Christian Negroes formed a highly peculiar group among the others. Perhaps in order to honour the English, their liberators, they wore high white starched stick-up collars, white scarves and waistcoats and cuffs in the same colour that all contrasted rather grotesquely with the black skin. All faces, however, of whatever colour and belonging to persons of whatever belief, shone from a deep inner joy and pure satisfaction, like the very shade of the luxuriant beam of the South, with which also the surrounding air, impregnated by the glow of the rising sun, began to suffuse every object, nearby or far away . . .

As the swarm moved away and the streets grew empty, the city began to acquire a dull appearance. Also I mounted a horse and left for the country riding along the feet of the Devil's Peak. At Rondebosch it was still too close to the city. Already in shady green Wynberg small parties could be seen below the trees. But on the road to Simon's Bay, around Rathfeller's and even further away, one could see, in the plains or around the scattered houses, innumerable crowds playing, laughing, making noise, drinking, singing and dancing, either out in the sun or in the shadow of their large waggons.[6]

[5] *De Zuid-Afrikaan*, 7 Dec. 1838, cited in Mason, ' "Fit for Freedom" ', 542.
[6] 'Den 1 December i Kap', *Wiborg: Tidning för Litteratur, handel och ekonomi*, 30 Jan. 1857; I am grateful to the National Library of Finland, Helsinki, for sending me a copy of this article, and to Thomas Lindblad for translating it from Swedish. Wiborg is now Wyborg, in Russian Karelia.

Figure 4 Procession on the anniversary of the Slaves Liberation, Cape Town. George Duff (*MuseuMAfricA, Johannesburg*)

By the late nineteenth century (if not earlier), New Year's Day was once again receiving the attention that it had had before emancipation.[7] Eventually, Emancipation Day would disappear from Cape Town's ritual calendar, until it was revived in the mid-1990s. Its spirit would survive, though, in the New Year's parades which came to be known as the Coon Carnival, South Africa's greatest Saturnalia.[8]

Such collective celebrations of emancipation were rare, if not entirely absent, outside Cape Town. At emancipation itself, or with the *de facto* ending of slavery with the expiry of the period of Apprenticeship four years later, some slaves went to church. There they heard sermons based on appropriate texts like: 'But now that you have been set free from sin and have become slaves of God, the return you get is sanctification and its end, eternal life',[9] preached by the Rev. Isaac Bisseux at Wellington in 1834, or, at Hankey in the Eastern Cape four years later, 'For it is God's will that by doing right you should put to silence the ignorance of foolish men. Live as free men, yet without using your freedom as a pretext for evil; but live as servants of God.'[10] In Grahamstown, just after midnight on 1 December 1838, they sang, with 'no ordinary fervour', the hymn 'Praise God from whom all blessings flow'.[11] Others again, or perhaps the same people, used the occasion of emancipation to get married. One woman who did so recalled at the end of her long life that the dominee of Durbanville, the Rev. J. J. Beck, was overrun by former slaves who wanted their unions sanctified. In his annual report to the Cape Synod at the time, however, Beck did not mention this, and only commented on the extent to which the freedmen and women were attracted to Islam.[12]

The years following emancipation in the Western Cape were marked by the attempts of the newly free to establish new relations of production upon and outside the farms and the ultimately more successful striving of their former owners to minimise the changes brought about by the new legal status of their labourers.[13] This was closely linked, as we have seen, to the

[7] Bickford-Smith, 'Meanings of Freedom', 297–8.

[8] Shamil Jeppie, 'Popular Culture and Carnival in Cape Town: The 1940s and 1950s', in Shamil Jeppie and Craig Souden (eds.), *The Struggle for District Six: Past and Present*, Cape Town, Buchu Books, 1990, 67–87.

[9] Bisseux to Directors, 23 Dec. 1834, *JME*, 10, 1835, 113–14. The text is Romans 6:22. See further Ross, 'Social and Political Theology', 97–8.

[10] Edward Williams to LMS, 20 Dec. 1838, LMS-SA 16/2/C, cited in Mason, '"Fit for Freedom"' 541. Following Mason, I have quoted the Revised Standard Version of this text (1 Peter 2:15–16); Williams was presumably preaching from a Dutch Bible.

[11] *Graham's Town Journal*, 6 Dec. 1838, cited in Mason, '"Fit for Freedom"', 540.

[12] Robert C.-H. Shell (ed.), 'Katie Jacobs: An Early Oral History', *QBSAL*, 46(3), 1992, 94–9; Godsdienstverslagen, NGK archives, now in the CA, R1/3.

[13] Mason, '"Fit for Freedom"', ch. 8; Nigel Worden, 'Between Slavery and Freedom: The Apprenticeship Period 1834–8'; Ross, '"Rather Mental than Physical"', both in Worden and Crais, *Breaking the Chains*, 146–69.

building of new forms of kinship and family among the free.[14] It was not accompanied, so far as I know, by the repeated collective celebration of emancipation. There were occasional individual demonstrations. Rosina van der Caab, who has already been met kissing her former owner in the streets of Caledon, used to read the Emancipation Act under his window every 1 December.[15] In general, though, the harshness of the rural Cape after 1838 limited such displays to the boldest of the former slaves.

Ordinance 50 and after

Apparently only in the Kat River was Ordinance 50 marked by an annual celebration.[16] Elsewhere, John Philip's progress into Bethelsdorp, and the great dinner which followed it, were isolated occurrences.[17] Khoikhoi defiance of the ruling class of the Eastern Cape was less ritual, and more verbal. In the period between 1830 and 1850, some of the mission Khoi began to express what was probably the first South African ideology of resistance to be formulated within the terms provided by their rulers. It has become known as 'Hottentot nationalism'.[18]

This movement was centred around the Kat River Settlement, if only because very many of the most articulate and energetic of the residents of the old missionary stations had moved to this valley, from which Maqoma's Xhosa had been expelled in 1829. The land had been set aside for Khoikhoi, to act as a buffer between the Colony proper and the Xhosa and to give some (small) chance for Ordinance 50 to be more than an empty statement of intentions.[19] In 1834, its inhabitants were still revelling in the freedom and comparative prosperity they enjoyed there. Nevertheless, they felt threatened by the proposals to introduce a Vagrancy Act, a measure which they believed would annul their freedom of movement and undo the advantages they had at least acquired from Ordinance 50. In the event their protests, channelled through the missionaries, were successful, and the Act was quashed by the Colonial Office in London, on the ground that it only applied to coloureds and was thus incompatible with Ordinance 50 – a view which was tacitly admitted even by its proponents, one of whom allowed that there were no white vagrants in the Colony.[20]

---

[14] Scully, *Liberating the Family?*, *passim*, and, 'Private and Public Worlds', 201–24; see above, chs. 6 and 7.   [15] Duff Gordon, *Letters from the Cape*, 112.

[16] Read to Philip, 7 May 1838, LMS-SA 16/1/C.   [17] See above, pp. 118–19.

[18] Trapido, 'The Emergence of Liberalism', 34–60.

[19] On the Kat River, see Marais, *Cape Coloured People*, 216–45; Kirk, 'Progress and Decline'; Visagie, 'Katriviernedersetting'; Crais, *White Supremacy and Black Resistance*, 79–86, 159–85.

[20] J. M. Bowker, cited in Crais, *White Supremacy and Black Resistance*, 140. Not everyone agreed with his comments. Hendrick Hendricksze, the wily secretary to the Griqua

In a great meeting, spread over two days in August 1834, many of the inhabitants of the Kat River Settlement protested against the draft Vagrancy Act which had been proposed by the Government, probably largely in anticipation of the emancipation of slaves later that year. The form of the meeting was according to British ideas of political action. Seven resolutions were proposed, debated and passed. The main thrust of the arguments was the expression of the fear that the implementation of the Act by prejudiced officials and white farmers would nullify the advantages they had gained since the passing of Ordinance 50 and would put a break on the economic advance they were currently enjoying. Many of the speakers described the *de facto* servitude from which they had emerged, and one was able to provide a hypothetical example to demonstrate how the new law would put his own business, cultivating barley for sale at Port Elizabeth, at risk. It was, Andries Hatha believed, the ragged state of his jacket which would convince the magistrate that he was a vagrant.[21] Similar arguments were also propounded in a number of mission stations,[22] and across the country men and women expressed their fear of the new Act by moving onto the missions in great numbers, in the expectation of safety there.[23]

These sorts of arguments and actions, expressing pragmatic, secular politics, were accompanied, at least in the Kat River, by claims that the speakers were representing the views of the 'Hottentot nation' to the Government. It was a phrase used by the chairman, Dirk Hatha, when he opened the meeting, and by several other speakers, including James Read Snr. It was, moreover, a Christian nationalism. Andries Botha was reported as saying that: 'He was at a loss to know the sins of the Hottentot nation that they should have deserved such oppression as they have suffered from the hands of others. He had never heard that the Hottentot nation possessed or had taken another people's land, or had oppressed them.'[24] It was also a nationalism expressed in Dutch. Only one man, Jan Uithaalder, father of the future rebel leader Willem, spoke in the Khoi language, although Andries Stoffels, and possibly others, included Khoi expressions in their speeches.

Given this, it is difficult to know precisely what to make of this claim to be

Government of Philippolis, once threatened to arrest the Boers who trekked north of the Orange River into Griqua country as vagrants.
[21] The transcript of these meetings, translated into English, is printed in *SACA*, 2 Sept., 6 Sept. and 10 Sept. 1834. More frequently it is cited from CA Acc 50.
[22] The petitions in question, including those in favour of a Vagrancy Act, are to be found in CA LCA 6.
[23] Macmillan, *Cape Colour Question*, 238–9; *PA*, XIII, 190.
[24] *SACA*, 6 Sept. 1834; Maqoma and those of his followers who had been driven out of the Kat River valley might have disagreed, and it was significant that Hendrik Joseph, an 'old man', recollected visiting the valley in his youth and finding only Gona Khoi there.

a nation. Presumably Dirk Hatha, Andries Botha and the others were using the Dutch word *natie*, but I do not know whether this was a translation of a Khoi concept, and if so what exactly that entailed.[25] Nevertheless, two matters are evident. The first is that the speakers were announcing the unity of all those of Khoisan descent.[26] Like most such claims, this was a programme, an appeal, not a statement of fact. Indeed, just as the meeting was denouncing the draft Vagrancy Act, another group within the Kat River Settlement was presenting a memorial to the Government applauding it.[27]

During the early years of the Kat River Settlement, it was riven by factional conflict. The two parties were known as the 'Bastards' and the 'Hottentots'. This distinction was not in the first instance a matter of descent. Several of those claiming to be part of the 'Hottentot nation' commented that their fathers had been whites, though they then noted that they had not been treated as full members of their fathers' families. One man commented to an admittedly hostile observer that: 'It is true my father was a slave, but I look upon myself as a Hottentot.'[28] In any case, by the mid-1830s 'pure-bred' Khoi were rare in the Eastern Cape. Rather the distinction was determined by a combination of wealth, place of origin – the 'Hottentots' generally came to the Kat River from the old LMS mission stations and often had family connections with the Gona Khoi who had once lived in the area, while the 'Bastards' had often grown up on the farms of the Eastern Cape – and political and ecclesiastical choice, with the Bastards favouring the DRC ministered to by William Ritchie Thomson, while the 'Hottentots' themselves called James Read to be their minister.[29]

In the event, the distinction did not last. By the late 1840s, the politics of the two groups were identical and there were men of 'Bastard' as well as 'Hottentot' families among the rebels in 1850.[30] Obviously, this was in part the consequence of shared experiences, but it had also to do with the refusal of the Khoi to accept leadership from their own. James Read Jnr wrote of the matter in 1851:

---

[25] This ignorance cannot be remedied. Although related languages are still spoken in Namibia and the Northern Cape, Cape Khoi has died out. Even if it had not, the precise weight given to a word that could be translated as 'nation' is not likely to have remained constant.

[26] One of the speakers, Mr Bergman, was a 'Bushman', though he did not himself talk of the 'Hottentot nation'.

[27] CA LCA 6/62, 20 Aug. 1834; this memorial, written in Dutch by someone who had learnt to write very legibly but had never learnt to spell, gloriously refers to the 'Wiet gevende Raad'.   [28] CA VC 888 (Moodie, *Afschriften*, vol. 25), 19.

[29] Visagie, 'Katriviernedersetting', 45–71; Donovan Williams, *When Races Meet: The Life and Times of William Ritchie Thomson . . . 1794–1891*, Johannesburg, AB Publishers, 1967, 113–21; Elbourne, ' "To Colonise the Mind" ', 300–1.

[30] Speech by Robert Godlonton in the Legislative Council, 10 Mar. 1852, BPP 1636 of 1852–3, 227–8; Jeroen Roozendaal, 'Tussen loyaliteit en verzet: Reakties van de "Kleurlingen"-bevolking in Oostkaapland op de koloniale overheersing, 1828–1853', MA thesis, Leiden University, 1994, 42–3.

It is known that Hottentots are prone to despise their own countrymen and will show more obedience to Europeans than to them. This arises from political and social causes. All ranks and different grades of society were crushed when the Hottentots lost their nationality, and, all feeling that they are on the same level, some of them are intractable to orders from any of themselves. In ordinary circumstances they are very civil to each other; and as among the Boers, the young call their male seniors uncles (ooms) and their female, aunts (tantas). But it is different in command; on the least provocation you will hear a Hottentot exclaim, – I won't allow another Hottentot to say anything to me, – I won't allow myself to be drilled or governed by another Hottentot.[31]

Distinctions on the basis of wealth came into existence, not merely in the Kat River but in all the mission communities, and indeed among the Griquas to the north of the Orange River. These distinctions were then reflected in matters such as dress, housing, or indeed the appearance of the matching span of oxen 'of immense height, of a glossy, brindled yellow colour, and striped like tigers', which the Griqua Captain, Andries Waterboer, drove into the Colony.[32] Together with personal piety, they also influenced access to ecclesiastical office. Not surprisingly, for a group of people emerging from a life of powerlessness, they could not be translated into secular authority within the Colony.

James Read's advice was that European officers should always command the levies raised in the Kat River Settlement, as only then would they obey orders. In the military context this was no doubt accurate, but not otherwise. This was the second message of the meetings of August 1834. From Dirk Hatha and Andries Stoffels through Sol Plaatje and the early ANC, Anton Lembede and the Youth League, Steve Biko and Black Consciousness to the revolts of the 1980s and the great transformation of the 1990s, black nationalisms in South Africa have always been an assertion of individual self-determination and a rejection of servility. This is after all one of the prime messages of the Protestant Christianity of which, at least in the beginning, it formed a part, and for the Khoi at least it went back to the singing of the psalms under the tutelage of Van der Kemp.

This individuality was affirmed over and against the settlers. In one notable incident in 1838, one of Andries Botha's sons, fortified by brandy, entered the house and store of Richard Painter, near the Kat River, without knocking, began to abuse his wife, sat down in one of the chairs and continued the argument, until Painter forced him out. Botha left, threatening to blow Painter's brains out and burn his house down. The latter threat was indeed put into action a decade and a half later.[33] It was also affirmed

---

[31] James Read, *The Kat River Settlement in 1851*, Cape Town, A. S. Robertson, 1852, 56.
[32] George Nicholson, *The Cape and its Colonists . . . with Hints to Prospective Emigrants*, London, Henry Colburn, 1848, 89–90.
[33] Crais, *White Supremacy and Black Resistance*, 148.

against the government officials. Captain James Alexander noted 'a disgusting instance of Independent disrespect to His Majesty's representative' and commented how 'the sulky Hottentot [school]master, standing in the midst of his scholars, neither lifted his cap from his head, nor took his hands from his pockets, when the governor approached and addressed him'.[34] Later, the colonial officials in the Settlement were satirically described as 'Touch your hat, Sir'.[35]

They had, it should be emphasised, good reason to be disdainful of officials, of settlers, even of missionaries, at least of some, perhaps most, individuals in each category. During the second quarter of the nineteenth century, Cape society became, for want of a better term, more racist, or racist in a different sort of way. Before the 1830s, slaves who had been manumitted or Khoi who accepted the colonial way of life might be absorbed into colonial society. This was particularly the case for women, though of course many were simply exploited sexually, with no prospect of incorporation for themselves or their half-caste children. However, there was a great difference between the piecemeal, if regular, taking up of manumitted individuals and the challenge presented by the great numbers after 1828 and 1838. It was not that ex-slaves and Khoisan were not prepared, or able, to adapt to the norms of colonial society. Many, if not all, were. Rather, evidence for such adaptation was no longer accepted, or nor longer considered sufficient.

These processes can be best exemplified with regard to the Kat River, both because they manifested themselves most clearly there and because the resolution of many conflicts, in the form of the 1852 constitutional arrangements, was in many ways driven by the events around the Kat River. Even the missionaries were becoming intolerant and prejudiced. Symptomatic of this was a quarrel which erupted in 1844, largely between the two James Reads, father and son, and the mass of other missionaries on the frontier. The immediate cause of the rumpus is not relevant here; what produced the real explosion was the fact that the elder Read wrote a letter on the matter to Arie van Rooyen, one of the Kat River settlers who was an old friend, a deacon of the church and later to be one of the first of the Khoi descendants to be ordained.[36] In this letter, Read criticised some of his white fellow missionaries, an act they saw as 'treason'. John Philip, summing up the affair, wrote as follows to the Directors of the LMS:

[34] J. E. Alexander, *Narrative of a Voyage of Observation among the Colonies of Western Africa, in the Flagship* Thalia *and of a Campaign in Kaffir-land*, 2 vols., London, Henry Colburn, 1837, II, 234, 239–40, cited in Williams, *When Races Meet*, 126.

[35] J. Green, *The Kat River Settlement in 1851*, Grahamstown, Godlonton & White, 1853, xvi, cited in Williams, *When Races Meet*, 165.

[36] J. J. Freeman, *A Tour in South Africa*, London, John Snow, 1851, 163ff.

What is esteemed and practised as a virtue by the one [class of missionaries] is viewed as a crime in the eyes of the other. You will find the key to the secret in Calderwood's letter . . . 'We object', says he, 'to the kind of intercourse which [Read] has with the *coloured* people' . . . Both parties would do the coloured people good but in different ways. In order to raise the people James Read would treat them as brethren and to this Mr Calderwood says, 'We object.'[37]

On an earlier occasion, Read, who had lived for forty years among the Khoikhoi, had married one and thought of himself as more a 'Hottentot' than an Englishman,[38] wrote that his fellow missionaries were concerned with 'the danger and difficulty of bring[ing] the [Khoikhoi] to a state of equality!!'. He joked that 'Tis a thousand pities that by conversion Hottentots and others do not get white skins and long hair. I think wigs would be a good substitute for the last, but for the first there is no remedy. I think the Hottentots should get a number of peruke-makers out immediately.' But this joke could not cover his bitterness, both at the abrogation of the principles by which he had lived his life and because he saw the comments as an attack on his eldest son, James.[39]

Such attitudes were widely to be found among, and were perhaps imbibed from, the settlers, much more among the British than the Dutch. While to some extent the settlers were expressing the ideas of their class and age on Africans, in part, the conflict was economic. The colonists coveted the rich, well-watered land of the Kat River valley, as did the Xhosa who had been driven off it. They also believed the Khoi to be inveterate thieves. Coming from a country where wild animals dangerous to stock had long been eliminated, they tended unwarrantably often to blame their losses of cattle and sheep on humans rather than on 'Jackals, wolves and tigers'.[40] They also wanted the labour of the Khoi, naturally enough on terms and at a price that they determined themselves. But, like so much else, this too could be wrapped up in the language of civilisation. While some missionaries believed that civilisation would come from economic independence, coupled of course to Christianity, T. H. Bowker could write:

---

[37] Philip to LMS, 31 Mar. 1846, LMS-SA 22/1/D, cited in Noël Mostert, *Frontiers: The Epic of South Africa's Creation and the Tragedy of the Xhosa People*, London, Jonathan Cape, 1993, 836 (original emphasis); on the affair see also Le Cordeur and Saunders, *Kitchingman Papers*, 249–51; F. G. Kayser, *Journal and Letters*, edited by H. C. Hummel, Cape Town, Maskew Miller Longman for Rhodes University, Grahamstown, 1990, xx–xxiv, 164–76. The Rev. Henry Calderwood was a gifted but increasingly disillusioned LMS missionary who was soon to resign to become a magistrate among the Xhosa.

[38] Read to Kitchingman, 13 May 1844, in Le Cordeur and Saunders, *Kitchingman Papers*, 248.

[39] Read to Kitchingman, 2 Dec. 1840, in Le Cordeur and Saunders, *Kitchingman Papers*, 218.

[40] Theopolis petition against the Vagrancy Act, cited in Macmillan, *Cape Colour Question*, 239. In nineteenth-century South Africa, hyenas were known as wolves, and leopards as tigers.

If the native or Hottentot is to be civilized, he must be made as much like the white man as possible, who has already attained that civilization, and this can only be done by mixing him with those whom it is desirable he should imitate. Like the white man, he must become a good servant before he can raise himself to be a master.[41]

The Khoi knew what was being said about them, and objected to it, even if at least the men would not have taken umbrage at the supremely gendered vision of civilisation which Bowker expounded. In 1851, during what became known as the Kat River rebellion,[42] Nicholas Smit, LMS missionary in Grahamstown, defended himself and his fellows against the charge of inciting their charges to disaffection. He commented:

Many of the Hottentots attend the *public meetings of the English* at which they hear *enough* to satisfy their minds about the *real* state of feeling towards the coloured races. Many of them also *read the frontier papers* which with scarcely an exception, exhibit the very worst of feelings towards them and still more do they *hear* and *experience* in their daily intercourse with not a few of the whites.[43]

Indeed, the desertion to the rebels of large numbers of Khoi soldiers occurred after they had read an article in *De Zuid-Afrikaan* calling for the 'ultimate extinction of the worthless creatures', and copies of the paper were found in their camp.[44] Moreover, there was speculation that the Cape Colony would receive its own Representative Assembly and then

Many of the farmers and other white inhabitants, it is notorious, injudiciously and most improperly began to exult in the prospect of making their own laws, and boasted that they would establish vagrant laws, and bring the coloured classes into the required subjection. It is well known that these threatenings operated injuriously upon the minds of the coloured people, especially on the frontier. They were taunted with the new prospects opening for their masters, and were plainly told that they would be brought to their proper level when the Colonial Parliament was established.[45]

The Khoi did indeed not need to read the *Graham's Town Journal* to know what Bowker thought of them. In the late 1840s, he was a member of the conservative clique which had gained temporary control over the Colony. It was led by John Montagu, the Cape Colonial Secretary, who was notori-

---

[41] *Graham's Town Journal*, 18 Dec. 1847, cited in Crais, *White Supremacy and Black Resistance*, 140.

[42] This is one of those terms, of which history is full, which is entrenched in usage, despite being inaccurate. On the one hand, a minority of the inhabitants of the Kat River Settlement revolted; on the other, the rebels also included people from the mission stations of Theopolis and Shiloh, soldiers from the Cape Corps and many farm labourers.

[43] Smit to Freeman, 6 Aug. 1851, LMS-SA 26/2/A, cited in Williams, *When Races Meet*, 157–8 (emphasis in original).

[44] Memorandum by John Montagu, 2 Feb. 1852, BPP 1636 of 1852–3, 106.

[45] Memorandum by John Montagu, 2 Feb. 1852, BPP 1636 of 1852–3, 105.

ous for having commented, on looking down on a Tyume valley in Xhosaland, close to the Kat River, that: 'It's a pity that such black Devils should have such a fine country.'[46] Montagu arranged that first T. J. Biddulph and then J. H. Bowker should be appointed Justice of the Peace for the Kat River Settlement. Their actions while holding this office seem to have been calculated, probably unconsciously, to provoke a rebellion, which duly broke out, centred on the Kat River and the mission stations of Theopolis and Shiloh. In such of their statements of intent as have survived, many of the rebels saw their fight as against the English settlers, not the British Government, and specifically referred to the threatened reintroduction of the Vagrancy Act.[47]

This is of course not in any way a full account of the causation of the rebellion. Such an account would have to include the repeated devastation of the Settlement in the frontier wars, notably in the War of the Axe of 1846–7, the links between those Xhosa who had come into the valley, notably Hermanus Matroos, whose Xhosa name was Ngxukumeshe, with Maqoma and other Xhosa and the conditions on the farms where a majority of the rebels lived. It would also have to take account of the impulses of a Christian theology of liberation and explain why a considerable majority of the Kat River Khoi did not join the rebellion.[48] Nevertheless, there was one poignant moment in the early days of the rebellion, which illustrates the failure of some missionaries' attempts to win civil rights through the civilisation of their converts. On 22 January 1851, the Rev. W. R. Thomson went to the rebel camp in an attempt to persuade the Khoi to return to their old loyalties. The rebel leader, William Uithaalder, said to him:

Sir, you and Mr Read were both young when you came among us, and you are now both old, . . . and yet these oppressions won't cease. The missionaries have for years written, and their writings won't help. We are now going to stand up for our own affairs. We shall show the settlers that we too are men. We are not against the queen.[49]

---

[46] Stretch to Freeman, 11 June 1851, LMS-SA 26/1/D, cited in Williams, *When Races Meet*, 193.

[47] E.g. Memorandum by Montagu, 2 Feb. 1852, BPP 1636 of 1852–3, 105; see Uithaalder to Kok, 11 June 1851, enclosed in Warden to Garrock, 31 Aug. 1851, Free State Archives, HC 1/1/3, also printed in *Further Correspondence relative to the State of the Kaffir Tribes*, BPP 1428 of 1852, 152; Uithaalder *et al.*, to Cathcart, 17 Jan. 1855, in *Translation of a communication received by the Governor from certain rebel Hottentots now without the Colony, addressed jointly to the Governor and to the Parliament*, CPP, C6, 1855; Mostert, *Frontiers*, 1151–2; statement of Windvogel, 28 July 1851, cited in Crais, *White Supremacy and Black Resistance*, 185.

[48] For modern accounts, see Marais, *Cape Coloured People*, 230–45; Crais, *White Supremacy and Black Resistance*, 164–88; Roozendaal, 'Tussen loyaliteit en verzet', *passim*.

[49] Read, *Kat River Settlement*, 47.

Acceptance and rejection

The steady racialisation of the Cape's social classification did not merely entail arguments for the rejection of the mass of 'coloureds'. It also necessarily required that the anomaly of Europeans who were not behaving according to the norms of respectable society be addressed. Before 1850, there were three main areas of concern in this matter, at least outside of the slums of Cape Town and the scandals caused by those whites who converted to Islam.

The first related to those whose poverty was a cause of disgrace. At least until the mid-century, there were few if any destitute native-born whites. One well-travelled missionary commented in 1836 that he had only ever met one or two beggars in the Colony, and they were Irishmen.[50] There were of course many who were poor and propertyless, but they seem to have been able to find sustenance as *bywoners*, or through an extended kinship network. Equally, although bankruptcy was an increasingly common occurrence, and undoubtedly led to great hardship, it did not force those who so suffered to beg their bread in the streets of the country towns. The networks of social security were still effective enough.[51]

There was one group for whom the Cape was seen as an escape from destitution, namely the children, both boys and girls, who were sent to the Colony through assisted schemes of emigration from the London slums. Arriving in Cape Town in the early 1830s, these children were first housed in what was described in a British Parliamentary Paper as a 'clean, capacious and well-ventilated building, situated in the centre of the government gardens', which was almost certainly the old government slave lodge. If so, this is a most interesting euphemism.[52] As might be imagined of people whose early life had been spent in poverty in London, they were generally physically puny in comparison to the mass of white Cape colonists.[53] Nevertheless, they were in considerable demand as additions to the labour

---

[50] Evidence of the Rev. H. P. Hallbeck before the Select Committee on Aborigines, 20 Apr. 1836, BPP 538 of 1836, 344.

[51] P. H. Philip, 'The Vicissitudes of the Early British Settlers at the Cape', *QBSAL*, 40, 1986, 169–70; Dooling, 'Agrarian Transformations', stresses the frequency of bankruptcy among Cape farmers in the mid-nineteenth century.

[52] *Report from the Governor of the Cape of Good Hope to the Secretary of State for the Colonies, relative to the condition of the children sent out by the Children's Friend Society*, BPP 323 of 1840, 9, cited in Edna Bradlow, 'The Children's Friend Society at the Cape of Good Hope', *Victorian Studies*, 27(2), 1984, 161. See also M. M. Brown, 'Die Children's Friend Society in Engeland en die Kaap die Goede Hoop, 1830–1841', *AYB*, 57, 1994.

[53] See BPP 323 of 1840, 12–18; for a comment on the small stature of the London poor, see Roderick Floud, Kenneth Wachter and Annabel Gregory, *Health, Height and History: Nutritional Status in the United Kingdom, 1750–1980*, Cambridge, Cambridge University Press, 1990, 163–75.

force of the Western Cape's farms. What happened to them thereafter depended on their luck with the master to whom they were assigned. Some were treated as part of the white family; others effectively became part of the bonded labour force, lost such literacy as they may have possessed and blended into what was becoming the Colony's coloured population. They could not even benefit from the effective abolition of slavery in 1838, as their apprenticeships did not end when those which had been imposed on the ex-slaves did.

For all this, a few of them had managed to maintain sufficient political skills and resources to cause their treatment to be at least a minor scandal, though probably more in England than in South Africa. That London paupers had to work as agricultural labourers, and not receive training in any craft (though some did), was not such a problem. What caused much greater disquiet was that they did not receive the religious instruction which their evangelical sponsors had required, that their apprenticeships were liable to be sold on to the highest bidder and that in general they were 'falling in to the immoral habits and customs of the [now free] coloured population, with whom in common they labour daily throughout their apprenticeship'.[54] This was stretching the confusion of categories too far.

A second group of emigrants were the Dutch orphans and other poor children who arrived in the Cape in the late 1850s. Initially they were seen as strengthening the Dutch element within the Colony, and were welcomed in the streets of Cape Town as 'sturdy little genuine Hollanders walking about and enjoying themselves, not a few with cigars in their mouths puffing clouds like young burgomeesters'. The girls were dressed 'in the quaintest old-fashioned caps and kirtles'.[55] In the event, many of the youngsters deserted or stole from their bosses, and the girls, unobservant of colonial mores, went about with blacks or behaved as prostitutes. On the other hand, their masters often treated them as did they their other labourers, to the dismay of their Dutch sponsors and parents. The combination meant that the experiment was quickly ended.[56]

Secondly, there were the soldiers. Respectable Cape society had an ambivalent attitude towards the British army. It was recognised that the

[54] Napier to Russell, 24 Feb. 1840, BPP 323 of 1840, enclosure no. 5, cited in Bradlow, 'Children's Friend Society', 166.

[55] Cited in A. F. Hattersley, *The Convict Crisis and the Growth of Unity: Resistance to Transportation in South Africa and Australia*, Pietermaritzburg, University of Natal Press, 1965, 27.

[56] Ivo Sicking, *In het belang van het kind: Nederlandse kinderemigratie naar zuid-Afrikaq in de jaren 1856–1860*, Utrecht, Utrechtse Historische Cahiers, 16(1), 1995, 45–63; H. Reenders, ' "De jeugdige emigranten naar de Kaap": Een vergeten hoofdstuk uit de geschiedenis van het Nederlandse protestantse Réveil (1856–1860)', *Documentatieblad voor de Geschiedenis van het Nederlandse Zending en Overseese kerken*, 2, 1995, 27–61.

army saved the Colony occasionally from suffering even worse losses at the hands of the Xhosa, and continually from bankruptcy. Army salaries redressed the chronic deficit in the Colony's balance of trade, and army contracts provided a favoured few, particularly in Grahamstown, with the basis of their private fortunes. Equally, the high army officers were often of a status within Britain to which few if any colonists could aspire. Thus the 1820 settlers of Grahamstown could invite Colonel Henry Somerset to their dinners, and hold their fetes in his park, even though they gossiped that he went on campaign with a retinue of Khoi mistresses, and had several of his bastards recruited into the Cape Mounted Rifles, the regiment he commanded.[57] Somerset's high birth might allow him to get away with such conduct, or at least to be so blatant about it.

The other side of the attitude towards the soldiers was a rejection of their disreputable way of life, for all that the respectable were prepared to take their money. The old, unreformed British army of the 1830s and 1840s was as drunken and brutal as ever. Its officers might find some of the Cape colonists willing to join them as they hunted the jackal to hounds or organised horse races.[58] Indeed, horse-racing and the gambling associated with it formed a bridge between the low culture of the elite and that of the (ex-) slaves and Khoi. The respectable, both white and coloured, could be scandalised. The army realised the disdain in which they were held, and on occasion hit back in kind. On one occasion the Wesleyan Methodist chapel in the garrison town of Fort Beaufort, which James Read called 'the most dissipated place, perhaps, in the whole colony', was daubed with the graffito: 'Wines and Spirits Sold here during the Races'.[59] The common soldiers certainly felt that they were being ostracised. The memoirs of one of them noted that a certain Englishman was 'of the true Colonial stamp – hated the very name of a soldier'.[60] The hatred may have come from fear, or from an uncertainty about the place which a private in the British army, one moreover who may have been travelling with his Khoi concubine, should have in society.[61] But the regiments of the British army were too temporarily in South Africa, though one of course replaced the other, and the soldiers too well isolated in their barracks, for their disreputable actions to be too great a threat to the fabric of society. And of course, when they fought, they would be lauded as heroes, whatever they did.

The third set of taxonomic anomalies who had to be kept out of the

[57] Mostert, *Frontiers*, 1059, 1131,
[58] Hattersley, *Social History*, 114–16; Viney and Brooke Simons, *The Cape of Good Hope*, 191–4.
[59] John Philip, *Letter to the Directors of the London Missionary Society on the Present State of their Institutions in the Colony of the Cape of Good Hope*, Cape Town, G. J. Pike, 1848, xx; Gordon-Brown, *Narrative*, 275.   [60] Gordon-Brown, *Narrative*, 105.
[61] On Adams's Khoi Kaatje, see Gordon-Brown, *Narrative*, 249–51.

Colony were white convicts. The Children's Friend Society was careful to announce that those paupers it shipped to the Colony did not have criminal records.[62] At the end of the 1840s, however, the British Colonial Secretary, over the strong protests from the Cape Government, announced that the Cape was henceforth to be considered as a convict colony, and despatched a ship to Cape Town containing 282 ticket-of-leave prisoners, that is to say men who had served the bulk of their sentences and were now to be allowed to work in the Colony under minimal supervision. This action brought forth such a widespread campaign of protest, with the boycotting of all those who worked for, or supplied, the Government, that eventually the ship had to be sent on to Australia with the convicts still on board. The agitation, which included mass meetings on the Parade in Cape Town of over 5,000 people, marked the beginning of a new phase in Cape colonial politics.

The Cape colonists[63] were virtually unanimous in their rejection of the convicts; those who opposed the agitation did so more to maintain themselves in favour with the Government or because they disapproved of the tactics, and ulterior motives, of the protestors, than because they approved its actions.[64] In their own terms, they were justified. The Anti-Convict agitation was transformed into a weapon by which the colonists could appropriate powers previously held by the Governor and his officials, and ultimately by the Colonial Office in London. This, though, was only part of the matter. The rejection of the convicts was more or less universal, and visceral. It was driven by emotions, not in the first place by political calculation. This can be seen from the numerous petitions to Queen Victoria praying that she rescind the decision her ministers had made, and perhaps most clearly in two such from the ladies of Stellenbosch and Hottentots Holland.[65] The former, eighty strong, 'laying aside that modest reserve which they feel to be so becoming in their sex, most humbly implore your Majesty to protect this distant colony, preserve it from this dire pollution, and restore us to our former happy and contented condition'.[66] The latter, from 'Wives, Mothers, Daughters, and Sisters, of your Majesty's most loyal subjects', contained a great rhetorical flourish:

It is not because the conversion of this Colony into a Penal Settlement will endanger the lives and property of your Majesty's subjects, that we are compelled to approach your Majesty as suppliants; – they with whom we freely parted when their

---

[62] Bradlow, 'Children's Friend Society', 141.

[63] Including indeed the Kat River settlers, who presented a petition against the landing of the convicts. See *SACA*, 16 June 1849.

[64] Le Cordeur, *The Politics of Eastern Cape Separatism*, 216.

[65] Hottentots Holland is the region of the Western Cape now containing the towns of Somerset West and the Strand.   [66] *SACA*, 12 May 1849.

country's danger called them to face the savage foe, and shed their blood in its defence, will not leave us to the mercy of those lawless ruffians who will be turned loose upon a scattered and unprotected population. It is not because we apprehend that we shall be reduced to poverty and distress; – they whose labours, by the blessing of a gracious Providence, have hitherto procured for us bread enough and to spare, will still toil for us, and Heaven will smile upon their honest toil. There is an evil more to be deprecated than poverty and want – the loss of character; there is an injury far greater than any which the midnight thief, or assassin, can inflict – the destruction of virtuous principle. These are precisely the two evils which the experience of other unfortunate colonies authorizes us to fear will result from the operation of that measure, for the rescinding of which we earnestly supplicate your Majesty.

The dark cloud which hangs over our land, and whose very shadow fills every breast with dismay, assumes to us a peculiarly frightful aspect. To . . . our beloved Husbands, Fathers, Brothers, Sons, . . . it is fraught with injury, dishonor, and disgrace; – but to us, its black bosom is charged with ruin, pollution, and misery.[67]

The Colony, then, would be tainted by the coming of the convicts. All South Africans might be suspected of having been transported to the Cape, and their honour threatened by the presence of such miscreants. But there was, of course, more to the matter. Several of the petitions alluded to the danger of introducing European convicts into a Colony with a large ex-slave population and with unsubdued Africans just across the border.[68] They might teach the unsophisticated, but inherently criminal, inhabitants of the Colony new tricks. They might also make more difficult the establishment and maintenance of a new racial order, as those who had become free only a decade or so earlier would come to associate Europeans with criminals.

The panic of 1851

The virtual unanimity and the overreacting vigour of the Anti-Convict agitation suggest that in the years after abolition the whites in the Cape Colony were under some sort of collective strain. The ladies of Stellenbosch and Hottentots Holland may have accepted the ideas of female subservience entailed within the current ideology of gentility, or at the very least have been prepared to make use of them in petitioning Queen Victoria, as a fellow woman. However, they, and their male fellows, were not at ease with the way in which social relations in the colony were developing. The result was a major panic in the early summer of 1851 among the farmers of the Western Cape, particularly in the wheat-growing districts of the Swartland and along the southern coastal plains. They convinced them-

---

[67] *SACA*, 15 Sept. 1849.
[68] The petitions are most easily collected in *Despatches relative to the Reception of Convicts at the Cape of Good Hope*, BPP 1138 of 1850.

selves that their farm labourers had plotted to rise up and murder them, initially on 1 December, the anniversary of emancipation, though later rumours suggested that the date of the massacre would be on Christmas Day, as they came out of church, or on New Year's Eve. As a result they stockpiled ammunition. In Durbanville they crammed the women and children into a house and twenty-five armed men patrolled all night. Near Malmesbury, over 100 assembled at the farm of the veldcornet. The men went about their work by day, and gathered in a guarded rendezvous at night. In Clanwilliam district, many of the coloured labourers were dismissed in the middle of the harvest, and Europeans employed at higher wages, solely for the purpose of keeping guard. Many families took to sleeping in the bush, at a different place each night. In reaction to the alarm, and fearing that they would be lynched, the coloured people went about with scythe blades fixed to straight sticks for their defence. In the event, as a number of government enquiries held in October and November had predicted, nothing happened.[69]

The immediate triggers of the panic were twofold. In the first place, the Europeans believed that the Western Cape labourers had been snared into rebellion by the Kat River rebels. During the course of 1851, a number of levies, particularly from the missions, had been sent to the east, to fight against the Xhosa and the rebels. There is some evidence that the rebels had attempted to persuade the levies to desert to their cause, not entirely a hopeless cause as a number of the regular soldiers of the Cape Mounted Rifles had indeed done so. These overtures were refused.[70] However, the presence of Xhosa and Khoi prisoners of war in the Western Cape, held in a labour camp and engaged in building the road over Bain's Kloof, was thought to increase the temptation for an uprising.

The second such trigger was the presentation of an Ordinance 'to prevent the practice of settling or squatting upon Government lands' to the Colony's Legislative Council. While by the time virtually all the easily accessible and well-watered land in the Colony was in private hands, small communities of, largely, Khoi descent were still to be found in the kloofs of

---

[69] On this, see Edna Bradlow, 'The "Great Fear" at the Cape of Good Hope, 1851–2', *International Journal of African Historical Studies*, 23, 1989, 401–2; John Marincowitz, 'From "Colour Question" to "Agrarian Problem" at the Cape: Reflections on the Interim', in Hugh Macmillan and Shula Marks (eds.), *Africa and Empire: W. M. Macmillan, Historian and Social Critic*, London, Temple Smith for the Institute of Commonwealth Studies, 1989, 155–60. Marincowitz argues that there was a genuine plot; like me, Bradlow considers it to have been a groundless panic. The evidence on which they, and I, base their accounts is to be found in *Proceedings of Evidence given before the Committee of the Legislative Council respecting the Ordinance to Prevent the Practice of Squatting on Government Lands* (henceforth *Proceedings*), published by order of the Legislative Council, Cape Town, Saul Solomon, 1852, also in BPP 1636 of 1852–3, 8–95, particularly Smith to Grey, 12 Feb. 1852.   [70] Evidence of the Rev. G. W. Stegmann, *Proceedings*, 6.

the Western Cape mountains. More generally, there was still considerable open land in the Bokkevelds and the Roggeveld to the north, and in parts of the Eastern Cape, particularly to the south-west of Graaff-Reinet, parts of which were occupied by people without licence from the Government.[71] At the same time, those mission residents who had been able to accumulate cattle, largely by working as temporary agricultural labourers, grazed them in the mountains around the stations.[72] The communities living in these places were anathema to the settled farmers. In the words of the draft Ordinance, they were considered to be 'idle and ill-disposed persons, refusing to labour for their livelihood', and they were also generally considered to be thieves.[73] As had been the case with the Vagrancy Bills, this measure caused considerable alarm amongst the ex-slaves and Khoi. The farmers misinterpreted their concern as plotting mass murder, a fear which was accentuated when gangs of harvesters marched through Paarl on their way to the wheat fields of the Swartland, as no doubt they did every year in October and November.[74] On one farm in the Koeberg, for instance, the harvesters came from Genadendal, Groenkloof (Mamre), Stellenbosch, Paarl, Drakenstein, Somerset West and the Eerste Rivier.[75] At the same time, the very fact that the harvest had to be got in meant that the number of 'the black classes' on each farm in the Swartland would be much larger than usual.

So far as can be gathered, the instigator of the rumours was Adriaan Johannes Louw, a farmer in the Koeberg to the south of the Swartland. It was a region, and Louw came from a family, where uprisings were part of tradition. South Africa's closest approximation to a slave revolt, the march on Cape Town in 1809 led by Louis, a Mauritian, had begun on the farm of Petrus Gerhardus Louw, who was probably A. J. Louw's second cousin, and possibly his wife's uncle.[76] The march had then passed on through the Koeberg before being dispersed on the outskirts of Cape Town.[77] It was something that A. J. Louw may well have witnessed himself as a young man, and certainly remembered. He recalled it in a letter of warning which he

---

[71] *Proceedings*, 17–18 (evidence of H. D. Jenchen), 30 (J. C. Chase, Civil Commissioner of Uitenhage, to Secretary to Government, 29 Oct. 1851), 37–8 (G. W. Stegmann to the Rev. W. Thompson, 31 Oct. 1851), 40–1 (Charles Piers, Resident Magistrate of Tulbagh to Secretary to Government, 10 Nov. 1851); Saul Dubow, *Land, Labour and Merchant Capital in the Pre-Industrial Rural Economy of the Cape: The Experience of the Graaff-Reinet District (1852–72)*, Cape Town, Centre for African Studies, 1982, 63–84.

[72] M. McIntyre to W. Hawkins, 17 Nov. 1851, *Proceedings*, 42.

[73] *Proceedings*, 29; see also Piers to Secretary to Government, 11 Apr. 1849, in *ibid.*, 38.

[74] Evidence of the Rev. G. W. Stegmann, *Proceedings*, 7.

[75] Evidence of A. J. Louw, 24 Nov. 1851, *Proceedings*, 63.

[76] The genealogy of the Louw family in De Villiers, *Geslagsregisters*, contains at least one inconsistency, which makes the tracing of relationships an uncertain matter.

[77] Ross, *Cape of Torments*, 97–105.

sent round to his fellow farmers on 24 October 1851.[78] This letter, from a
man who as a former veldcornet was well respected in his neighbourhood,
sparked off the panic. Then, it spread with speed over some hundreds of
kilometres, though it seems not to have affected the wine-producing heart-
land of Stellenbosch, probably because in the early summer the travelling
labourers were not on the wine farms. Some indication of the way the
rumour could be confirmed can be gathered from the interrogation of
Hendrik February, a groom of slave descent (as his name would suggest)
living on the farm of Dirk Hanekom near Malmesbury. Hanekom ques-
tioned him on the projected uprising, and February replied: 'What could
the people[79] do, if they were inclined to act as King Louis did some years
ago, without a proper captain or leader?' He probably only meant this as a
prudent acquiescence in his *baas*'s views, and would later specifically deny
knowing anything about the uprising, but the jumpy Hanekom took it as
confirmation of his fears.[80]

Politics Deep and Politics High

The celebrations of emancipation, the Kat River rebellion, the Convict
Crisis, the panic of 1851, indeed virtually everything discussed in this book,
could be described as the expression of what John Lonsdale has called 'deep
politics', that is to say the politics of kinship and family, of gender, of the
relations between master and servant, of identity, of respect and so forth.[81]
In this sense, they are the politics inherent in the slogan that 'the personal
is political', though with a wider understanding of the personal than is
generally implied by that sentence. They can thus be set against high politics – the politics of formal institutions, parliaments, governments, the state
in general. Obviously, the two spheres are never completely separate from
each other, but there are moments at which their interaction is more evident
and more crucial than at others. In the history of the pre-industrial Cape,
the most salient such moment was the political crisis of the early 1850s.
Indeed, the distinction had become so blurred that the Governor, Sir Harry
Smith, blamed the panic on the machinations of those who were opposed
to the Legislative Council as then constituted. He believed that the opposition fomented the panic in order to prevent it from passing any legislation.[82]

[78] *Proceedings*, 31.
[79] Presumably *het volk*, words used in the Cape for the farm labourers.
[80] Interrogation of Dirk Andries Hanekom by the Commission of Inquiry, 28 Nov. 1851, and
of Hendrik February, 29 Nov. 1851, *Proceedings*, 69.
[81] John Lonsdale, 'The Moral Economy of Mau Mau: Wealth, Poverty and Civic Virtue in
Kikuyu Political Thought', in Bruce Berman and John Lonsdale, *Unhappy Valley: Conflict
in Kenya and Africa*, 2 vols., London, James Currey, 1992, 317.
[82] Smith to Grey, 12 Feb. 1852, BPP 1636 of 1852–3, 9.

He was mistaken in this analysis, but nevertheless the effect was the same and the Squatters Bill was abandoned in mid-passage.

The crisis derived from a widespread feeling among those just below the colonial elite – farmers, merchants, professional people and so forth – that they should be represented more directly in the government of the Colony. In 1834, the Legislative Council had been instituted with four official members and five to seven appointed by the Governor from among 'Chief Landed Proprietors and Principal Merchants' of the Colony.[83] Almost from that very moment, groups among the colonists began to agitate for a legislative assembly chosen through elections. Initially, the movement was a transparent attempt to maintain the control of the old slave-holding order in an international environment in which they saw slavery as a dying institution. In 1832, a well-attended meeting in Cape Town proposed the (very) gradual emancipation of slaves in exchange for the granting of a representative assembly. The conservatism inherent in such movements was too apparent. For instance, John Fairbairn, the liberal editor of the *SACA*, decided temporarily to oppose the gradual democratisation of the Cape's system of government on terms which, he rightly assumed, would have ensconced his opponents in power.[84]

By the late 1840s, the pressure for a representative assembly had grown considerably. As has been shown, those who might have stressed Dutch ethnicity had made a tacit, and tactical, decision not to do so, thereby removing one of the hindrances to the Cape Parliament which they confidently expected to dominate. Equally, it was increasingly felt that the fiscal conservatism of officialdom was preventing the investment necessary for colonial economic development.[85] It was this, coupled to his own parlous financial state, which induced John Fairbairn, for instance, to support the demands for a parliament. This change of heart was confirmed, for him and for many others, by the authoritarian actions of the Secretary to the Government, John Montagu, and especially by the actions of the officials, from the Governor down, during the Convict Crisis. Evidently, the Government was no longer acting in the best interests of the Colony as a whole, and needed to be controlled by a representative assembly.[86] Nevertheless, the objections to such a body which had been voiced by the British Colonial Secretary, Lord Stanley, in response to a petition from the Cape Town municipality in 1841, still had to be removed. In addition to certain matters of a technical nature, he saw the main difficulties as deriving from the composition of colonial society, 'the elements of which . . . are

[83] Government Proclamation, 24 Jan. 1834, in *Cape of Good Hope Government Gazette*.
[84] *De Zuid-Afrikaan*, 20 May 1832; Botha on Fairbairn.
[85] Kirk, 'Self-Government and Self-Defence'; Warren, 'Merchants, Commissioners and Wardmasters', 61–108.   [86] Botha, *John Fairbairn*, esp. chs., 7 and 8.

heterogen[e]ous, dissimilar and separated from each other by distinctions almost indelible'. He referred to the English, the Dutch, the 'free Aborigines', the 'Fingoes' and others who had recently entered the Colony, and the emancipated slaves. If a parliament was instituted,

> by what method is it proposed to secure for each of these component elements of society its due weight and influence in that body and no more? . . . I cannot regard as a matter of secondary concern the adjustment and balance of that authority in such a manner as may prevent its being perverted into a means of gratifying the antipathies of a dominant caste, or of promoting their own interests or prejudices at the expense of those of other and less powerful classes. Will the wealthy, the intelligent, and enterprising minority [the English] be content to find themselves overborne by a majority inferior to themselves in all respects except that of numerical strength? Or if their greater zeal and activity, and their greater proximity to the seat of government, should have the effect of giving to an English minority a preponderance in the Legislature over the numerical majority of the population, will there not be serious risk of extensive popular discontent? Will not questions continually arise, between them and the other classes in the colony, of rival interests and conflicting prejudices, the solution of which in a sense favourable to the English minority, will constantly aggravate the jealousies and embitter the alienation arising out of difference of race?[87]

The way out of the dilemmas expressed by Stanley was found through the setting of the franchise at a low level. All adult males who had occupied fixed property worth £25 for at least a year would be eligible to vote.[88] This was a figure which was proposed almost at the beginning of the protracted discussions on a new Cape constitution, and was maintained until the end.[89] Nevertheless, the matter was a question of continued debate in which the various tensions within the Colony became peculiarly apparent. It is valuable to discuss them in detail.

First, there was the question whether a franchise granted only to occupiers of property should be countenanced. The alternative – effectively universal manhood suffrage – was denounced by the Attorney-General, William Porter, as threatening the Colony with 'communism, socialism and red republicanism which had caused so much mischief in France' in the Revolution of 1848.[90] This was sufficient to quash any such aspirations, if they seriously existed among those engaged in making the decision.

Secondly, there was the general fear that any parliament, on whatever basis it might be elected, would entrench power in the Colony in the hands

---

[87] Stanley to Napier, 15 Apr. 1842, BPP 1137 of 1850, 91; Stanley, then Colonial Secretary, would later accede to the Earldom of Derby.

[88] The provision that individuals had to have been resident for a year was seen as providing 'the great moral and social advantage of encouraging a fixity of domicile'. Darling to Pakington, 25 Apr. 1852, BPP 1656 of 1852–3, 179.

[89] In general on this, see Trapido, 'Origins of the Cape Franchise Qualifications'.

[90] Speech in Legislative Council, 13 Feb. 1850, BPP 1362 of 1851, 41.

of the oppressors of the Khoikhoi and ex-slaves. This, as has been shown, was the motive ascribed by the Colonial Secretary, John Montagu, for the rebellion of the Eastern Cape Khoi.[91] He may have been somewhat self-serving in this. At the time he made the statement, he was struggling to postpone the introduction of a representative assembly, and thus prolong his own dominance over colonial affairs.[92] Nevertheless, such feelings were demonstrably held both by the rebels and by a considerable number of mission-station residents (and no doubt others) who remained loyal. For instance, the missionaries of Genadendal believed themselves to be expressing the general fear of their flock that a parliament would come into the hands of farmers with hostile feelings towards the coloured population. Their only protection had come from 'Her Majesty's Government and officers appointed by it'. They therefore requested that 'in the new constitution, such provisions may be made, by which the coloured classes are secured against any oppressive laws and enactments of the new Legislature, depriving them of rights and privileges of British subjects'.[93] Similar ideas were also expressed among the inhabitants of Zuurbraak, a mission village in the Southern Cape.[94] The experience of the Parliament after 1854, particularly when it sharpened the Master and Servants Act, demonstrated that such fears were in no way groundless.[95]

The same political position was reached from the other end of the political spectrum, by those who saw the establishment of a representative assembly as leading to the end of British political hegemony at the Cape. This was a continual undercurrent in conservative and official thought, but could rarely be expressed in public after the British Government had announced that such an assembly would eventually come. In private, matters were different. For instance, T. B. C. Bayley, a noted horse-breeder living near Caledon who would later introduce petitions for a high franchise, wrote to Richard Southey during the Convict Crisis as follows:

The real object of Wicht, Truter and Co. is to promote Dutch ascendancy and accustom the Afrikaner to public meetings, agitation and political feuds. I should like to know what Sir Harry [Smith] thinks now of a *Representative Assembly*, and

---

[91] See above, p. 157.   [92] Kirk, 'Self-Government and Self-Defence', esp. ch. 11.

[93] Petition of C. L. Teutsch *et al.*, 5 Nov. 1850, BPP 1362 of 1851, 141. They did not seek the 'hundreds of signatures' they believed they could have obtained for this petition, as they thought it 'not becoming for ministers of the Gospel to instil in our congregations, feelings of hatred against the farmers as their oppressors, or excite suspicion against the future legislature of their country, and contrary to the direction of the apostle, put them in mind [not] to be subject to principalities and powers to obey magistrates'. They are of course referring to Romans 13:1.

[94] *SACA*, 6 Apr. 1852; Petition of Kaalkop Hendricks and forty-two others, 30 Mar. 1852, BPP 1636 of 1852–3, 294.

[95] Colin Bundy, 'The Abolition of the Master and Servants Act', *South African Labour Bulletin*, 2, 1975.

what kind of a thing it would be if established now. The same machinery which rules the acute Convict Association (so called) would ensure the return of nineteen Afrikaners and one Englishman, *and what would be the result?*[96]

Thirdly, there were those who considered the sum of £25 to be too low. There were indeed those who considered the Colony not yet ripe for a representative assembly. Benjamin Moodie, a leading landowner from a notably conservative family, for instance, accepted the Governor's nomination to the Legislative Council in 1851 because it would enable him to 'join in stemming the torrent of democracy with which we have been threatened'.[97] Others were more self-serving, essentially arguing for a parliament so constituted that they, and their allies, could monopolise it. The 'resident householders' of Port Elizabeth were afraid of a franchise which would 'open the door to almost every hutholder as well as householder'.[98] In two petitions from the 'landowners of Caledon', led by T. B. C. Bayley, it was argued, first, in 1851, that 'all Hottentots, Fingoes, and other coloured people residing in missionary institutions, shall not be allowed votes in the election, as such persons must be considered as liable to be influenced in whatever way the missionaries choose, and not as free agents'.[99] A year later, they returned to the theme, arguing, as summarised by John Montagu (whose views they by this time probably represented) that under the low franchise 'a body of ignorant coloured persons, whose mere numbers would swamp the wealthy and educated portion of the community, would enjoy votes which would be turned to account by political partisans'. This would be particularly galling since there were numbers of English and 'country-born European[s]' who would be excluded from the vote because they had no fixed property, but lived with their employers while working as 'confidential clerk, commercial assistant, steward, bailiff, gardener, artisan or field labourer'. Such an arrangement would have been intolerable since, to their racist minds, 'the superior education and intelligence and capacity of political discrimination of the Europeans of any class residing in this Colony, will be readily conceded'.[100] Other conservatives were perhaps somewhat less blatant, but were also somewhat less consistent. Robert Godlonton, for instance, initially supported the measure, as did John Montagu, but both

[96] Bayley to Southey, 11 Dec. 1849, cited from Alex Wilmot, *The Life and Times of Sir Richard Southey KCMG etc. . . .,* London, Sampson, Low Marston & Co., 1904, 86, cited in Kirk, 'Self-Government and Self-Defence', 272.

[97] Moodie to Montagu, 4 Oct. 1851, BPP 1427 of 1852, 8.

[98] Report of the Committee of Resident Householders of Port Elizabeth, accepted at a Public Meeting, 14 Oct. 1850, BPP 1362 of 1852, 138.

[99] Petition from Caledon landowners, undated, enclosed in Smith to Grey, 21 Jan. 1851, BPP 1362 of 1851, 150.

[100] Petition of landowners, agriculturalists and other British subjects, residing in the district of Caledon, enclosed in Montagu to Peel, 28 Feb. 1852, BPP 1636 of 1852–3, 133–4.

changed their position in the course of 1851 and 1852. The reason for this, at least in Godlonton's case, was the Kat River rebellion. He should not have been surprised at the rebellion he had done much to foment. However, he could make use of the opportunity it presented to continue his vendetta against the Settlement and the missionaries associated with it. This had been made worse not merely by the rebels' destruction of property and their killing of one of his relatives, but also because in the elections which had been held in 1850 he himself had not received a single vote from the Kat River. This he attributed to the interference of James Read – he did not name him, but William Porter later did so for him – thus demonstrating, to his satisfaction and to that of those many in the Eastern Cape who agreed with him, that the mission station inhabitants were unfit to exercise the franchise.[101]

Fourthly, there was the view which eventually prevailed. The express reason for the £25 franchise was to give the vote to a substantial number of coloured men, particularly those resident on the mission stations. The men of the Kat River appreciated this. At a meeting held in Philipton on 21 October 1850, thus a few months before the outbreak of the rebellion, the leaders of the community, men who would not rebel, noted

that they engaged with mixed feelings of hope and fear in the duties attending the framing of representative institutions, for whilst on the one hand they are glad to see such institutions confirmed on Her Majesty's subjects as their peculiar birthright, they are not without forebodings about the working of a South African Parliament. They feel like children leaving their father's home to begin the world for themselves.

The subject of the franchise was to them of deep interest, and hence their satisfaction in finding that it had been fixed at £25 fixed property by the 'late Legislative Council'. Memorialists have, however, seen with concern and alarm an opposition on the frontier to this permission, by which many of the coloured people will be considered electors.[102]

Once the sum had been determined, it became a fixed part of the programme of those who were agitating to achieve the establishment of a legislative assembly, especially Sir Andries Stockenstrom, John Fairbairn, Christoffel Brand and F. W. Reitz, the four men who resigned from the Council because it did not proceed immediately to take that step. Some of those who supported the low franchise may have done so because they had done their sums and realised that there was no division of the Colony in which the coloured voters could return a Member of Parliament on their own strength. Certainly, William Porter, the Attorney-General who made

---

[101] Speeches by Godlonton and Montagu, Legislative Council, 10 Mar. 1852, BPP 1636 of 1852–3, 225–37.   [102] BPP 1362 of 1852–3, 138.

a succession of speeches in defence of the £25 franchise after the resignation of the 'popular four', appreciated this fact. He only believed that the
coloured vote would lead to the election of more moderate men, and
thereby temper extremism.[103] He compared the ideas of those who excluded
the Khoikhoi from the vote with homeopathy, with the view that 'the way
to cure a diseased body was to apply the very treatment which would in a
healthy body produce the same disease'. Whatever its medical efficacy, he
was wholly opposed to the extension of this practice to politics. He could
never agree that 'the way to cure a rebellious people of disloyalty was to
treat them in such a way as would drive a loyal people into rebellion'.
Rather, the coloureds had to be incorporated, and thus disarmed. In the
greatest ringing phrase to come out of the debate, he declaimed: 'I would
rather meet the Hottentot at the hustings, voting for his representative, than
meet the Hottentot in the wilds with his gun on his shoulder.' It was a sentence spoken when there were still Khoikhoi in the wilds of the Eastern
Cape, with their guns on, or at, their shoulders, and it is one whose implica-
tions were not fully appreciated in South Africa until 1994.[104]

By 1852, politics in the Colony had become deadlocked. The conservatives under John Montagu dominated the Legislative Council, after the
resignation of the 'popular four' and the appointment in their stead of men
guaranteed to vote with Montagu. Montagu had also packed the civil
service with individuals who supported his policies and who controlled the
flows of information to London. Against this, the opposition to the
Government, particularly from the Cape Town municipality, continued
unabated. The impasse that this created was broken in the next two years
primarily by the actions of the new Lieutenant -Governor, Charles Darling,
who arrived in the Cape in March 1852 as part of a new team to replace Sir
Harry Smith, who was seen in London, correctly, as having failed both to
end the war on the Eastern Frontier and to create conditions for the
establishment of a Cape parliament. From the beginning, Darling saw the
importance of maintaining the low franchise. After only a month in South
Africa, he wrote to his superiors in London that

nothing is more notorious than upon the present, as well as upon former occasions,
large numbers of [the coloured population] have taken arms for [the] purpose [of
defending the Colony against enemies and rebels]. It is difficult to discover either
the justice or the policy which would exclude from the franchise those who have
been found innocent of having afforded any ground for the panic which arose

[103] Speech of 23 Oct. 1852, BPP 1656 of 1852–3, 246. See also Stanley Trapido, 'White Conflict
and Non-White Participation in the Politics of the Cape of Good Hope, 1852–1910', Ph.D.
thesis, University of London, 1963, esp. 379–448.
[104] Speech of 9 Mar. 1852, BPP 1236 of 1852–3, 220.

among a particular class of their fellow colonists; but would leave that privilege in the hands of the very class who have been declared to have committed an aggression, both unjust and inimical upon them.[105]

It would take two years of hard political work, cleansing the civil service and exposing their financial malpractices, before Darling could achieve his objectives. In this he was aided by the retirement and death of Montagu and by a change of administration in Great Britain. Nevertheless, on 1 July 1854, the Cape Parliament met for first time, elected, as the Cape liberals had hoped, on a low franchise.[106]

[105] Darling to Pakington, 25 Mar. 1852, BPP 1636 of 1852–3, 178.
[106] This paragraph relies on Kirk, 'Self-Government and Self-Defence', ch. 12.

8 Conclusion

The 1853 constitution put a figure on respectability. Men whose property was worth £25 were within the limits, as were their families. The rest were not, and had no say in the government of the country. This was a formalisation, and thus a simplification, of the rules by which high politics was henceforth to operate.

It would be a mistake to underestimate the importance of the constitution. At the time it was just about the most democratic in the world. This might seem remarkable, given the racial tensions in South Africa at the time, until it is realised that it was created precisely to alleviate those tensions. Of course it had its faults, by modern measures. It was far from universal manhood suffrage, and women did not have the vote at all – not altogether surprisingly since no-one proposed this as a possibility. But it would be anachronistic in the extreme to blame the makers of the 1853 constitution for failing to be, at the least, forty years ahead of their time.

The criticisms which can, and should, be made of the constitution of 1853 refer not to its principles but rather to its implementation. It is usually commented that no 'coloured' or African men were ever elected to the Cape Parliament. How far this is true is a matter of definition. There were two MPs who received hereditary titles from the British crown. One, Sir Andries Stockenström, Bt., was the grandson of a slave, and while he himself was quite light-skinned, his sister, who was married to the Civil Commissioner of Beaufort West, was not.[1] The other, John Henry, Baron de Villiers, was described as 'that old brown man' in the *Straatpraatjes* in 1909.[2] These sketches, almost certainly written by Dr Abdurahman and published in the newspaper of the (predominantly coloured) African Political Organisation, give an idea of how the coloured elite of Cape Town saw some of those who

---

[1] See, for example, J. B. Brain (ed.), *The Cape Diary of Bishop Patrick Raymond Griffith for the Years 1837 to 1839*, Mariannhill, Southern African Catholic Bishops' Conference, 1988, 162. Stockenström had of course received his baronetcy before he was elected to the Cape Parliament.

[2] Mohamed Adhikari (ed.), *Straatpraatjes: Language, Politics and Popular Culture in Cape Town, 1909–1922*, Pretoria, J. L. van Schaik, and Cape Town, Buchu Books, 1996, 34.

ran the Colony. Moreover, Stockenström and De Villiers were only the most distinguished of those MPs who, in later terminology, would be disparaged by those classified as 'coloureds' as 'try-for-whites'. On the other hand, no African was elected to the Cape Parliament until after Union in 1910, when it ceased to be a sovereign entity and had become merely the Cape Provincial Council.

It is a measure of the genuine importance attached to the franchise that regular attempts were made to change or dilute it. In 1887, the Registration Act made it harder for Africans and coloureds to get on the roll, and in 1892 the Franchise and Ballot Act raised the property qualification from £25 to £75. Nevertheless, by this stage some 15 per cent of voters were African and twice that number were coloured.[3] At about the same time, the threatened election of a Muslim in Cape Town brought about a change of the electoral rules to make the tactical voting which might have brought this about impossible. Union was only brought about because it was agreed to maintain the then current franchise arrangements in the four provinces. This of course had the effect of diluting the importance of the black vote, as the other three provinces had racially defined franchises.[4] Even at that stage, however, there were plans to give the vote to white (but not black) women, so that the relative weight of African and coloured voters would be diminished.[5] In 1930, this indeed happened. Thereafter, Afrikaner nationalists made consistent attempts to remove first African and then coloured voters, first from the common role and then from all participation in electing the country's rulers. In 1960, they finally achieved their object.

Even among its supporters, Cape liberalism, which was symbolised by the low franchise, was not always a whole-hearted creed. To be charitable, it should be pointed out that politicians, particularly those whose power base is not strong, need to trim in order to achieve anything. It is always a nice calculation whether it is better to compromise on principles or to hold firm and risk a total defeat. Perhaps the liberals in the Cape Parliament were too ready to take the former option. In general their sticking point was with regard to the rule of law, not with regard to individual rights. In so doing, however, they managed to preserve a considerable good for the South Africa of the twentieth century.[6]

[3] T. R. H. Davenport, *South Africa: A Modern History*, London and Basingstoke, Macmillan, 1977, 83.

[4] *De jure* in the Transvaal and the Orange Free State; *de facto* in Natal.

[5] L. M. Thompson, *The Unification of South Africa, 1902–1910*, Oxford, Clarendon Press, 1960, 222–3.

[6] Phyllis Lewsen, 'Cape Liberalism in its Terminal Phase', in D. C. Hindson (ed.), *Working Papers in Southern African Studies*, Johannesburg, Ravan, 1983, III; T. R. H. Davenport, 'The Cape Liberal Tradition to 1910', in Jeffrey Butler, Richard Elphick and David Welsh (eds.), *Democratic Liberalism in South Africa: Its History and Prospect*, Middletown, Conn., Wesleyan University Press, 1987.

Nevertheless, there were at root two problems which Cape liberalism faced, and failed to escape. The first was inherent in the terms within which it was expressed. As Martin Legassick has written, 'abstractions of freedom and equality existed in, served to reproduce, and were unable to explain, capitalist society as a class society'.[7] Put in another way, liberalism was and is predicated upon the autonomy of individuals, or at the most nuclear families. In this, of course, it gelled well with evangelical protestantism, with its stress on individual calling and salvation. It could not cope with the consequences of identity politics – racial, linguistic, national or whatever – with their inevitable tendency to lump people, rather than address them as the individuals with which liberalism was required by its own precepts to work. It required little disguise for measures which had a discriminatory effect to pass through the wide mesh of liberal acceptance.

The second problem was that the political base of the Cape liberals was meagre, within the confines of the electoral process. Afrikaner support for the low franchise, mobilised by Sir Andries Stockenström and F. W. Reitz in particular, was not translated into permanent Dutch rural backing for a liberal programme.[8] In electoral terms, Cape liberalism relied on three groups. The first were the artisans of Cape Town, together with a number of merchants and so forth. Their parliamentary representative for years was Saul Solomon, the spiritual heir of Philip and Fairbairn – he was a printer and publisher who had been apprenticed to Fairbairn's partner, George Greig, and his brother at least had been brought up in Philip's household.[9] Secondly there were the residents of mission stations, such as Genadendal and Elim, who together made up three-quarters of the electorate of the constituency, Caledon, which long returned John Fairbairn. Thirdly, there were the African peasant farmers of the Eastern Cape, increasingly enfranchised and in alliance with the merchant groups who relied on their trade. These voters might influence various contests, and might provide the balance between two candidates each enjoying equal amounts of white support, but rarely if ever could they determine a contest in any given constituency, let alone in the Colony as a whole.[10]

There is a mirror side to this argument, though. The adherents of the Cape liberals were themselves the African and coloured elites who were the initiators of black political nationalism. That is the danger of rhetoric; it can be believed and acted upon by those to whom it is targeted. There is a

---

[7] Martin Legassick, 'The State, Racism and the Rise of Capitalism in the Nineteenth-Century Cape Colony', *SAHJ*, 28, 1993, 338.

[8] André du Toit, 'The Cape Afrikaners' Failed Liberal Moment', 43–8.

[9] Solomon, *Saul Solomon*, 11, 15.

[10] Stanley Trapido, ' "The Friends of the Natives": Merchants, Peasants and the Political and Ideological Structure of Liberalism at the Cape, 1854–1910', in Marks and Atmore, *Economy and Society*, 247–74.

direct historical line from Van der Kemp and James Read to the ANC from 1912 onwards, although of course this was only one strand in its ancestry.[11] It is not just that the Christian basis for political action which they propagated, and which Willem Uithaalder in the Kat River put into practice, has many parallels in modern South Africa, notably in the United Democratic Front (UDF) of the 1980s.[12] In addition, the idea that respectability entails representation lay at the basis of so much black political activism. It was only in its rejection that it was transformed into a more inclusive political ideology.

That this argument was possible was in part the consequence of the propaganda of Christian missionaries and their allies. All the same, this could never have worked if their message had not been taken up by Africans, Khoisan and ex-slaves. Certainly for the latter two groups the alternative may have been even harsher. Nonetheless they struggled with success to maintain a respectable way of life even though the rewards they received for so doing were intangible, and to a large extent only accrued to their distant descendants. Their achievements were not recognised, and were continually threatened by the sharpening racism of South African society. That was their tragedy. All the same, without the daily efforts of many thousands of men and women to realise the way of life after which they sought, against very considerable odds, the political history of South Africa would have been much harsher even than it eventually was. The men and women in question were not ignorant of the immediate political import of their personal lives. They could not have known the longer term results which their struggles would bring.

[11] These two individuals would have been among the few whites in nineteenth-century South Africa to have voted unequivocally for the ANC in 1994, if such an anachronistic parlour game may be allowed. One would give much to hear Van der Kemp's denunciation of the National Party's failure to live up to the Christian ideals it propagated. It would have been more uninhibited than that of any of the party's actual critics. Other members of that select club would have included the Colenso family in Natal and, only somewhat facetiously, Cecil Rhodes, the latter on the principle that he would have recognised sooner than anyone the need to 'square Mandela' and acted accordingly.

[12] Peter Walshe, 'Christianity and the Anti-Apartheid Struggle: The Prophetic Voice within Divided Churches', in Elphick and Davenport, *Christianity in South Africa*, 383–99.

Bibliography

OFFICIAL PUBLICATIONS

BRITISH PARLIAMENTARY PAPERS

Report from the Select Committee on Aborigines (British Settlements), 538 of 1836
Report of the Select Committee on Aborigines (British Settlements), 638 of 1837
Report from the Governor of the Cape of Good Hope to the Secretary of State for the Colonies, relative to the Condition of the Children sent out by the Children's Friend Society, 323 of 1840
Despatches relative to the Reception of Convicts at the Cape of Good Hope, 1138 of 1850
Further Correspondence relative to the State of the Kaffir Tribes, 1428 of 1852

CAPE PARLIAMENTARY PAPERS

Translation of a communication received by the Governor from certain rebel Hottentots now without the Colony, addressed jointly to the Governor and to the Parliament, C6, 1855
Report of a Commission appointed to inquire into and report upon the Government Educational System of the Colony, G16, 1863
Report on the Law of Inheritance for the Western Districts, G15, 1865

OTHER

Cape of Good Hope, *Documents Relative to the Question of a Separate Government for the Eastern Districts of the Cape Colony*, Grahamstown, Godlonton & White, 1847
Cape of Good Hope, Legislative Council, *Master and Servant: Addenda to the Documents on the working of the Order in Council of 21st July 1846*, Cape Town, Saul Solomon, 1849
Cape of Good Hope, Legislative Council, *Proceedings of Evidence given before the Committee of the Legislative Council respecting the Ordinance to Prevent the Practice of Squatting on Government Lands*, Cape Town, Saul Solomon, 1852

GENERAL

Abel, Richard L., *Politics by Other Means: Law in the Struggle against Apartheid*, New York and London, Routledge, 1995

Adhikari, Mohamed (ed.), *Straatpraatjes: Language, Politics and Popular Culture in Cape Town, 1909–1922*, Pretoria, J. L. van Schaik, and Cape Town, Buchu Books, 1996

Akyeampong, Emmanuel, 'What's in a Drink? Class Struggle, Popular Culture and the Politics of *Akpeteshie* (Local Gin), in Ghana, 1930–67', *JAH*, 37(2), 1996

Alexander, J. E., *Narrative of a Voyage of Observation among the Colonies of Western Africa, in the Flagship* Thalia *and of a Campaign in Kaffir-land*, 2 vols., London, Henry Colburn, 1837

Ayliff, John, *Memorials of the British Settlers of South Africa*, Grahamstown, Robert Godlonton, 1845

Backhouse, James, *Narrative of a Visit to the Mauritius and South Africa*, London, Hamilton, Adams & Co., 1844

Baines, Gary, 'The Origins of Urban Segregation: Local Government and the Residence of Africans in Port Elizabeth, c. 1835–1865', *SAHJ*, 22, 1990

Balie, Isaac, *Die Geskiedenis van Genadendal, 1738–1988*, Cape Town and Johannesburg, Perskor, 1988

Bank, Andrew, *The Decline of Urban Slavery at the Cape, 1806 to 1843*, Cape Town, Centre of African Studies, UCT, Communication no. 22, 1991

'The Great Debate and the Origins of South African Historiography', *JAH*, 38(2), 1997

'Liberals and their Enemies: Racial Ideology at the Cape of Good Hope, 1820–1850', Ph.D. thesis, University of Cambridge, 1996

Barrow, John, *Travels into the Interior of Southern Africa*, 2 vols., London, Cadell and Davies, 1801–4

Beinart, William, '*Amafelandawonye* (the Die-hards): Popular Protest and Women's Movements in Herschel District in the 1920s', in William Beinart and Colin Bundy, *Hidden Struggles in Rural South Africa: Politics and Popular Movements in the Transkei and Eastern Cape, 1890–1930*, London, Berkeley, Los Angeles and Johannesburg, James Currey, University of California Press and Ravan, 1979

'The Night of the Jackal: Sheep, Pastures and Predators in the Cape', *Past and Present*, 158, 1998

Belich, James, *Making Peoples: A History of the New Zealanders from Polynesian Settlement to the End of the Nineteenth Century*, Harmondsworth, Allen Lane for the Penguin Press, 1996

Berman, Bruce, *Control and Crisis in Colonial Kenya: The Dialectic of Domination*, London, James Currey, 1990

Beyers, Coenraad, *Die Kaapse Patriotte gedurende die laatste kwart van die agtiende eeu en die voortlewing van hul denkbeelde*, 2nd edn, Pretoria, J. L. van Schaik, 1967

Bickford-Smith, Vivian, 'Dangerous Cape Town: Middle-class Attitudes to Poverty in Cape Town in the Late Nineteenth Century', *Studies in the History of Cape Town*, 4, 1981

Ethnic Pride and Racial Prejudice in Victorian Cape Town: Group Identity and Social Practice, 1875–1902, Cambridge, Cambridge University Press, 1995

'Meanings of Freedom: Social Position and Identity among ex-Slaves and their Descendants in Cape Town, 1875–1910', in Worden and Crais, *Breaking the Chains*

Bird, W. W., *State of the Cape of Good Hope in 1822*, London, John Murray, 1823, reprinted Cape Town, Struik, 1966

Böeseken, Anna, 'Die Nederlandse Commissarisse en die 18de eeuse sameleving aan die Kaap', *AYB*, 7, 1944

Boniface, C. E., *De Nieuwe Ridderorde, of de Temperantisten*, Cape Town, P. A. Brand, 1832

Booyens, B., 'Kerk en Staat, 1795–1853', *AYB*, 28, 1965
Nagmaalsweek deur die jare: 'n kerkhistoriese studie, Cape Town, N. G. Kerk-Uitgevers, 1982

Borcherds, P.B., *An Autobiographical Memoir*, 1861, reprinted Cape Town, African Connoisseurs Press, 1963
'Over het belang der Geschiedenis als de beste bron van algemeen onderwys', *NZAT*, 16, 1839

Boshoff, Anlen, 'Die interieur van 'n 19de eeuse Kaapse Moslemhuis na aanleiding van dokumentêre bronne', *Bulletin of the South African Cultural History Museum*, 11, 1990

Bosman, D. B. and H. B. Thom (eds.), *Daghregister gehouden by den Oppercoompman Jan Anthonisz van Riebeeck*, 3 vols., Cape Town, Balkema, 1952–7

Bosman, F. C. L., *Drama en Toneel in Suid-Afrika*, I: *1652–1855*, Cape Town and Pretoria, HAUM and J. H. de Bussy, 1928

Botha, H. C., 'Die rol van Christoffel J. Brand in Suid-Afrika, 1820–1854', *AYB*, 40, 1977
John Fairbairn in South Africa, Cape Town, Historical Publication Society, 1984

Bowker, John Mitford, *Speeches, Letters, and Selections for Important Papers*, Grahamstown, Godlonton and Richards, 1864

Bradlow, Adil, 'Imperialism, State Formation and the Establishment of a Muslim Community at the Cape of Good Hope, 1770–1840: A Study in Urban Resistance', MA thesis, UCT, 1988

Bradlow, Edna, 'Children and Childhood at the Cape in the 19th Century', *Kleio*, 20, 1988
'The Children's Friend Society at the Cape of Good Hope', *Victorian Studies*, 27(2), 1984
'The Culture of a Colonial Elite: The Cape of Good Hope in the 1850s', *Victorian Studies*, 29, 1986
'The "Great Fear" at the Cape of Good Hope, 1851–2', *International Journal of African Historical Studies*, 23, 1989
'Mental Illness or a Form of Resistance: The Case of Soera Brotto', *Kleio*, 23, 1991
'Women and Education in Nineteenth-Century South Africa: The Attitudes and Experiences of Middle-Class English-Speaking Females at the Cape', *SAHJ*, 28, 1993
'Women at the Cape in the Mid-nineteenth Century', *SAHJ*, 19, 1987

Brain, J. B. (ed.), *The Cape Diary of Bishop Patrick Raymond Griffith for the Years 1837 to 1839*, Mariannhill, Southern African Catholic Bishops' Conference, 1988

Bredekamp, H. C., and J. L. Hattingh (eds.), *Das Tagebuch und die Briefe von Georg Schmidt: Dem ersten Missionar in Südafrika*, Bellville, Wes-Kaaplandse Instituut vir Historiese Navorsing, 1981

Bremmer, Jan, and Herman Roodenburg (eds.), *A Cultural History of Gender*, Ithaca, NY, Cornell University Press, 1991

Brown, M. M., 'Die Children's Friend Society in Engeland en die Kaap die Goede Hoop, 1830–1841', *AYB*, 57, 1994

Bruijn, J. R., F. S. Gaastra and I. Schöffer, *Dutch-Asiatic Shipping in the 17th and 18th Centuries*, 3 vols., The Hague, Martinus Nijhoff, 1987

Bryer, Lynne, and Keith Hunt, *The 1820 Settlers*, Cape Town, Don Nelson, 1984

Buchanan, Eben. J., *Cases decided in the Supreme Court of the Cape of Good Hope during the Year 1879*, Cape Town, Port Elizabeth and Johannesburg, J. C. Juta, 1894

Bundy, Colin, 'The Abolition of the Master and Servants Act', *South African Labour Bulletin*, 2, 1975

  The Rise and Fall of the South African Peasantry, London, Heinemann, 1979

Burchell, W. J., *Travels in the Interior of South Africa*, edited by I. Schapera, 2 vols., London, Batchworth Press, 1953

Bushman, Richard L., *The Refinement of America: Persons, Houses, Cities*, New York, Alfred A. Knopf, 1992

Cairns, Margaret, 'Geringer and Bok; a Genealogical Jig-saw', *Familia*, 13, 1976

Casalis, Eugène, *My Life in Basutoland*, reprinted Cape Town, Struik, 1971

Changuion, A. N. E., *De Nederduitsche Taal in Zuid-Afrika hersteld: Zijnde eene handleiding tot de kennis dier taal naar de plaatselijke behoefte van het land gewijzigd*, 2nd edn, Rotterdam, J. van der Vliet, 1848

Chanock, Martin, 'Writing South African Legal History: A Prospectus', *JAH*, 30, 2, 1989

Chaveas, L. M., 'A Study of the Quilted and Corded Kappies of the Voortrekker Women and their Resemblance to French White Work Quilting of the 17th and 18th Centuries', *Navorsinge van die Nasionale Museum, Bloemfontein*, 1993

Cock, Jacklyn, *Maids and Madams: A Study in the Politics of Exploitation*, Johannesburg, Ravan, 1980

Cole, Alfred W., *The Cape and the Kafirs: Or Notes of Five Years Residence in South Africa*, London, Richard Bentley, 1852

Colley, Linda, *Britons: Forging the Nation, 1707–1837*, New Haven and London, Yale University Press, 1992

  'Whose Nation? Class and National Consciousness in Britain 1750–1830', *Past and Present*, 113, 1986

Comaroff, Jean and John, *Of Revelation and Revolution: Christianity, Colonialism and Consciousness in South Africa*, I, Chicago and London, University of Chicago Press, 1991

Crais, Clifton C., 'Slavery and Emancipation in the Eastern Cape', in Worden and Crais, *Breaking the Chains*

  White Supremacy and Black Resistance in Pre-Industrial South Africa: The Making of the Colonial Order in the Eastern Cape, 1770–1865, Cambridge, Cambridge University Press, 1992

Crass, David Colin, and C. Garth Sampson, ' "A Few Old Clothes": 19th Century European Attire adopted by the Seacow River Bushmen', *Africana Notes and News*, 30(6), 1993

Cronwright-Schreiner, C. S., *The Life of Olive Schreiner*, London, T. Fisher Unwin, 1924

Cunningham, Hugh, 'The Language of Patriotism, 1750–1914', *History Workshop Journal*, 12 (1981)

Currie, Marion Rose, 'The History of Theopolis Mission, 1814–1851', MA thesis, Rhodes University, Grahamstown, 1983

Da Costa, Yusuf, and Achmat Davids, *Pages from Cape Muslim History*, Pietermaritzburg, Shuter & Shooter, 1994

Dale, Sir Langham, 'The Cape and its People', in R. Noble (ed.), *The Cape and Its People*, Cape Town, J. C. Juta, 1869

Dangor, S., 'In the Footsteps of the Companions: *Sheykh* Yusuf of Macassar (1626–1699)', in Da Costa and Davids, *Pages from Cape Muslim History*

Davenport, T. R. H., *The Afrikaner Bond: The History of a South African Political Party, 1880–1911*, Cape Town, Oxford University Press, 1966

   'The Cape Liberal Tradition to 1910', in Jeffrey Butler, Richard Elphick and David Welsh (eds.), *Democratic Liberalism in South Africa: Its History and Prospect*, Middletown, Conn., Wesleyan University Press, 1987

   South Africa: A Modern History, London and Basingstoke, Macmillan, 1977

Davidoff, Leonore, and Catherine Hall, *Family Fortunes: Men and Women of the English Middle Class, 1780–1850*, London, Hutchinson, 1987

Davids, Achmat, 'The Afrikaans of the Cape Muslims from 1815 to 1915: A Sociolinguistic Study', MA thesis, University of Natal, 1991

   'Alternative Education: *Tuan Guru* and the Formation of the Cape Muslim Community', in Da Costa and Davids, *Pages from Cape Muslim History*

   'The "Coloured" Image of Afrikaans in Nineteenth Century Cape Town', *Kronos: Journal of Cape History*, 17, 1990

   The History of the Tana Baru: The Case for the Preservation of the Muslim Cemetery at the top of Longmarket Street, Cape Town, Committee for the Preservation of the Tana Baru, 1985

   The Mosques of Bo-Kaap: A Social History of Islam at the Cape, Athlone, South African Institute of Arabic and Islamic Research, 1980

   'Muslim–Christian Relations in Nineteenth Century Cape Town, 1825–1925', *Kronos: Journal of Cape History*, 19, 1992

   'The Origins of the *Hanafi-Shafi'i* Dispute and the Impact of Abu Bakr Effendi', in Da Costa and Davids, *Pages from Cape Muslim History*

De Graaf, H. J., 'De herkomst van de Kaapse "Chalifah"', *Tydscrif vir Wetenkap en Kuns*, 10, 1950

De Haan, F., *Oud Batavia*, 2nd edn, 2 vols., Bandung, Nix, 1935

De Jong, Cornelius, *Reizen naar de Kaap de Goede Hoope, Ierland en Norwegen in de Jaren 1791 tot 1797*, 3 vols., Haarlem, François Bohn, 1802–3

De Jong, J. J., *Met goed fatsoen: De elite in een Hollandse stad, Gouda, 1700–1780*, Amsterdam, De Bataafse Leeuw, 1985

De Kock, Victor, *Those in Bondage: An Account of the Life of the Slave at the Cape in the Days of the Dutch East India Company*, Pretoria, Union Booksellers, 1963

De la Caille, Nicolas Louis, *Travels at the Cape: 1751–53*, translated and edited by R. Raven-Hart, Cape Town and Rotterdam, Balkema, 1976

'Den 1 December i Kap', *Wiborg: Tidning för Litteratur, handel och ekonomi*, 30 Jan. 1857

Denyssen, D., 'Voorlezing in de Algemene Vergadering der Maatschappy ter Uitbreiding van Beschaving en Letterkunde', *NZAT*, 12, 1835

Desmond, Adrian, and James Moore, *Darwin*, London, Michael Joseph, 1991

De Villiers, C. C., *Geslagsregisters van die Ou Kaapse Families*, edited by C. Pama, 3 vols., Cape Town and Amsterdam, Balkema, 1966

De Vries, Jan, *The Dutch Rural Economy in the Golden Age*, New Haven and London, Yale University Press, 1974

Dooling, Wayne L., 'Agrarian Transformations in the Western Districts of the Cape Colony, 1838–c. 1900', Ph.D. thesis, Uinversity of Cambridge, 1996

   Law and Community in a Slave Society: Stellenbosch District, South Africa c. 1760–1820, Centre for African Studies, UCT, Communication No. 23, 1992

Dreyer, A., *Die Kaapse Kerk en die Groot Trek*, Cape Town, Van de Sandt de Villiers, 1929

Dreyer, A. (ed.), *Boustowwe vir die Geskiedenis van die Nederduits-Gereformeerde Kerke in Suid-Afrika*, III: *1804–1836*, Cape Town, Nasionale Pers, 1936

Dubow, Saul, 'Colonial Nationalism, the Milner Kindergarten and the Rise of "South Africanism", 1902–1910', *History Workshop Journal*, 43, 1997

   Land, Labour and Merchant Capital in the Pre-industrial Rural Economy of the Cape: The Experience of the Graaff-Reinet District (1852–72), Cape Town, Centre for African Studies, UCT, 1982

Duff Gordon, Lady, Lucy, *Letters from the Cape*, annotated by Dorothea Fairbridge, London, Oxford University Press, 1927

Du Plessis, I. D., *The Cape Malays: History, Religion, Traditions, Folk Tales: The Malay Quarter*, 2nd edn, Cape Town, Balkema, 1972

Du Plessis, I. D., and C. A. Lückhoff, *The Malay Quarter and its people*, Cape Town, Race Relations Series of the Sub-Department of Coloured Affairs, Department of the Interior, 1963

Du Plessis, J., *The Life of Andrew Murray of South Africa*, London, Marshall Bros., 1920

   'Colonial Progress and Countryside Conservatism: An Essay on the Legacy of Van der Lingen of Paarl, 1831–1875', MA thesis, Stellenbosch, 1988

Du Toit, André, 'The Cape Afrikaners' Failed Liberal Moment: 1850–1870', in Jeffrey Butler, Richard Elphick and David Welsh (eds.), *Democratic Liberalism in South Africa: Its History and Prospect*, Middletown, Conn., Wesleyan University Press, 1987

Du Toit, André, and Hermann Giliomee, *Afrikaner Political Thought: Analysis and Documents*, I: *1780–1850*, Cape Town and Johannesburg, David Philip, 1983

Elbourne, Elizabeth, ' "To Colonize the Mind": Evangelical Missionaries in Britain and the Eastern Cape, 1790–1837', D.Phil. thesis, University of Oxford, 1991

   'Early Khoisan Uses of Mission Christianity', in Henry Bredekamp and Robert Ross (eds.), *Missions and Christianity in South African History*, Johannesburg, Witwatersrand University Press, 1995

Elbourne, Elizabeth, and Robert Ross, 'Combatting Spiritual and Social Bondage: Early Missions in the Cape Colony', in Elphick and Davenport, *Christianity in South Africa*

Elks, Katherine, 'Crime, Community and the Police in Cape Town', 1825–1850, MA thesis, UCT, 1986

Ellman, Stephen, *In a Time of Trouble: Law and Liberty in South Africa's State of Emergency*, Oxford, Clarendon Press, 1992

Elphick, Richard, and Rodney Davenport (eds.), *Christianity in South Africa: A Political, Social and Cultural History*, Claremont, David Philip, 1997

Elphick, Richard, and Hermann Giliomee (eds.), *The Shaping of South African Society, 1652–1840*, 2nd edn, Cape Town, Maskew Miller Longman, 1989

Elphick, Richard, and V. C. Malherbe, 'The Khoisan to 1828', in Elphick and Giliomee, *Shaping*

Elphick, Richard, and Robert Shell, 'Intergroup Relations: Khoikhoi, Settlers, Slaves and Free Blacks, 1652–1795', in Elphick and Giliomee, *Shaping*

Elton, G. R., *Return to Essentials: Some Reflection on the Present State of Historical Study*, Cambridge, Cambridge University Press, 1991

Enklaar, Ido H., *Life and Work of Dr J. Th. van der Kemp, 1747–1811: Missionary Pioneer and Protagonist of Racial Equality in South Africa*, Cape Town and Rotterdam, Balkema, 1988

Erlank, Natasha, 'Letters Home: The Experiences and Perceptions of Middle Class British Women at the Cape 1820–1850', MA thesis, UCT, 1995

Fagan, G. and G., *Church Street in the Land of Waveren*, Tulbagh, Tulbagh Restoration Committee, 1975

Fast, Hildegard H. (ed.), *The Journal and Selected Letters of Rev. William J. Shrewsbury, 1826–1835: First Missionary to the Transkei*, Johannesburg, Witwatersrand University Press for Rhodes University, Grahamstown, 1994

Faure, Abraham, *Redevoering bij het tweede Eeuw-feest ter herinnering aan de vestiging der Christelijke Kerk, in Zuid-Afrika, gehouden in de Groote Kerk, in de Kaapstad op dinsdag den 6 April, 1852*, Kaapstad, Van de Sandt de Villiers & Tier, 1852

February, V. A., *Mind Your Colour: The 'Coloured' Stereotype in South African Literature*, London and Boston, Kegan Paul International, 1981

Ferguson, W. T., and R. F. M. Immelman, *Sir John Herschel and Education at the Cape, 1834–1840*, Cape Town, Oxford University Press, 1961

Findlay, Joan (ed.), *The Findlay Letters*, Pretoria, Van Schaik, 1954

Floud, Roderick, Kenneth Wachter and Annabel Gregory, *Health, Height and History: Nutritional Status in the United Kingdom, 1750–1980*, Cambridge, Cambridge University Press, 1990

Franken, J. L. M., ''n Kaapse huishoue in de 18de eeu uit von Dessin se briefboek en memoriaal', *AYB*, 3, 1940

Fransen, Hans, and Mary Alexander Cook, *The Old Buildings of the Cape*, Cape Town, Balkema, 1980

Freeman, J. J., *A Tour in South Africa*, London, John Snow, 1851

Gerber, Hilda, *Traditional Cookery of the Cape Malays*, Amsterdam and Cape Town, Balkema, 1957

Gerstner, Jonathan Neil, *The Thousand Generation Covenant: Dutch Reformed Covenant Theology and Group Identity in Colonial South Africa, 1652–1814*, Leiden, New York, Copenhagen and Cologne, Brill, 1991

Giliomee, Hermann, 'The Eastern Frontier, 1770–1812', in Elphick and Giliomee, *Shaping*

Die Kaap tydens die Eerste Britse Bewind, 1795–1803, Cape Town and Pretoria, HAUM, 1975

A Question of Survival: A Social History of the Afrikaners, forthcoming

Giliomee, Hermann, and Richard Elphick, 'The Origins and Entrenchment of European Dominance at the Cape, 1652–c. 1840', in Elphick and Giliomee, *Shaping*

Gleanings in Africa, London, James Cundee, 1806

Godlonton, Robert, *Memorials of the British Settlers of South Africa*, Grahamstown, Robert Godlonton, 1844

Gordon-Brown, A. (ed.), *James Ewart's Journal*, Cape Town, Struik, 1970

  The Narrative of Private Buck Adams, 7th (Princess Royal's) Dragoon Guards on the Eastern Frontier of the Cape of Good Hope, 1843–1848, Cape Town, Van Riebeeck Society, 1941

Green, J., *The Kat River Settlement in 1851*, Grahamstown, Godlonton & White, 1853

Groenveld, S., *Was de Nederlandse Republiek verzuild? Over segmentering van de samenleving binnen de Verenigde Nederlanden*, Leiden, Leiden University Press, 1995

Grose, Kelvin, 'Dr Halloran's Secret Life at the Cape', *QBSAL*, 41, 1987

Gutsche, Thelma, *The Bishop's Lady*, Cape Town, Howard Timmins, 1970

Hall, Martin, 'The Secret Lives of Houses: Women and Gables in the Eighteenth-Century Cape', *Social Dynamics*, 20, 1994

Hanekom, T. N., *Helperus Ritzema van Lier: Die Lewensbeeld van 'n kaapse Predikant uit die 18de Eeu*, Cape Town and Pretoria, N. G. Kerk-Uitgewers, 1959

Harris, W. Cornwallis, *The Wild Sports of Southern Africa*, London, Henry G. Bohn, 1852

Hattersley, A. F., *The Convict Crisis and the Growth of Unity: Resistance to Transportation in South Africa and Australia*, Pietermaritzburg, University of Natal Press, 1965

  An Illustrated Social History of South Africa, 2nd edn, Cape Town, Balkema, 1973

  A Victorian Lady at the Cape, 1849–51, Cape Town, Maskew Miller [1951]

Hattingh, J. L., *Die Eerste Vryswartes van Stellenbosch, 1679–1720*, Bellville, Wes-Kaaplandse Instituut vir Historiese Navorsing, 1981

Heese, H. F., *Groep sonder Grense (die rol en status van die gemengde bevolking aan die Kaape 1652–1795)*, Bellville, Wes-Kaaplandse Instituut vir Historiese Navorsing, 1984

Heuman, Gad, *The Killing Time: The Morant Bay Rebellion in Jamaica*, London and Basingstoke, Macmillan, 1994

Hofmeyr, Isabel, 'Building a Nation from Words: Afrikaans Language, Literature and Ethnic Identity', in Shula Marks and Stanley Trapido, *The Politics of Race, Class and Nationalism in Twentieth Century South Africa*, London and New York, Longman, 1987

Hofmeyr, S., 'Mijne reis door den Graaff-Reinetschen ring – herinneringen, gedachten en opmerkingen', *Elpis*, 2(4), 1858

Hogan, Neville, 'The Posthumous Vindication of Zacharias Gqishela: Reflections on the Politics of Dependence at the Cape in the Nineteenth Century', in Marks and Atmore, *Economy and Society*

Hoge, J., 'Die Geskiedenis van die Lutherse Kerk aan die Kaap', *AYB*, 1(2), 1938

Holt, Thomas C., *The Problem of Freedom: Race, Labor, and Politics in Jamaica and Britain, 1832–1938*, Baltimore and London, Johns Hopkins University Press, 1992

Hont, Istvan, and Michael Ignatieff, 'Needs and Justice in *The Wealth of Nations*: an Introductory Essay', in Hont and Ignatieff, *Wealth and Virtue: The Shaping of Political Economy in the Scottish Enlightenment*, Cambridge, Cambridge University Press, 1983

Host, Elizabeth Anne, 'Die Hondje Byt: Labour Relations in the Malmesbury District, c. 1880 to 1920', Honours thesis, UCT, 1987

Hugo, A. M., *The Cape Vernacular*, Cape Town, UCT, 1970

Hugo, A. M., and J. v. d. Bijl, *Die Kerk van Stellenbosch, 1686–1965*, Cape Town, Tafelberg, 1963

Hunt, Keith S., 'The Development of Municipal Government in the Eastern Province of the Cape of Good Hope, with Special Reference to Grahamstown (1827–1862)', *AYB*, 14, 1963 for 1961

    Sir Lowry Cole, Governor of Mauritius 1823–1828, Governor of the Cape of Good Hope 1828–1833: A Study in Colonial Administration, Durban, Butterworths, 1974

Hutton, C. W. (ed.), *The Autobiography of the late Sir Andries Stockenström, Bart.*, 2 vols., Cape Town, J. C. Juta, 1887

Introduction to the History of the Dutch Republic for the Last Ten Years, reckoning from the Year 1777, London, M. C. Miller, 1788

Israel, Jonathan I., *The Dutch Republic: Its Rise, Greatness and Fall, 1477–1806*, Oxford, Oxford University Press, 1995

Japha, Derek and Vivienne, *The Landscape and Architecture of Montagu*, Cape Town, School of Architecture and Planning, UCT, 1992

Jeffreys, K. M. (ed.), *Kaapse Archiefstukken*, 7 vols., Cape Town and Pretoria, Cape Times and Staatsdrukker, 1926–38

Jeppie, M. Shamil, 'Historical Process and the Constitution of subjects: I. D. du Plessis and the Reinvention of the "Malay"', BA Hons. thesis, UCT, 1987

    'Leadership and Loyalties: The Imams of Nineteenth Century Colonial Cape Town, South Africa', *Journal of Religion in Africa*, 26(2), 1996

    'Popular Culture and Carnival in Cape Town: The 1940s and 1950s', in Shamil Jeppie and Craig Souden (eds.), *The Struggle for District Six: Past and Present*, Cape Town, Buchu Books, 1990

Johnson, David, *Shakespeare and South Africa*, Oxford, Clarendon Press, 1996

Judges, Shirley, 'Poverty, Living Conditions and Social Relations: Aspects of Life in Cape Town in the 1830s', MA thesis, UCT, 1977

Kapp, P. H., 'Dr John Philip: Die Grondlegger van Liberalisme in Suid-Afrika', *AYB*, 48, 1985

Kayser, F.G., *Journal and Letters*, edited by H. C. Hummel, Cape Town, Maskew Miller Longman for Rhodes University, Grahamstown, 1990

Keegan, Timothy, *Colonial South Africa and the Origins of the Racial Order*, Cape Town and Johannesburg, David Philip, 1996

    'The Making of the Orange Free State, 1846–1854: Sub-imperialism, Primitive Accumulation and State Formation', *Journal of Imperial and Commonwealth History*, 17(1), 1988

Kennedy, F.R., *Johannesburg Africana Museum Catalogue of Pictures*, 7 vols., Johannesburg, Africana Museum, 1966

Keppel-Jones, Arthur (ed.), *Philipps, 1820 Settler*, Pietermaritzburg, Shuter & Shooter, 1960

Kirby, P. R., *The Musical Instruments of the Native Races of South Africa*, London, Oxford University Press, 1934

Kirk, Tony, 'Progress and Decline in the Kat River Settlement, 1829–1854', *JAH*, 14(3), 1973

'Self-Government and Self-Defence in South Africa: The Inter-relations between British and Cape Politics, 1846–1854', D.Phil. thesis, Oxford, 1972

Klopper, Sandra, 'George French Angas' (Re)presentation of the Zulu in *The Kafirs Illustrated*, *South African Journal of Cultural and Art History*, 3, 1989

Kollisch, Maximillien, *The Mussulman Population at the Cape of Good Hope*, Constantinople, Levant Herald Office, 1867

Kooijmans, L., *Onder regenten: De elite in een Hollandse stad, Leiden, 1700–1780*, Amsterdam, De Bataafse Leeuw, 1985

Koolhof, Sirtjo, and Robert Ross, 'Upas, September and the Bugis at the Cape of Good Hope: The Context of a Slave's Letter', *SARI: A Journal of Malay Studies*, forthcoming

Krüger, Bernhard, *The Pear Tree Blossoms: A History of the Moravian Mission Stations in South Africa, 1737–1869*, Genadendal, Genadendal Printing Works, 1966

Le Cordeur, Basil A., *The Politics of Eastern Cape Separatism, 1820–1854*, Cape Town, Oxford University Press, 1981

Le Cordeur, Basil, and Christopher Saunders (eds.), *The Kitchingman Papers: Missionary letters and journals, 1817 to 1848 from the Brenthurst Collection Johannesburg*, Johannesburg, Brenthurst Press, 1976

Le Feuvre, Philip, 'Cultural and Theological Factors affecting Relationships between the Nederduitse-Gereformeerde Kerk and the Anglican Church (of the Province of South Africa) in the Cape Colony, 1806–1910', Ph.D. thesis, UCT, 1980

Legassick, Martin, 'The Northern Frontier to c. 1840: The Rise and Decline of the Griqua People', in Elphick and Giliomee, *Shaping*

'The State, Racism and the Rise of Capitalism in the Nineteenth-Century Cape Colony', *SAHJ*, 28, 1993

Leibbrandt, H. C. V. (ed.), *Precis of the Archives of the Cape of Good Hope*, 17 vols., Cape Town, Richards, 1896–1906

Lester, Alan, 'The Margins of Order: Strategies of Segregation on the Eastern Cape Frontier, 1806–c. 1850', *JSAS*, 23(4), 1997

'"Otherness" and the Frontiers of Empire: The Eastern Cape Colony, 1806–c. 1850', *Journal of Historical Geography*, 24, 1998

Lewcock, Ronald, *Early Nineteenth Century Architecture in South Africa: A Study in the Interaction of Two Cultures, 1795–1837*, Cape Town, Balkema, 1963

Lewsen, Phyllis, 'Cape Liberalism in its Terminal Phase', in D. C. Hindson (ed.), *Working Papers in Southern African Studies*, III, Johannesburg, Ravan, 1983

Lichtenstein, H., *Travels in Southern Africa in the Years 1803, 1804, 1805 and 1806*, trans. A. Plumtre, 2 vols., 2nd edn, Cape Town, Van Riebeeck Society, 1928–30

Lister M. H. (ed.), *Journals of Andrew Geddes Bain*, Cape Town, Van Riebeeck Society, 1949

Lloyd, Christopher, *Mr Barrow of the Admiralty*, London, Collins, 1970

Loff, Chris, 'The History of a Heresy', in De Gruchy and Villa-Vicencio (eds.), *Apartheid is a Heresy*, Grand Rapids, Mich., Eerdmans, 1983

Lonsdale, John, 'The Moral Economy of Mau Mau: Wealth, Poverty and Civic Virtue in Kikuyu Political Thought', in Bruce Berman and John Lonsdale,

Unhappy Valley: Conflict in Kenya and Africa, 2 vols., London, James Currey, 1992

Ludlow, Elizabeth Helen, 'The Work of the London Missionary Society in Cape Town, 1812–1841', BA hons. thesis, UCT, 1981

McCracken, J. L., *New Light at the Cape of Good Hope: William Porter, the Father of Cape Liberalism*, Belfast, Ulster Historical Publications, 1993

McGinn, M. J., 'J. C. Chase – 1820 Settler and Servant of the Colony', MA thesis, Rhodes University, Grahamstown, 1975

McKenzie, Kirsten, 'The *South African Commercial Advertiser* and the Making of Middle Class Identity in Early Nineteenth-Century Cape Town', MA thesis, UCT, 1993

Maclennan, Ben, *A Proper Degree of Terror: John Graham and the Cape's Eastern Frontier*, Johannesburg, Ravan, 1986

Macmillan, W. M., *Cape Colour Question*, London, Faber & Gwyer, 1927

Malan, Antonia, 'Households of the Cape, 1750–1850: Inventories and the Archaeological Record', Ph.D. thesis, UCT, 1993

Malherbe, V. C., 'The Cape Khoisan in the Eastern Districts of the Colony before and after Ordinance 50 of 1828', Ph.D. thesis, UCT, 1997

Manuel, G. M., and B. Frank, *District Six*, Cape Town, Longman, 1967

Marais, J. S., *The Cape Coloured People, 1652–1937*, reprinted Johannesburg, Witwatersrand University Press, 1968

Marais, Maria M., 'Armesorg aan die Kaap onder die Kompanjie, 1652–1795', *AYB*, 6, 1943

Marincowitz, John, 'From "Colour Question" to "Agrarian Problem" at the Cape: Reflections on the Interim', in Hugh Macmillan and Shula Marks (eds.), *Africa and Empire: W. M. Macmillan, Historian and Social Critic*, London, Temple Smith for the Institute of Commonwealth Studies, 1989

    'Rural Production and the Labour in the Western Cape, 1838 to 1888, with Special Reference to the Wheat Growing Districts', Ph.D. thesis, University of London, 1985

Marks, Shula, and Anthony Atmore (eds.), *Economy and Society in Pre-Industrial South Africa*, London, Longman, 1980

Marks, Shula, and Stanley Trapido, ' "A White Man's Country"? The Construction of the South African State and the Making of White South African "Nationalisms", 1902–1914' (as yet unpublished)

Mason, John Edwin, ' "Fit for Freedom": The Slaves, Slavery and Emancipation in the Cape Colony, South Africa, 1806 to 1842', Ph.D. thesis, Yale University, 1992

Maxwell, W. A., and R. T. McGeogh (eds.), *The Reminiscences of Thomas Stubbs*, Cape Town, Balkema for Rhodes University, Grahamstown, 1978

Mayson, John, *The Malays of Cape Town*, reprinted Cape Town, Africana Connoisseurs Press, 1963

Mentzel, O. F., *A Geographical and Topographical Description of the Cape of Good Hope*, trans. H. J. Mandelbrote, 3 vols., Cape Town, Van Riebeeck Society, 1921, 1924, 1944

    Life at the Cape in the mid-Eighteenth Century, being the Biography of Rudolph Siegfried Allemann, trans. Margaret Greenlees, Cape Town, Van Riebeeck Society, 1919

Merriman, N. J., *The Cape Journals of Archdeacon Merriman*, edited by D. H. Varley and H. M. Matthew, Cape Town, Van Riebeeck Society, 1957

Meyer, Birgit, 'Translating the Devil: An African Appropriation of Pietist Protestantism: The Case of the Peki Ewe in Southeastern Ghana, 1847–1992', Ph.D. thesis, University of Amsterdam, 1995

Millar, A. K., *Plantagenet in South Africa: Lord Charles Somerset*, Cape Town, London and New York, Oxford University Press, 1965

Missive van Bewindhebberen der Oost-Indische Compagnie geschreven den 13 October 1785, met copie van alle de stukken, brieven, resoluties &c. relatief tot het werk van de Caab, 4 vols., The Hague, for the VOC, 1785

Mitford-Barberton, I., and Violet White, *Some Frontier Farmers: Biographical Sketches of 100 Eastern Province Families before 1840*, Cape Town and Pretoria, Human & Rousseau, 1968

Mitra, Sidha M., *The Life and Letters of Sir John Hall*, London, Longman, 1911

Moodie, Donald (ed.), *The Record: Or a series of Official Papers relative to the Condition and Treatment of the Native Tribes of South Africa*, Cape Town, 1838–41, reprinted Amsterdam and Cape Town, Balkema, 1960

Moodie, J. W. D., *Ten Years in South Africa*, 2 vols., London, Richard Bentley, 1835

Mostert, Noël, *Frontiers: The Epic of South Africa's Creation and the Tragedy of the Xhosa People*, London, Jonathan Cape, 1993

Muller, C. F. J., *Die Britse Owerheid em Die Groot Trek*, Johannesburg, Simondium, 1963

Murray, Joyce (ed.), *In Mid-Victorian Cape Town: Letters from Miss Rutherfoord*, Cape Town, Balkema, 1968

Mrs Dale's Diary, Cape Town, Balkema, 1966

Nahuys van Burgst, H. C., *Adventures at the Cape of Good Hope in 1806*, Cape Town, South African Library, 1993

Nash, M. D., *Bailie's Party of 1820 Settlers: A Collective Experience in Emigration*, Cape Town, Balkema, 1982

Naudé, S. D. (ed.), *Kaapse Plakkaatboek*, III, Cape Town, Cape Times, 1949

Newman, Gerald, 'Anti-French Propaganda and British Liberal Nationalism in the Early Nineteenth Century: Suggestions toward a General Interpretation', *Victorian Studies*, 18, 1975

The Rise of English Nationalism: A Cultural History, 1740–1830, London, Weidenfeld & Nicolson, 1987

Newton-King, Susan, 'The Labour Market of the Cape Colony, 1807–28', in Marks and Atmore, *Economy and Society*

'The Rebellion of the Khoi in Graaff-Reinet, 1799 to 1803', in Susan Newton-King and V. C. Malherbe, *The Khoikhoi Rebellion in the Eastern Cape (1799–1803)*, Cape Town, Centre for African Studies, UCT, 1981

Nicholson, George, *The Cape and its Colonists . . . with Hints to Prospective Emigrants*, London, Henry Colburn, 1848

Odendaal, André, *Vukani Bantu: The Beginnings of Black Protest Politics in South Africa to 1912*, Cape Town and Johannesburg, David Philip, 1984

Pama, C., *Regency Cape Town*, Cape Town, Tafelberg, 1975

Wagon Road to Wynberg, Cape Town, Tafelberg, 1979

Peires, J. B., 'The British and the Cape, 1814–1834', in Elphick and Giliomee, *Shaping*

The House of Phalo: A History of the Xhosa People in the Days of their Independence, Johannesburg, Ravan, 1981

Penn, Nigel G., 'Anarchy and Authority in the Koue Bokkeveld, 1739–1779', *Kleio*, 17, 1985

Percival, Robert, *An Account of the Cape of Good Hope*, London, C. Andr. Baldwin, 1804

Philip, John, *Letter to the Directors of the London Missionary Society on the Present State of their Institutions in the Colony of the Cape of Good Hope*, Cape Town, G. J. Pike, 1848

Researches in South Africa illustrating the Civil, Moral and Religious Condition of the Native Tribes, 2 vols., London, James Ducan, 1828

Philip, P. H., 'The Vicissitudes of the Early British Settlers at the Cape', *QBSAL*, 40, 1986

Picton-Seymour, Desirée, *Victorian Buildings in South Africa, including Edwardian and Transvaal Republican Styles*, Cape Town and Rotterdam, Balkema, 1977

Pitt-Rivers, J., 'On the Word "Caste" ', in T. O. Beidelman (ed.), *The Translation of Culture: Essays to E. E. Evans-Pritchard*, London, Tavistock, 1971

Ponelis, Fritz, *The Development of Afrikaans*, Frankfurt-on-Main, Pieter Lang, 1993

Postma, Johannes Menne, *The Dutch in the Atlantic Slave Trade, 1600–1815*, Cambridge, Cambridge University Press, 1990

Prak, M., *Gezeten burgers: De elite in een Hollandse stad, Hoorn, 1700–1780*, Amsterdam, De Bataafse Leeuw, 1985

Pringle, Thomas, *Narrative of a Residence in South Africa*, reprinted Cape Town, Struik, 1966

Quispel, Chris, *Dienaar en Bruut: Studies over laat-negentiende-eeuws racisme, in het bijzonder in het Zuiden van de Vereenigde Staten*, Leiden, Centrum voor Moderne Geschiedenis, 1995

Radford, Dennis, 'South African Christian Architecture', in Elphick and Davenport, *Christianity in South Africa*

Randall, Peter, *Little England on the Veld: The English Private School System in South Africa*, Johannesburg, Ravan, 1982

Ranger, Terence, 'The Local and the Global in Southern African Religious History', in Robert W. Hefner (ed.), *Conversion to Christianity: Historical and Anthropological Perspectives on a Great Transformation*, Berkeley, Los Angeles and Oxford, University of California Press, 1993

Rassool, Ciraj, and Leslie Witz, 'The 1952 Jan Van Riebeeck Tercentenary Festival: Constructing and Contesting Public History in South Africa', *JAH*, 34(3), 1993

Read, James, *The Kat River Settlement in 1851*, Cape Town, A. S. Robertson, 1852

Reenders, H., ' "De jeugdige emigranten naar de Kaap": Een vergeten hoofdstuk uit de geschiedenis van het Nederlandse protestantse Réveil (1856–1860)', *Documentatieblad voor de Geschiedenis van het Nederlandse Zending en Overseese kerken*, 2, 1995

Roozendaal, Jeroen, 'Tussen loyaliteit en verzet: Reakties van de "Kleurlingen"-bevolking in Oostkaapland op de koloniale overheersing, 1828–1853', MA thesis, Leiden University, 1994

Rose, Cowper, *Four Years in Southern Africa*, London, Richard Bentley, 1829

Ross, Andrew, *John Philip (1775–1851): Missions, Race and Politics in South Africa*, Aberdeen, Aberdeen University Press, 1986

Ross, Robert, *Adam Kok's Griquas: A Study in the Development of Stratification in South Africa*, Cambridge, Cambridge University Press, 1976

Beyond the Pale: Essays on the History of Colonial South Africa, Hanover, N.H. and London, Wesleyan University Press for the University Press of New England, 1993

Cape of Torments: Slavery and Resistance in South Africa, London, Routledge & Kegan Paul, 1982

'Donald Moodie and the Origins of South African Historiography', in *Beyond the Pale*

'The Occupations of Slaves in Eighteenth Century Cape Town', *Studies in the History of Cape Town*, 2, 1980

'Paternalism, Patriarchy and Afrikaans', *SAHJ*, 32, 1995

' "Rather Mental than Physical": Emancipations and the Cape Economy', in Worden and Crais, *Breaking the Chains*

'The Relative Importance of Exports and the Internal Market for the Agriculture of the Cape Colony, 1770–1855', in G. Liesegang, H. Pasch and A. Jones (eds.), *Figuring African Trade: Proceedings of the Symposium on the Quantification and Structure of the Import and Export and Long Distance Trade of Africa in the Nineteenth Century*, Berlin, Kolner Beitrage zur Afrikanistiek, 1985

'The Rule of Law at the Cape of Good Hope in the Eighteenth Century', *Journal of Imperial and Commonwealth History*, 9, 1980

'The Social and Political Theology of Western Cape Missions', in Henry Bredekamp and Robert Ross (eds.), *Missions and Christianity in South African History*, Johannesburg, Witwatersrand University Press, 1995

'The Top Hat in South African History: The Changing Significance of an Article of Material Culture', *Social Dynamics*, 16, 1990

'The "white" Population of South Africa in the Eighteenth Century', *Population Studies*, 29, 1975

Saaltink, H. W., 'Om de plaats van het graf', *Holland*, 19, 1987

Sachs, Albie, *Justice in South Africa*, London, Heinemann for Sussex University Press, 1973

Sahlins, Marshall, *Culture and Practical Reason*, Chicago and London, University of Chicago Press, 1976

Schama, Simon, *The Embarrassment of Riches: An Interpretation of Dutch Culture in the Golden Age*, London, W. Collins, 1987

Patriots and Liberators: Revolution in the Netherlands, 1780–1813, New York, Alfred A. Knopf, 1977

Schoeman, Karel, *A Debt of Gratitude: Lucy Lloyd and the 'Bushman Work' of G. W. Stow*, Cape Town, South African Library, 1997

Die dood van 'n Engelsman: Die Cox-moorde van 1856 en die vroeë jare van die Oranje-Vrystaat, Cape Town, Pretoria and Johannesburg, Human & Rousseau, 1982

'Elizabeth Rolland (1803–1901), pioneer van kindertuinonderwys in Suid-Afrika', *QBSAL*, 40(1), 1985

Olive Schreiner, 'n lewe in Suid-Afrika, 1855–1881, Cape Town, Human & Rousseau, 1989

'A Thorn Bush that Grows in the Path': The Missionary Career of Ann Hamilton, 1815–1823, Cape Town, South African Library, 1995

'Voersis, Bafta en Molvel: 'n Aantekening oor westerse kleredrag in de Oranjerivier-Soewereiniteit, 1850–1854', Africana Notes and News, 30(2), 1992

Schoeman, Karel, (ed.), The Recollections of Elizabeth Rolland (1803–1901), Cape Town and Pretoria, Human & Rousseau, 1987

Scholtz, J. du P., Die Afrikaner en sy taal, 1806–1875, Cape Town, Nasionale Pers, 1939

Schutte, G. J., 'Tussen Amsterdam en Batavia: De Kaapse samenleving en de Calvinistische kerk onder de Compagnie', unpublished paper presented to the Conference of Dutch and South African Historians, Johannesburg, 1997

Schutte, G. J. (ed.), Briefwisseling van Hendrik Swellengrebel jr oor Kaapse sake, 1778–1792, Cape Town, Van Riebeeck Society, 1982

Scott, Patricia E., 'An Approach to the Urban History of Early Victorian Grahamstown 1832–53, with Particular Reference to the Interiors and Material Culture of Domestic Dwellings', MA thesis, Rhodes University, Grahamstown, 1987

Scully, Pamela, The Bouquet of Freedom: Social and Economic Relations in the Stellenbosch District, South Africa, c. 1870–1900, Cape Town, Centre for African Studies, UCT, no. 17, 1990

Liberating the Family? Gender and British Slave Emancipation in the Rural Western Cape, South Africa, 1823–1853, Oxford, James Currey, 1997

'Liquor and Labor in the Western Cape, 1870–1900', in Jonathan Crush and Charles Ambler (eds.), Liquor and Labor in Southern Africa, Athens and Pietermaritzburg, Ohio University Press and University of Natal Press, 1992

'Private and Public Worlds of Emancipation in the Rural Western Cape, c. 1830–42', in Worden and Crais, Breaking the Chains

Semple, Robert, Walks and Sketches at the Cape of Good Hope, 1805, 2nd edn, Cape Town and Amsterdam, Balkema, 1968

Shaw, Barnabas, Memorials of South Africa, 2nd edition, London, Adams & Co, 1840, reprinted Westport, Conn., Negro Universities Press, 1970

Shell, Robert C.-H., 'Between Christ and Mohammed: Conversion, Slavery, and Gender in the Urban Western Cape', in Elphick and Davenport, Christianity in South Africa

Children of Bondage: A Social History of the Slave Society at the Cape of Good Hope, Hanover, N.H. and London, Wesleyan University Press, 1994

De Meillon's People of Colour: Some Notes on their Dress and Occupations, with special reference to Cape Views and Customs: Water-colours by H.C. de Meillon in the Brenthurst Collection, Johannesburg, Brenthurst Press, 1978

'The Establishment and Spread of Islam at the Cape from the Beginning of Company Rule to 1828', BA Hons. thesis, UCT, 1974

'The March of the Mardijckers: The Toleration of Islam at the Cape, 1633–1861', Kronos: Journal of Cape History, 22, 1995

'Rites and Rebellion: Islamic Conversion at the Cape, 1808–1915', SHCT, 5, 1984

'S. E. Hudson's "Slaves"', Kronos: Journal of Cape History, 9 (1984)

Shell, Robert C.-H., (ed.), 'Katie Jacobs: An Early Oral History', QBSAL, 46(3), 1992

Sicking, Ivo, *In het belang van het kind: Nederlandse kinderemigratie naar zuid-Afrikaq in de jaren 1856–1860*, Utrecht, Utrechtse Historische Cahiers, 16(1), 1995

Smith, A. H., *Cape Views and Costumes: Water-Colours by H. C. de Meillon*, Johannesburg, Brenthurst Press, 1978

Smith, K. W., *From Frontier to Midlands: A History of the Graaff-Reinet District, 1786–1910*, Grahamstown, Institute of Social and Economic Research, Occasional Paper 20, 1976

Solomon, W. E. Gladstone, *Saul Solomon: THE Member for Cape Town*, Cape Town, Oxford University Press, 1948

South Africa, Archives Commission, *Kaapse Plakkaatboek, 1652–1806*, 6 vols., Cape Town, Cape Times, 1944–51

Sparrman, Anders, *A Voyage to the Cape of Good Hope, towards the Antarctic Polar Circle, round the World and to the Country of the Hottentots and the Caffers from the Year 1772–1776*, edited by V. S. Forbes, trans. J. and I. Rudner, 2 vols., Cape Town, Van Riebeeck Society, 1975–6

Spierenburg, Peter, *The Spectacle of Suffering: Executions and the Evolution of Repression; from a Preindustrial Metropolis to the European Experience*, Cambridge, Cambridge University Press, 1984

Spilhaus, M. Whiting, *South Africa in the Making*, Cape Town, Juta, 1966

Spoelstra, C., *Bouwstoffen voor de Geschiedenis der Nederduitsch-Gereformeerde Kerken in Zuid Africa*, 2 vols., Amsterdam, Hollandsch Afrikaansche Uitgevers Maatschappij, 1907

Stavorinus, J. S., *Voyages to the East Indies*, trans. S. H. Wilcocke, 3 vols., London, G. G. and J. Robinson, 1798

Steytler, F. A., (ed.), 'Minutes of the First Conference held by the African Missionaries at Graaff-Reinet (1814)', *Hertzog-Annale van die Suid-Afrikaanse Akademie vir Wetenskap en Kuns*, 3, 1956

Steytler, John George, 'Remembrances from 1832–1900', *QBSAL*, 25, 1971

Strutt, Daphne H., *Fashion in South Africa, 1652–1900*, Cape Town and Rotterdam, Balkema, 1975

Stuart, Doug, '"Of Savages and Heroes": Discourses of Race, nation and Gender in the Evangelical Missions to Southern Africa in the Early Nineteenth Century', Ph.D. thesis, University of London, 1994

Sturgis, James, 'Anglicisation at the Cape of Good Hope in the Early Nineteenth Century', *Journal of Imperial and Commonwealth History*, 11, 1982

Suasso de Lima, J., *The Chalifa Question: Documents connected with the Matter*, Cape Town, Van de Sandt de Villiers, 1857

De Taal der Kapenaren, tegen de schandelijke aanranding derzelver van Professor Changuion, verdedigd, Cape Town, J. Suasso da Lima, 1844

Swaving, J. G., *J. G. Swavings zonderlinge ontmoetingen en wonderbaarlijke lotswisselingen na zijne vlugt uit Delft*, Dordrecht, Blussé and Van Braam, 1830

Tamarkin, Mordechai, *Cecil Rhodes and the Cape Afrikaners: The Imperial Colossus and the Colonial Parish Pump*, London, Frank Cass, 1995

Taylor, Miles, 'The Beginnings of Modern British Social History?', *History Workshop Journal*, 43, 1997

Teenstra, M. D., *De Vruchten Mijner Werkzaamheden gedurende mijne Reize over de*

Kaap de Goede Hoop, naar Java, en Terug, over St Helena, Naar de Nederlanden, edited by F. C. L. Bosman, Cape Town, Van Riebeeck Society, 1943

Terwen, J. J., 'De ontwerpgeschiedenis van de Marekerk te Leiden', in *Opus Musivum*, Assen, 1964

Theal, George McC. (ed.), *Belangrijke Historische Dokumenten verzameld in de Kaap Kolonie en elders*, 3 vols., Cape Town and London, 1896–1911

Records of the Cape Colony, 36 vols., London, Swan Sonnenschien, 1897–1905

Thompson, E. P., *The Making of the English Working Class*, 2nd edn, Harmondsworth, Penguin, 1968

Thompson, F. M. L., *The Rise of Respectable Society: A Social History of Victorian Britain*, London, Fontana, 1987

Thompson, Leonard, *The Political Mythology of Apartheid*, New Haven and London, Yale University Press, 1985

Survival in Two Worlds: Moshoeshoe of Lesotho, 1786–1870, Oxford, Clarendon Press, 1975

Thompson, L. M., *The Unification of South Africa, 1902–1910*, Oxford, Clarendon Press, 1960

Thunberg, C. P., *Travels at the Cape of Good Hope, 1772–1775*, edited by V. S. Forbes, Cape Town, Van Riebeeck Society, 1986

Tolstoy, L. N., *Anna Karenin*, trans. Rosemary Edmonds, Harmondsworth, Penguin, 1954

Trapido, Stanley, 'The Emergence of Liberalism and the Making of 'Hottentot Nationalism', 1815–1834', *SSA*, 17, 1992

'"The Friends of the Natives": Merchants, Peasants and the Political and Ideological Structure of Liberalism at the Cape, 1854–1910', in Marks and Atmore, *Economy and Society*

'The Origins of the Cape Franchise Qualifications of 1853', *JAH*, 5(1), 1964

'White Conflict and Non-White Participation in the Politics of the Cape of Good Hope, 1852–1910', Ph.D. thesis, University of London, 1963

Tutu, Desmond, *The Rainbow People of God: South Africa's Victory over Apartheid*, London, Doubleday, 1994

Vail, Leroy (ed.), *The Creation of Tribalism in Southern Africa*, London, Berkeley and Los Angeles, James Currey, University of California Press, 1989

Valentyn, Francois, *Description of the Cape of Good Hope with the Matters Concerning it*, edited by R. H. Raven-Hart, 2 vols., Cape Town, Van Riebeeck Society, 1971 and 1973

Valkhoff, Marius F., *Studies in Portuguese and Creole, with Special Reference to South Africa*, Johannesburg, Witwatersrand University Press, 1966

Van Arkel, Dik, 'The Growth of the Anti-Jewish Stereotype: An Attempt at a Hypothetical Deductive Method of Historical Research', *International Review of Social History*, 30, 1985

Van Arkel, D., G. C. Quispel and R. J. Ross, 'Going Beyond the Pale: on the Roots of White Supremacy in South Africa', in Ross, *Beyond the Pale*

Van der Chijs, J. A. (ed.), *Nederlandsch-Indisch Plakkaatboek 1602–1811*, 16 vols., Batavia and The Hague, Landsdrukkerij and M. Nijhoff, 1885–97

Van der Merwe, J. P., *Die Kaap onder die Bataafse Republiek, 1803–1806*, Amsterdam, Swets & Zeitlinger, 1926

Van Heyningen, Elizabeth, ' "Gentoo" – A Case of Mistaken Identity', *Kronos: Journal of Cape History*, 22, 1995
  'The Social Evil in the Cape Colony, 1868–1902: Prostitution and the Contagious Diseases Act', *JSAS*, 10(2), 1984
Van Rooden, Peter, 'Nineteenth-Century Representations of Missionary Conversion and the Transformation of Western Christianity', in Peter van der Veer (ed.), *Conversion to Modernities: The Globalization of Christianity*, New York and London, Routledge, 1996
Van Ryneveld, Tessa, 'Merchants and Missions: Developments in the Caledon District, 1838–1850', BA Hons. thesis, UCT, 1983
Van Swigchem, T., T. Brouwer and W. C. A. van Oss, *Een Huis voor het Woord: Het protestantse kerkinterieur in Nederland tot 1900*, The Hague, Staatsuitgeverij, 1984
Van Zyl, D. J., *Kaapse Wyn en Brandewyn, 1795–1860*, Cape Town and Pretoria, Hollandsch Afrikaansche Uitgevers Maatschappij, 1974
Viney, Graham, and Phillida Brooke Simons, *The Cape of Good Hope, 1806–1872: Aspects of the Life and Times of British Society in and around Cape Town*, Johannesburg, Brenthurst Press, 1994
Visagie, J.C., 'Die Katriviernedersetting, 1829–1839', Ph.D. thesis, UNISA, 1978
  'Willem Fredrik Hertzog, 1792–1847', *AYB*, 37, 1974
Wagenaar, E. J. C., 'A Forgotten Frontier Zone – Settlements and Reactions in the Stormberg Area between 1820–60', *AYB*, 45, 1982
Wagenaar, Gerard, 'Johannes Gysbertus van Reenen – Sy aandeel in die Kaapse geskiedenis tot 1806', MA thesis, University of Pretoria, 1976
Walshe, Peter, 'Christianity and the Anti-Apartheid Struggle: The Prophetic Voice within Divided Churches', in Elphick and Davenport, *Christianity in South Africa*
  The Rise of African Nationalism in South Africa: The African National Congress, 1912–1952, London, Hurst, 1970
Walton, James, *Cape Cottages*, Cape Town, Intaka, 1995
Warner, Brian, (ed.), *Lady Herschel: Letters from the Cape, 1834–1838,* Cape Town, South African Library, 1991
Warren, Digby, 'Merchants, Commissioners and Wardmasters: Municipal and Colonial Politics in Cape Town, 1840–1854', *AYB*, 55, 1992
Watermeyer, E. B., and William Porter, *Community of Property and the Law of Inheritance at the Cape of Good Hope*, Cape Town, Saul Solomon, 1859
Watson, R. L, *The Slave Question: Liberty and Property in South Africa*, Hanover, N.H. and London, University Press of New England, 1990
Williams, Donovan, *When Races Meet: The Life and Times of William Ritchie Thomson . . . 1794–1891*, Johannesburg, AB Publishers, 1967
Williams, Raymond, *Marxism and Literature*, Oxford, Oxford University Press, 1987
Wilmot, Alex, *The Life and Times of Sir Richard Southey KCMG etc. . . . ,* London, Sampson, Low Marston & Co., 1904
Winberg, C., 'The "Ghoemaliedjes" of the Cape Muslims: Remnants of a Slave Culture', unpublished paper, UCT, 1992
Worden, Nigel, 'Between Slavery and Freedom: The Apprenticeship Period 1834–8', in Worden and Crais, *Breaking the Chains*

Slavery in Dutch South Africa, Cambridge, Cambridge University Press, 1985

'Violence, Crime and Slavery on Cape Farmsteads in the Eighteenth Century', *Kronos: Journal of Cape History*, 5, 1982

Worden, Nigel, and Clifton C. Crais (eds.), *Breaking the Chains: Slavery and its Legacy in the Nineteenth-Century Cape Colony*, Johannesburg, Witwatersrand University Press, 1994

Young, Mary (ed.), *The Reminiscences of Amelia de Henningsen (Notre Mère)*, Cape Town, Maskew Miller Longman for Rhodes University, Grahamstown, 1989

Index

196

Other books in the series